THE ESSENTIA
HAROLD CRUS

THE ESSENTIAL HAROLD CRUSE

A READER

Edited by William Jelani Cobb

Foreword by Stanley Crouch

palgrave

CONTENTS

P A R T   O N E

Early Writing

E S S A Y S

C O R R E S P O N D E N C E

P A R T   T W O

From
The Crisis of the Negro Intellectual
(1967)

PART SIX

From
Plural but Equal
(1987)

PART SEVEN

Interview with Harold Cruse

This book is dedicated to Nandi Ayeesha, my favorite person—whose restless nine year-old's curiosity and ceaseless stream of "whys?" represent an intellectual tradition all her own.

ACKNOWLEDGEMENTS

Anyone who has ever labored through the acknowledgments of a first-time author or editor knows that the "thank-yous" can run longer than an Academy Award acceptance speech. And this one is no different. There are a number of people whose critical engagement, dialogue, and friendship greatly enhanced this book. My most immediate thanks go to family members, Mary Cobb, Valerie, William, Terrence, and Natasha Foster.

I owe much of my perspective and development as a historian to Elizabeth Clark Lewis of Howard University. The members of my dissertation committee have been immeasurably insightful: David Levering Lewis, David Oshinsky, Daryl Scott, and Steve Lawson. I am particularly indebted to another committee member, Robin Kelley, who is responsible for the Harold Cruse Papers housed at the Tamiment Library of New York University and who provided key information during the formative stages of this project. Angela Ards generously shared her wit, her time, and her opinions. She was invaluable in helping this project move from the abstract to the concrete.

My "Washington connections"—Kenneth and Joy Carroll, Joel Dias-Porter, Eric Easter and Tina Hamilton-Easter, Brian Gilmore, Elanna Haywood, Bridget and Todd Warren of Vertigo Books, Simba Sana and Sunny Sumpter of Karibu Books, and Marcia Davis—contributed to the book in their own unique ways. I have also benefited from the constructive criticism and friendship of colleagues and professors at Rutgers University: Khalil Muhammad and Stephanie Lawson-Muhammad, Carolyn Brown, Kim Butler, Jen Brier, Dan Katz, Peter Lau, Tiffany Gill, Aminah Pilgrim, Stephanie Simms, Kelena Reed, and Amrita Myers.

Several other people granted me their time and attention and made those undefinable offerings that helped this book along: Mali Fleming and Alejandro Smith; Travis Ray; Ena Gomez; Martha Jones; April Silver; Akanke Washington; Alejandro Bodipo-Memba, who graciously provided housing accommodations during my sojourns to Michigan; Don Sinkfield; Ta-Nehesi Coates; Damita Baez Coats; David Carr; Kate Tuttle; Kay Shaw; Victoria Valentine; Steven Newsome; Camille Acey; Alondra Nelson; and the distinguished minds of the

Afrofuturism listserv. Asale Angel-Ajani, Jean Fairfax, Tonya Bolden (a millennial race woman), Natalie Bullock Brown, Sherman Brown, Mark Mason, Minkah Makalani, Claudia Menza, Robyn Spencer, the Morris family—Tracy, Cherry, and John—Natasha Tarpley, Diane Dickenshied, Imani Wilson and Edda Fields (whose wisdom exceeds her years), and Al-Yasha I. Williams, all helped this project (and its editor) along in innumerable ways.

Finally, there is a trio without whom this book would have remained a good idea stranded on my hard drive: Victoria Sanders, Asha Bandele, and Deborah Gershenowitz. I owe a debt of infinite thanks to them for their collective faith in this project and my abilities as a historian and writer.

BLUES FOR BROTHER CRUSE

BY STANLEY CROUCH

Even these many years later, the bulk of what Harold Cruse has written remains surprising. That is because it is always surprising to read anyone who thinks about Negro Americans as both part of a particular cultural development and part of the overall question of American identity. Far, far too often there is a segregated vision of black Americans as though they could have lived in this country—as chattel or not—for close to four hundred years yet function forever outside of the context of the nation. Due to that both uninformed and irresponsible vision, there is little argument, analysis, and deduction about the virtues and the troubles of color within the contexts of the aesthetic, the social, the political, and the economic planes of human life. There is no sense of the varieties and victories and failures of engagement within the mobile and not-so-mobile realities of American life. A set of cliches once dominated and continues to dominate discussion, the only changes amounting to newly shaped bottles for old slop.

Cruse did not have that problem because he was always thinking about something far more complex than what was expected in the discussion of racial matters. His work—while sometimes right and sometimes either wrong or optimistically naïve or incomplete—was much more consistently insightful or substantial in its reporting than what could be expected from those who condescendingly considered themselves "radical" or "progressive." I am referring to those who were always willing to resort to a theoretical basis for taking on the problems of American life. This was true even if those theories were not based in the facts of that very life they assumed would change for the better if the ideology to which these "progressives" adhered took over the terms of thought and action. Which, as we know, never happened.

Today, it is easy to talk about so-called black or so-called white but one almost never reads any discussion of what Cruse takes on when looking at the matrix of what he calls "white protestants, white Catholics, and white Jews," obviously alluding to the fact that there are black versions of all three. This is

THE ESSENTIAL HAROLD CRUSE

especially profound because it makes it clear that there has never been the kind of monolithic ethnicity based solely on color some would have us believe. This means that we have to look at how ethnic backgrounds and Americana at large combine to create certain points of view—with all the possibilities for surprise that human nature makes nearly inevitable.

The reason that almost no one would talk of such a matrix now is not because it has disappeared but because to suggest that Jews, in particular, have any kind of cultural power, especially in the world of the arts, is to run the risk of being accused of anti-Semitism. That is because there are those who remember well the Black Power years when, among its most hysterical advocates, anti-Semitism became an article of racist faith. (LeRoi Jones almost singlehandedly introduced this into Black politics and it is, therefore, quite interesting to read how Cruse assessed him and the saxophonist Archie Shepp, who were both married to white women, living in New York's East Village, and working out what was then a stage animus indicative of the pollution to come.) So any mention of Jews having power and influence now zooms us back to that low point in aspects of our national discourse focussed on the dilemmas wrought by color prejudice or misdirected support or cultural envy. Cruse, however, was not promoting bigotry, he was trying to understand how we all contribute to the majesty and the morass of Americana. He was intent on solving or delineating a riddle with assessments based upon actual experience and very close observations of the varied ethnic worlds in which he lived and moved. This thinker was not willing to have a theory handed to him after he came to maturity.

Cruse was also unafraid to call forth opinions and observations from a world far too often veiled by stereotypes or inadequate assessment. Negroes did actually think things and did actually agree and disagree and did actually have allegiance to or hostility towards each other on the basis of what classes they were from and what parts of the country they were from and whether or not they were actually natives or came into this country with all the prejudices that black colonials could have toward the black descendants of people who had been central to the making of American culture. In short, no matter how far removed from so-called intellectual consensus what he heard among black people might have been, Cruse was willing to put it on the table and move from there, giving us much to think about within the parameters of the periods in which he was writing. He raises very serious aesthetic questions when discussing the work, the thought, the politics, and the careers of Gilbert Seldes, Lorraine Hansberry, Josephine Baker, James Baldwin, Nat Cole, and Harry Belafonte, as examples. Those questions move from the arena of art and entertainment to the complex of regions of race, convention, aspirations, individual and group identity, and so on.

If he is talking about Greenwich Village forty years ago, Cruse lets us in on the dynamics that dictated the behavior that was once rebellious and isolated but is now, we can easily see, part of the popular menu in which dissent from certain social conventions has become no more than another commodity pumped out by MTV and BET. At the time, however, Cruse moved into very fresh areas by putting bohemian rebellion within an overall American frame. He saw—as no American novelists or screenwriters or playwrights then did—that the social and sexual freedoms of Greenwich Village were taken seriously by some and were no more than slumming rights for others. Those who were serious were attracted to a world less racially repressive or intellectually vacant. Some such Negroes were only on the make for the kinds of whites ready to jump into bed and "go native" in the Village bush. Cruse also added to the record the fact that Negroes had been downtown for a few hundred years and, therefore, were not newcomers to that part of Manhattan, which sent up the idea that they were social interlopers. Then, as now, there was no interest on the part of white liberals in the Americanness of Negroes. That Americanness almost inevitably predates the ancestry of those given the opportunity by skin tone to look down on those with far deeper historical and cultural roots.

We can, therefore, see in this gathering of work that Cruse was on the case long before the 1967 publication of his monumental work, *The Crisis of the Negro Intellectual.* In fact, when we look at his other work, we understand how he was able to bring off so important a work as *Crisis,* which dwarfed almost all other books of the period when it came to bringing together politics, art, and social movements related to or inspired by the Afro-American condition. With that book, Cruse did, in his own way, what Ralph Ellison and Albert Murray have become either well known or barely known for arguing. He recognized that the call and response between the Negro and America at large is central to what Negroes became and what this nation became.

But when *The Crisis of the Negro Intellectual* was published, there was no plethora of black studies programs across the country, there was hardly any recognition of the fact that anything like a black intellectual even existed. In 1967, however, Ellison published his extraordinary collection of essays, *Shadow and Act,* which took the discussion of the Negro and of America to such heights that Stanley Edgar Hyman deemed him the finest critic of American culture at large. Murray's reputation was years away and still remains small, even though he produced far more material than Ellison did while living—one novel and two books of essays.

Harold Cruse, however, was not necessarily in dialogue with either man. He was announcing that there was a crisis in the world of the Negro intellectual and that its causes were far from simple. At this point, we can understand how poorly understood meanings of culture and cultural life and group independence can create a reductive vision shared by both the layperson and the intellectual. The crisis Cruse was onto 35 years ago has spread out into Afro-American culture at large and is presently celebrated as some sort of a liberation from "white middle class values," meaning that thug scum, whorish behavior, drooling materialism, and all of the dictates of "street knowledge" somehow provide an alternative to restrictive, external values. Cruse understood how all of that is wound up in the American quest for something beyond where someone starts, which is a quintessential issue. He surely recognized how color and career and class and art and economic support and sex and pretension and would-be radical politics all fuse in the arena of identity—lawd, lawd, lawd. That recognition makes this collection, whatever one's disagreements with particular parts might be, a truly powerful addition to understanding who we are and where we came from and, perhaps, where we are going.

Stanley Crouch is the author of *Don't the Moon Look Lonesome,* which Susan DiSesa, former Senior Editor of the Modern Library, called "One of the most profound novels in the English language." He has also published three books of essays: *Notes of a Hanging Judge; The All-American Skin Game;* and *Always in Pursuit.*

WHAT IS LEFT? AN INTRODUCTION

The America of 1967 found itself stranded at a bitter crossroads. The nation was mired in that turbulent middle ground between the brutal assassination of John F. Kennedy and impending deaths of Martin Luther King Jr. and Robert F. Kennedy. The tenor of American politics took on an increasingly radical edge as the nation lurched past the threshold of innocence. The social momentum of the nonviolent civil rights movement was dwindling—and looming on the horizon were apocalyptic riots, a rising antiwar movement, and the indelible, chaotic images of the Chicago Democratic Party Convention.

It was in this context that Harold Cruse's brilliant tome *Crisis of the Negro Intellectual* was first published. Written in lucid, bold prose and delivered into the crucible of post-Watts America, the book was immediately recognized as a benchmark in Afro-American scholarship. The book was a monumental analysis of the politics, personalities, and aesthetics that had defined Black America for the preceding four decades—and the reasons for their collective failure.

Swimming against the tide of prevailing opinion, Cruse indicted civil rights integrationists for their inability to recognize the essentially "pluralist" dynamics of American society. In short, America was a nation in which the guiding ethic was "every group for itself," and integration was tantamount to social suicide for Black America. Not only was integration inept as social policy, Cruse argued, but an integrationist *aesthetic* had corrupted the talent of otherwise respected artists like Paul Robeson and Lorraine Hansberry. Giving no intellectual quarter, Cruse laid the blame for this state of affairs at the feet of liberals—black and white—who'd had their origins in the Communist Party activism of the 1930s.

In *The Crisis of the Negro Intellectual* and his two successive works, *Rebellion or Revolution* and *Plural and Equal,* Professor Cruse detailed the impact of ethnic, religious, and corporate "blocs" in American society and called for the creation of an artistic and political bloc to define and advance the agenda of Black America.

In the final sentence of *The Crisis of the Negro Intellectual,* Cruse delivers a parting injunction against forgetting. Sampling a line from the philosopher George Santayana, he warns the reader that "Those who cannot remember the past are condemned to repeat it." As punctuation on 565 pages of analysis, the statement illustrates the overarching concern, the central theme of Harold Cruse's intellectual career. It is easy to forget, at this distant remove, that Harold Cruse's body of work has overwhelmingly concerned itself with the contradictions, oversights, and shortcomings that have undermined anti-oppression movements in Black America. A survey of the objective conditions of black lives in this country, a random sampling of the indices of incarceration, HIV infection, deindustrialization, and racial hostility would lead us to conclude that there is much work to be done. And despite the scathing ad hominem indictments that characterized it, *The Crisis of the Negro Intellectual* merits its position as a central text in the anti-oppression literature of the twentieth century.

Yet, for over three decades, *Crisis* has remained as controversial as it is indispensable in its analysis of the politics and culture of Black America. It is also one of those rare books that elicits response and reinterpretation by successive generations of readers. Consider these opinions:

- In 1968 critic Christopher Lasch wrote that "When all the manifestoes and polemics of the Sixties are forgotten, this book will survive as a monument of historical analysis."
- In 1980 historian Mark Naison wrote in his book *Communists in Harlem during the Depression* that Harold Cruse has "had a profound influence on black and white intellectuals" in this country.
- In 1988 the music critic and writer Nelson George referred to *The Crisis of the Negro Intellectual* as an "essential technical and intellectual guide."
- Professor Jerry Gafio Watts wrote in his 1992 book *Heroism and the Black Intellectual,* "Twenty-five years after its initial publication, *The Crisis of the Negro Intellectual* must by now be considered a classic text in Afro-American cultural studies, for it remains one of the most provocative and suggestive treatments of the political behavior and beliefs of twentieth-century Afro-American intellectuals."
- In 1998 sociologist Winston James remarked in his book *Holding Aloft the Banner of Ethiopia* that "Harold Cruse deserves credit for raising big and important questions and should be praised for attempting to discuss the political questions of the day within the wider historical experience of Afro-Americans."

To be sure, the book is an intellectual period piece. Cruse asserted as much when he wrote in 1971 that "I knew this book had flaws when it was published.

There were flaws in organization, lack of thoroughness in research . . . half-developed ideas. If I had postponed my book [it] would never have appeared in time to witness the demise of the Sixties euphoric expectations." Coming as it did, in the crucible of post-Watts America and on the cusp of the insurgent Black Power movement, *Crisis* was both timely and intensely relevant. In the months following its publication, the book elicited hostile response from such influential figures in African American cultural life as Julian Mayfield, Ernest Kaiser, and Robert Chrisman.[1]

Winston James, in fact, has argued at great length that *Crisis* is deeply anti-Caribbean and a reflection of the author's own biases against West Indians. While praising Cruse's brand of high-octane polemic, James's sentiment is that *Crisis* is mired in a subjective response that undermines its own authority. Jerry Gafio Watts went on to score Cruse for his reliance on an axis of nationalism and integrationism, an error that he asserts caused him to "underestimate the degree to which the most vehement black nationalist intellectual was fundamentally American." Mark Naison devotes an essay in his book to refuting the idea that Jewish Communists held sway over their Black comrades—an idea that, at least in part, has its origins in Cruse's treatise. Kevin Gaines's essay "The Cold War and the African American Expatriate Community in Nkrumah's Ghana" charges that Harold Cruse erroneously conflates "left internationalism" and "integrationism" in his analysis, thereby making him an unwitting ally of Cold War liberals. And importantly, feminist scholar Beverly Guy-Sheftall has raised enduring criticisms regarding Cruse's omission of an entire segment of the Black intellectual lineage—Black women.[2] Given the aggregate *weight* of these charges, one must ask why Cruse remains relevant to African Americans. Why collect this scholar's work? What reason is there to return to so flawed a thesis? In a phrase, what is left?

Much of the criticism of Cruse has originated among the academic left. And his ambivalent status within the canon of black thinkers is at least as much a product of the ascent of the academic left at the same time that Black nationalist thought finds itself in a quagmire. Given the fact that the prime exemplar of Black nationalism in our time is Louis Farrakhan, this state of affairs is perhaps understandable. The caliber of nationalist thought has most certainly declined since Malcolm X issued his "Ballot or the Bullet" ultimatum. And save the intellectual pot liquor of Afrocentrism, Black nationalism is out of vogue—denigrated for its patriarchal and homophobic excesses (problems that, it should be noted, were far from absent within Black liberal and integrationist quarters). Intellectually soldered to the onerous concept of racial "essentialism," Black nationalist thought has fallen into disfavor in an era where race is routinely dismissed as a "social construct." But for most black people in the United States, society is a *racial* construct, a fact that was apparent to Cruse three and a half decades ago. That is to say, irrespective of its specious biological origins, race remains a central axis of black—and thereby white—life in America in a way that no amount of deconstruction has altered. In the binary racial logic of American life, Cruse's idea that individual rights in America were inextricably linked to group status remains a valid thesis.

Further, in making the case for his nationalist politic, Cruse consistently cited the escapist, utopian, and contradictory tendencies that had been (and remain) characteristic of Black nationalism. Cruse is virtually alone among his generation of intellects in that he created an agenda and provided an intellectual blueprint for a movement—in this instance, the Black Power project of the 1970s. Further—Cruse along with Hubert Harrison, Malcolm X, and John Henrik Clarke—represents a tradition of Harlem autodidacts. As a product of the Harlem intellectual tradition, he concerned himself with real, three-dimensional issues of power, organization, culture, and progress— in contrast to the deconstructive word games that characterize much of the current discourse. And like Malcolm X and John Henrik Clarke, Cruse arrived in Harlem from rural America. Much of his life, in fact, can be read as somehow emblematic of broader historic trends in black life. Cruse had first-person experience of the Great Migration, the depression era and its attendant radicalism, World War II, the civil rights and Black Power movements. In the midst of these historic junctures, he was also a critic and culture-producer, having written a novel and several plays before turning his attention to the subject of Negro leadership.

Born in Virginia at the beginning of World War I, Cruse was among that number of hopeful Negroes who made their way North in the interwar years. The Harlem Renaissance and Popular Front activities of the Depression years formed a critical backdrop to his youth. The vivid artistic recollections in essays like "Interludes with Duke Ellington" were gleaned from his weekly sojourns with an aunt from their Queens home up to the vaudeville shows of Harlem.

The coming of World War II and Cruse's service as a supply trooper in Italy brought him into contact with Italian communists in the antifascist underground, a connection that presaged his entry into the Communist Party in postwar Harlem. Cruse took his advanced degrees from the street-corner academies of Harlem oratory where, as he put it, "you were considered a goddamned dummy" if you couldn't expound on the finer points of Marxist theory. That informal boulevard curriculum was given ballast when he began taking classes at the George Washington Carver school in Harlem, the uptown adjunct of the radical Jefferson School.

His entry into the Communist Party—and his resignation some seven years later—were driven by a web of motives, both personal and intellectual. In his rendering of those events, his experiences during the world war left him with a favorable view of communism—although he began to question its efficacy as an uplift strategy shortly after he joined the party in 1947. He entered the CP ranks during that brief entente between black liberals and the radical left that splintered with the onset of the Cold War. His exit took place amid the political repression of the McCarthy era. Cruse was asked by government sources to consider rejoining the party as an informant. He did not do so and, effectively exiled from the network of communist social relations, he began to concentrate on his artistic interests. The second half of the 1950s, the period discussed in his "Race and Bohemianism in Greenwich Village" essay, found Cruse living downtown, writing plays, and interacting socially with intellectuals of the Washington Square set.

Unsuccessful in his attempts to have any of his four plays produced, he turned his attention to nonfiction and criticism. Although he had begun his writing career filing short reviews for the *Daily Worker,* it was not until the early 1960s that longer, bolder, and far more provocative prose work began to appear under his byline. This evolving approach to what might be termed "critical history" was apparent in the unpublished 1960 essay "A Negro Looks at Cuba" and "James Baldwin, the Theater and His Critics," which was written in 1963. As one of a handful of black intellectuals and activists invited to Cuba by Fidel Castro, Cruse's views on the newborn revolutionary state are of some historic import.

By the mid-1960s, Cruse had completed a manuscript on black politics and culture. Responding to the publisher's request for an introduction, he began summarizing the nature of Black America's politico-cultural dilemma. The resulting 1,000 pages were revised and the publisher decided to shelve the original manuscript (which, sadly, is not included among Cruse's papers). The massive introduction was published as *The Crisis of the Negro Intellectual.* The book, along with Fanon's *Wretched of the Earth* and Malcolm X's autobiography, became required reading among Black Powerites. In the wake of the book's success, he became involved with Amiri Baraka (with whom he'd visited Cuba) and taught history at the Black Arts Movement institutions in Newark, New Jersey. The following year he produced *Rebellion or Revolution,* which expounded on the themes of *Crisis.*

The rising cry for black studies had, by the late 1960s, resulted in the formation of embryonic centers for the study of the black world. After accepting a position at the University of Michigan, Ann Arbor, in 1971, Cruse became one of the first generation of black studies faculty and devoted a great deal of intellectual energy to creating a methodology for the field. By the 1980s, he had enough historical distance to evaluate the successes of the near-century-old civil rights strategy vis à vis the economic rights approach. He raised these questions in *Plural but Equal,* concluding that Great Society–type programs and allegiance to the Democratic Party should be consigned to the dustbin of history. Taken in total, his contribution to African American letters and his critical assessments remain formidable.

Moreover, he is one of a handful of intellectuals who wrote comfortably outside the parameters of discipline and genre. *Crisis of the Negro Intellectual* and *Rebellion or Revolution* can only uneasily be categorized as "history" books. His body of work synthesized historical research, cultural criticism, and political analysis into a provocative new whole. In placing culture in the foreground of his analysis, Cruse, like Amilcar Cabral and W. E. B. Du Bois, was expanding the parameters of the "political" arena.

Nevertheless, no work of analysis, however insightful, remains unweathered by the passage of time. Cruse's demand for cultural and intellectual autonomy, while valid, failed to grapple with the complexities of cultural output. Just as the younger generation of Harlem Renaissance aesthetes and intellectuals created a cultural product that was often at odds with the political prescriptions of their forebears, the current crop of hip-hop cultural workers frequently is anything but aesthetically correct.

On the opening page of this new millennium, hip-hop is the primary cultural export of the United States. And contrasting the problem of autonomy that Cruse cited, the global dissemination of African American urban culture is facilitated by black-owned record labels, magazines, and communications outlets such as Black Entertainment Television (BET) and BlackPlanet.com. Yet the nominal independence of these culture-producers from the type of liberal-Jewish paternalism that Cruse found so problematic has yielded less than revolutionary returns. Of particular irony is the recent controversy over the labor practices of BET and the enlistment of the entertainment establishment and a number of liberal Jews in an effort to force a black company to pay black actors and comedians a decent wage. And despite significant numbers of black filmmakers, the product has not tremendously widened the horizons of African American cinematic depiction.

Further, the intraracial class conflicts in Black America are not fully charted in *The Crisis* or Cruse's subsequent work. Insightful in his dissection of the cultural tendencies and social marginality of the alleged Negro bourgeoisie,

Cruse was less than definitive on who the black working class was (and is) and what its historic role was vis-à-vis the Black world. To his credit, Cruse extended the ideas of thinkers like Du Bois and George Padmore who grappled with the thorny implications of racialized capitalism and the problem of class during the red years of the Great Depression. In recent years, reams of analysis have been dedicated to charting the speculative borders of "whiteness" as a social and class identity. Certainly Harold Cruse merits mention among those theorists who were at the forefront of understanding race as a class identity. In the essay "Revolutionary Nationalism and the Afro-American" he writes:

> [American Marxists] have never been able to understand the implications of the Negro's position in the social structure of the United States. They have no more been able to see the Negro as having revolutionary potentialities in his own right than European Marxists could see the revolutionary aspirations of their colonials as being independent of, and not subordinate to, their own . . . the belief in a political alliance of Negroes and whites is based upon a superficial assessment of the Negro's social status: *the notion that the Negro is an integral part of the American nation in the same way as is the white working class . . . Negroes have never been equal to whites* of any class *in economic, social, cultural or political status.*[3]

Ergo, class is simultaneously race, and the glorified appeals to "unity of the working class" were to founder time and again on the shoals of American racism. Nevertheless, pluralism as espoused by Cruse critiqued American epidermal politics but left open the question of what exactly a black working class agenda would look like. In the era of globalization, deindustrialization, and the diminished influence of labor unions, that question remains paramount.

These issues notwithstanding, there has been a resurgence of interest in Cruse's work of late—interestingly enough, among younger left thinkers. In light of the ideas of hegemony and the matrices of oppression, the newer generation has noted that Cruse's pluralist ideas are not entirely incompatible with Marxism—a particular irony considering the fact that the Communist Left spent two decades creating labyrinthine arguments for Negro nationality. In this vein, Cruse wrote:

> The living facts of the world revolution today are more persuasive than any revolutionary theory that came out of western Europe after the death of Marx. We do not hold Marx accountable for any deviations or distortions that either history or men have imposed to detract from his doctrine. He was a towering

product of his times and his conclusions about the society of men tore away the veil that hid the profound forces that moved societies. His forecasts have been negated by the very dialectical process he revealed; yet to say, nay, insist, that history should act just the way Marx thought it would is to do an injustice to a great thinker and to imply that dialectics is a philosophical fraud, as many have tried to do (even some who called themselves Marxists).[4]

In writing that Marx's "forecasts have been negated by the very dialectical process he revealed," Cruse was attempting to bridge the chasm between orthodox ideology and his own contemporary reality. Faced with the truth of revolution in the preindustrial states of Russia, China, and Vietnam and in that semicolonial American vassal, Cuba, Cruse raised the idea that there are no perfect doctrines. And if such is the case, the class-over-race prescriptions of American communists were subject to question. A strong case can be made that Cruse was far more dismissive of Marxists than of Marxism. In the big picture, his writings on nationalism, pluralism, and culture might well be indispensable to our understanding of the intersection of race and class. Thus, we again return to the question: What is progressive? What is left?

To be sure, it is no small accomplishment to write a book that elicits praise thirty-five years after publication—and perhaps, as is the case with *Crisis,* it is even more difficult to write one that inspires lacerating criticism in that same span of time. This collection is something of a coda to Cruse's massive body of work, an attempt to chart his intellectual trajectory over nearly half a century. This reader was culled from hundreds of pages of unpublished work housed in the Tamiment Library of NYU alongside hundreds of pages of previously published work. (Although a substantial amount of Harold Cruse's papers is housed at the Auburn Avenue Research Center in Atlanta, this collection is, unfortunately, unprocessed and unavailable to scholars.) As with any collection spanning such a long period, there are evolutions, subtle and grand: Lorraine Hansberry is excoriated in the pages of *Crisis of the Negro Intellectual;* by 1980, Cruse was praising *A Raisin in the Sun* for singlehandedly breaking the white liberal stranglehold over the creation of "black" theatrical characters. Some of the early essays were written for the Communist Party USA newspaper *The Daily Worker;* his latter essays appeared in such mainstream outlets as *The Los Angeles Times.*

Many of the essays that appear in *The Essential Harold Cruse: A Reader* were excerpted from larger works. In the case of essays that do not appear in their entirety, a set of bracketed ellipses indicate where text has been omitted. The most extensively edited are three of the previously unpublished pieces, "The New Negro History of John Hope Franklin," "On Robert Brustein's Theater Visions" (published here as

"The Racial Origins of American Theater"), and "James Baldwin, the Theater and His Critics." The first two essays were prohibitively long in their original form, the essay on James Baldwin was, with the permission of Harold Cruse, edited from the three drafts of it that are in the Cruse Collection at the Tamiment Library of New York University. In a small number of instances, text has been edited for clarity; these edits are also encased by brackets.

As a means of maintaining fidelity to Professor's Cruse's work, most of his footnotes have been kept as they appeared in the original manuscripts. However, in the interest of clarity and consistency, all strictly bibliographical notes have been converted to chapter endnotes and renumbered accordingly. The contents of Professor Cruse's notes have not been altered, unless indicated. Brackets have been placed around notes contributed to the text by earlier editors. My own editorial notes have been incorporated into the introductions to the essays.

This volume is divided into five chronological sections. The first, "Early Writings," contains essays and reviews written by Cruse in the 1950s and early 1960s—a period that spanned his membership and resignation from the Communist Party and his years as a playwright in Greenwich Village. The second section contains excerpts from *The Crisis of the Negro Intellectual*. The third section, "Black Power Era," contains work that Cruse produced during the turbulent years of the late 1960s for publications like *Black World* and his lengthy analysis of Eldridge Cleaver. The fourth section, *Rebellion or Revolution*, contains a number of essays that were also written during the Black Power period and compiled in his follow-up to *Crisis*. His "Post Black Power Writings" section covers the period following the demise of the National Black Political Convention after the Little Rock gathering of 1974 and extends to his correspondence in the mid-1980s and the publication of *Plural but Equal*, an excerpt from that book constituting the fifth section. The "afterword" consists of an interview with Cruse that appeared in *Radical History Review* in 1997. On its most obvious level, Cruse's work during the period covered by this collection moves from contemporary criticism of the burgeoning civil rights movement to critical exposition of the Black Power concept to retrospective analysis of the net gains and losses of those movements. His is a vital perspective on race in the second half of the alleged American century.

It has often been said of Harold Cruse that his body of work has raised more questions than it has successfully answered. If such is indeed the case, we would do well to revisit these questions, many of which remain looming before us. The final line of *Plural but Equal* offers this statement: "What is lacking is the quality of black leadership capable of harnessing black potential." As this state of affairs is sadly persistent, *The Essential Harold Cruse: A Reader,* is offered as an overview of this problem and one thinker's contributions toward the task of resolving it.

William Jelani Cobb
Brooklyn & Atlanta

NOTES

1. Harold Cruse, "Black and White: Outlines of the Next Stage," *Black World,* January 1971, 22. See also Julian Mayfield "A Challenge to a Bestseller: Crisis or Crusade?" *Negro Digest,* June 1968; Ernest Kaiser, "The Crisis of the New Intellectual," *Freedomways* 9, December 1969; and Robert Chrisman, "The Crisis of Harold Cruse," *The Black Scholar,* vol. 1, no. 1 (1969).
2. See Kevin Gaines, "The African American Expatriate Community in Nkrumah's Ghana" in *Universities and Empire,* Christopher Simpson, ed., *The New Press* (1998), 135-158. Also, Beverly Guy-Sheftall, "Reconstructing a Black Female Intellectual Tradition: Commentary on Harold Cruse's *The Crisis of the Negro Intellectual*"in *Voices of the African Diaspora,* vol. IX, no. 1, Winter 1994 (publication of the University of Michigan, Ann Arbor: Center for Afroamerican and African Studies).
3. "Revolutionary Nationalism and the Afro-American," *Rebellion or Revolution* (New York: William Morrow, 1968) pp. 76-77.
4. "Marxism and the Negro," *Rebellion or Revolution,* pp. 152-53.

PART ONE

Early Writing

CHAPTER ONE

Salute to Josephine Baker, Magnificent Negro Artist

(*Daily Worker*, March 14, 1951)

The name of Josephine Baker when mentioned has always conjured up many facts, real and imagined, relating to the career of this famous Negro artist of the international entertainment world.

To those in the United States who knew her personally, she is a friend, fellow artist, colleague. Between them there exist close bonds that have endured twenty years or more and are yet as strong as ever in spite of the fact that she, long, long ago, became a citizen of France. Her first appearance in France was in the 1925 Folies Bergère. To others in our country who never knew her personally, and they are many thousands, Josephine Baker has always been a legend flavored by sights and sounds and visions of Paris where she has reigned supreme. To most Negroes she is the outstanding example of the native daughter who made good far, far from home.

This reviewer remembers hearing of the personality of Josephine Baker so many years ago that it would be impossible to say just when. But it was not until the years of 1942-1943 that it was my pleasant good fortune to see and hear this marvelous woman.

It was during the North African campaign of World War II that the name Josephine Baker found its way into consciousness of many soldiers, Negro and white, who had never heard of her. After working in the French underground resistance movement during those first years of the German Occupation, she had escaped to North Africa and was reported living in Marrakech, Morocco.

Rumor had it that she was at first ill, seriously ill, even dead. The Army newspaper *Stars & Stripes* carried many stories about her and then finally reported that she was not dead but had recovered from a serious illness and would be around soon on an entertainment junket. And so one starry night near the edge of the great Sahara, Josephine Baker sang and performed for my regiment. For this reviewer it was a never to be forgotten experience.

She was, at that time, thin and wasted from her illness, but so vibrant and vital that her physical condition was soon lost sight of. She sang several American and French songs, one of which was the famous "J'ai Deux Pays" (Two Loves Have I: My Country and Paris). The GIs swooned and she was the topic of conversation for many, many, months after.

And so, for this viewer, seeing Jo Baker again at the Strand was in the nature of a second triumph, a repeat performance, even better than the one seven years ago. It is an experience that surpasses anything describable in mere words. What she sings, what she says in words, expresses in movement of body, in dance motions and pantomime, constitute an art of such magnificence and individuality that it is not enough to talk about it. She must be seen.

She must be seen, not merely for the splendor of lavish gowns designed by Balanciaga, Dior, Dessès, and Madame Schiaparelli and Jacques Fath which alone would make a fashion show. She must be seen to partake of what she communicates across the boards to an audience. She creates an atmosphere alive with quiet and then audible wonder, tense and then vocal appreciation, an electric charge of spontaneous endearment. And you become lost in a rapport that centers around this personality, captivated by this Negro Woman who personifies an institution in France.

A little note in *The New York Times*, May 10, 1943, quoted Josephine Baker as saying that she would never return to the U.S. but would return to France as soon as the war was over. One need not go into the reasons why she made that statement. No doubt she has expressed the same sentiment many times before and since.

Rather, it is a tribute to this artist who adopted another country, that she did not thereby become a rootless, declassed cosmopolitan spurning forever the tap-source of her talents—the Negro Cultural Idiom. So her return to this country is truly a triumph.

A triumph for herself and a triumph for the American Negroes who were drawn to the Strand by the magic mention of this fabulous personality. And there is a logic in all this, for the road that leads an individual to fight with resistance forces of a mother country against an invader is not the road that leads one away from one's nativity.

And this is the fine thing about Josephine Baker. That is the persistence of her native Negro idiom which she never lost and which predominates what she does artistically. Rather, it has enriched, and has been enriched by an acquired French and Latin flavor. When she sang the famous "J'ai Deux Pays" in French and English it was symbolic of a woman who, while having achieved integration on a high level, has never lost her touch.

This is how one must view Josephine Baker, and it is wished that American audiences, particularly white audiences, could grasp the full meaning of the story behind this statuesque Negro woman.

For here is a story of life, art, fame and fortune, that America, Jo Baker's native home, would not offer. There is, then, a real irony in the fact that Americans must know her by virtue of newspaper notices that speak of a fame she fashioned in another country. Her native countrymen's children will never speak the name of Josephine Baker with the fond familiarity that French children speak of her in France and in French colonies where her name is practically a household word.

I wonder if the audience at the Strand comprehended what was happening when she stood on the stage and with consummate art reached out through the haze of American "show me" attitude at the beginning of her show, and clasped the reluctant ones to her person. Caressed them, indulged them in their lukewarm unfamiliarity, fondled them out of their standoffishness, then having won them, electrified them and sent them home after resounding applause agreeing with each other that they had just experienced something extraordinary.

Throughout her performance this reviewer's mind kept going across the sea to North Africa and back again to the Strand setting, linking up the two events over the span of years.

After the performance, I waited at the stage door with several other admirers for her appearance. Her manager appeared finally and said that she was too tired for any more interviews for the night. However, when she did emerge she stopped to exchange greetings with the group that waited for her.

It was then that I approached her and asked her to remember a certain performance she gave in North Africa to a certain Negro regiment at a certain place. With a light of recognition she clasped my hand and said, "Oh, how well I remember that. North Africa? How could I ever forget!"

This is part of the story of a world figure who since returning to these shores has not shrunk from a consistent fight in her field of work and art against discrimination. She made history when recently, in Miami Florida, at the Copa City Club, a rule of no Jimcrow was enforced and her audiences were Negro and white. She has recently turned down other offers for appearances which did not promise a non-discriminatory policy. She also spoke out sharply against the legal lynching of the Martinsville Seven.

Let us all salute Josephine Baker, Negro woman, artist, soldier fighter against discrimination, former lieutenant, French Resistance Army, and a citizen of the world.

CHAPTER TWO

A Negro Looks at Cuba

(Unpublished 1960)

In 1960 Harold Cruse traveled to Cuba as part of a delegation of Afro-American intellectuals and artists invited to witness the spectacle of a postrevolutionary society. In the early days of the "new Cuba"—prior to Fidel Castro's affiliation with the Soviet Union—the revolution was seen as part of the global movement of Third World peoples to shake off the dead hand of imperialism. Not surprisingly, Cruse saw the Cuban revolution as an anticolonial uprising that more closely resembled the 1804 Haitian revolution than the Russian revolution which had taken place just forty-three years earlier. His statement that "the Cuban revolution is an un-Marxian revolution and was carried out by non-Marxists" could only have been made during that brief window of time when intellectuals, artists, and politicians aligned with the emerging nations of the Caribbean and Africa and envisioned a world free of the domination of larger Western nations—and of Eastern as well.

The Cuba of the age of Fidel Castro is so close to Mississippi, Georgia et al that it almost became part of the slave empire of the South just prior to the Civil War. This abortive attempt on the part of slave-holding adventurers to capture Cuba is not commonly known in the general tradition of American folklore about slavery. If Cuba had been annexed when several Southern American expeditions tried to land there, it would have been part of the U.S. at the end of the Civil War. In that case the Cuban agrarian question would have developed along the same lines as the agrarian problem in the South and there certainly would have been no agrarian revolutionary reforms as have been carried out under Castro.

This bit of history is worth mentioning in connection with Cuba and the U.S. inasmuch as social progress is a thing that must be assessed in terms of historical factors. When the slave states were defeated in the American Civil War, certain Northern statesman attempted to carry out agrarian reform in the South by breaking up the former plantations of former slaveholders and dividing the land among the freedmen. In fact, the slogan "Forty Acres and a Mule" became the hope of every former Negro slave. This agrarian reform was subverted and finally defeated, allowing most of the former slaveholders to retain their property. Thus, the former slaves became sharecroppers and tenant farmers instead of land-owning farmers. From that time down to the present, practically all the ills of the race problem in the South can be traced to the failure to carry through the Northern victory to its logical conclusion—agrarian reform which would have stripped the slaveowners of their economic and political power for all time. As a direct result of this failure, American democratic processes, in and out of Congress, have been hamstrung and undermined by a long line of Southern reactionaries—the political progeny of the slaveowners, the Bilbos, Rankins, Talmadges, Eastlands, etc.

But Cuba today has achieved agrarian reform—a revolutionary transition without which no nation can really become a real democracy. This is the first instance of complete democratization of agriculture in the history of the western hemisphere. The irony of all this is that seen against the background of Cuban-U.S. relations going back to the 1840's, the Cuban revolution has brought both countries into a serious conflict of interests. Castro has become an enemy of American concepts of "freedom" but [the Eastlands and Talmadges have not].

These are the thoughts I was thinking on the morning of July 26, 1960, as I was on a train speeding through central Cuba headed for the province of Oriente and the Sierra Maestre mountains. I could not help think of Mississippi as the surprisingly flat terrain of Cuba sped by my window. I saw the rich earth of Cuba, the extreme poverty of its peasants, the green wealth of its sugar cane ripening under the intense sun for the next harvest. One can see in Cuba today vast stretches of fertile acreage which has lain fallow for decades while peasants and the nation as a whole were held in economic bondage by single-crop agriculture. To witness this and then to see the condition of Cuban peasants one understands clearly the necessity of Cuba's agrarian reform. This is, moreover, a strange commentary on progress in our western hemisphere—Cuba, which narrowly missed becoming a slave state, is now more advanced than Mississippi.

As an American Negro, all of this has special meaning to me. Cuba is a racial mixture of Spanish white, Negro and Indian. Aside from the support the overwhelming majority of Cubans have thrown behind Fidel Castro, the Cuban Negro (Afro-Cuban) has a special stake in the reforms of the Cuban revolution. This is not to imply that inter-racial relations in Cuba are to be equated with our North American racial practices. Quite the opposite is true. In Cuba, despite economic and class discrimination, racial intermingling has been the rule. The numerically dominant class is the mestizo or the Spanish-Indian mixture. While the Negro has not been racially absorbed into a class of mulattoes, the unmixed Negro is pretty well integrated in lower-class society. The discrimination heretofore practiced against "people of color" has been economic since the lower-class Cubans of whatever color all suffered the same fate of existing in a semi-colonial, underdeveloped society. In other words, racism as we know it in the U.S. is not endemic in Cuba.

Race relations being what they are in the U.S., Fidel Castro does not have to be a political genius to realize that there might be a more profitable market in American Negro goodwill towards his revolution than the market that vanished with the Cuban sugar quota. We recall that in pursuit of this possibility, the Cuban government, some months ago, launched a tourist program to attract American Negroes to Cuba's discrimination-free hotels and resorts. The Cuban Institute of Tourism even entered contractual agreements with Joe Louis, ex-champion of boxing, and his public relations firm to promote Negro tourism in Cuba. The New York newspapers gave Louis' venture hostile coverage, forcing him to break off a $287,000 annual contract with the Cuban Institute of Tourism. This was, in effect, a cruel slap in the face to the ambitions of our Negro middleclass for whom opportunities to make the grade in American business and trade are precious few. Moreover, it makes a mockery of our American pretensions about the sanctity of "free enterprise." However, the reactions of Joe Louis and his Negro advisors prove that the Castro government did make an error in thinking that it could win support from the Negro middleclass for the revolution. There are no greater patriots in the U.S. than our elite members of E. Franklin Frazier's "Black Bourgeoisie" who never were and never will be "revolutionaries" even on the question of their "civil rights." Every American white-owned firm that hasn't yet been nationalized by the Cuban government is still doing business in Cuba. *The New York Times* of August 22 reported that "While U.S. exports to Cuba have fallen sharply, the Caribbean country has continued to import a sizable amount of essential items from this country despite hostile political relations." This was evident to me in Havana whose stores are still stocked with every conceivable item of U.S. imports. Of course, we understand that American tourism now becomes a political question in Cuba-U.S. relations but for the Negro it is also a civil rights question. The newspaper attack on Joe Louis' business dealings with Cuba was a clear case of discrimination against the Negro in trade and commerce, but the NAACP wouldn't touch it with a legal brief a mile long. During my stay in Havana, *The New York Times* of July 31 had a front page story describing how Henry Lee Moon, Public Relations director of the NAACP, had turned down an invitation by the Cuban government to visit [and] see what a real revolutionary middleclass looks like. Moon refused which explains a lot about the NAACP which might loom as some sort of revolutionary bugbear to Sen. Eastland and company but which is in reality as safely conservative as the typical American bourgeois. There was much discussion of this *Times* article in Havana (the Sunday *Times* sells for 90 cents down there) and I said to some Cuban intellectuals that the NAACP is so busy trying to make the promises of our two American revolutions (1776 and 1861) come true that they don't have time to take on the Cuban revolution. All of which is quite puzzling to many Cubans who are acquainted with the NAACP and the civil rights issue in the U.S. Many of the Negroes in my group that were invited to Cuba are members of the NAACP and the group as a whole reflected a variety of levels of political and social awareness. In the last analysis, however, it must be said that the Castro government is not so far wrong in its feelings about the American Negro even if it has made the error of assuming that all American Negroes think like the NAACP which the majority does not. The NAACP has some 350,000 members out of an estimated 16 to 20 million Negroes in America. Even though this great body of Negroes resides in the U.S. they are to be counted among the underprivileged colored peoples of the world. Try as the Negro might to become 100 percent qualified American with all the privileges and emoluments associated thereto, the pressures of world events (especially in Africa and Latin America) will more and more aggravate his already untenably marginal position in American society. This is already happening. Although it is not generally publicized, there is an increasing number of Negroes who are beginning to look towards Africa because they have despaired of any promise that the U.S. will ever solve its racial problems. As for Latin America, I have already mentioned the strong influences of African Negro cultural charac-teristics. A Cuban writer revealed to me in Havana that if it were not for the Afro-Cuban elements in island life, Cuba's present cultural renaissance would be pretty lacking in creative spirit. This was a white Cuban speaking and it says much for the American Negro in regards to the possibilities of a new phase of inter-American cultural relations involving those of African descent. In fact, my group in Cuba had several Negro writers among them, which already establishes the first beginnings of this cultural exchange program between American Negroes and Cubans. This is only natural, for the Negroes in the western hemisphere whether in the U.S. or Cuba or Brazil or Honduras all came originally from the same African source.

The two weeks I spent in Cuba were one of the most inspiring experiences I have ever had. Here I do not propose to speak for the other Negro writers in my group since the visit evoked different responses in each of us. Out of a group of fourteen there were four writers and one painter—all Negroes but with different points of view and social background. We had all been influenced to one degree or another by the picture of Cuba painted in the American press. But we found a Cuba that is being irrevocably transformed into an economically sovereign nation. I have no doubts that this signals further changes of the same sort all over Latin America and it is my strong opinion that we Americans will have to learn to live with these changes.

As an American Negro, I welcome what is happening in Cuba's economic, social and cultural spheres. I must morally and intellectually support Cuba's newly achieved sovereignty because I belong to a minority group in the U.S. which has never been sovereign within the community of American national groupings politically, economically or culturally. To meet the people of Cuba is to meet a nation embracing sovereignty with all the fervent enthusiasm of being released from bondage. Americans born into freedom from birth have never experienced what this means.

In Havana, my group was under the direct sponsorship of the Casa de las Americas (House of the Americas) which is, in effect, the cultural ministry of the Cuban government. In addition to directing the cultural life of new Cuba, Casa de las Americas also sponsors inter-cultural exchange between the sister countries of Latin America and the United States. We were met at the airport by representatives of Casa de las Americas and given our first taste of Cuban hospitality—a musical trio playing Latin music and a table stacked with exquisite daiquiris. Reporters and photographers were on hand for on-the-spot interviews, and the next day films of our arrival were shown on TV. In short, we were treated like visiting dignitaries.

From there we were sped into Havana in three taxis and put up in the Hotel Presidente, a privately managed establishment of the conservative family type. I describe this hotel only to reveal that free enterprise is much in evidence in Cuba. It is only the big tourist hotels which have been nationalized—the Havana Hilton (now Havana Libre), the Riviera, the Hotel St. John, and the ultra swank Hotel Nacional, the former resort of the international "400." It was told to us that American influence prevented Cuban Negroes from even working in the Hotel Nacional, not to speak of living there. Our group was honored with a dinner party at this hotel as guests of Srs. Enrique Bienavides and Rafael Gorostiza, both Cuban Negroes. Sr. Bienavides is now the manager of the nationalized Hotel St. John and Sr. Gorostiza is one of his associates in the Cuban Institute of Tourism.

The next day began a round of interviews with the under-secretaries of various government ministries which soon acquainted us with the actual reforms being carried out in the fields of education, labor, social welfare, agrarian reform, culture, savings and bonds, housing and tourism. These interviews revealed a social transformation that was astounding—and from the lips of those directly responsible for these achievements. The guides and translators assigned to us from Casa de las Americas informed us beforehand that we did not have to go on these interviews if we did not want to. We were at liberty to tour Havana on our own if we so desired. Casa de las Americas would not have it said that we were limited to guided tours. We chose to accept Casa's planned itinerary and thus were able to match official claims about Cuba's plans and progress with the ordinary citizen's estimate of conditions. We found that the man on the street was even more vocal and enthusiastic about the achievements of the Cuban revolution than were the officials. The officials are sober in their optimism, matter-of-fact in stating the problems, intensely aware and preoccupied with the immense scope of their work. These Cuban leaders are social pioneers of the first order for they are social engineers who have unleashed a dam of human energy that has been pent up for generations and they are channelling this energy into constructive projects which would amaze any American. Each ministry is alive with hundreds of clerical workers, aides, militiamen, orderlies and civilians seeking information, assistance and guidance.

The charts, graphs, diagrams and statistics cited by leaders spoke volumes of Cuban sociological data, but this was better conveyed to us by Cubans—taxi-drivers, hotel workers, street-cleaners, waiters, tavern-keepers, bus-drivers, etc., whose leading question was "Ah, an American. Say, how do you like our revolution?" In this manner our first few days in Havana acquainted us with the general outlines of Cuba's New Deal and we were wonder-struck. To attempt to report on each ministry is impractical. Statistics make for dry reading, which is why our interview with the Minister of Social Welfare, a young woman, Dr. Raquel Perez de Miret, I found most enlightening because this ministry has to do with the basic human imperatives of the Cuban revolution.

The revolutionary government inherited all the social evils compounded by a history of national growth stunted by economic imperialism. There are those who are sound in mind and body who can make revolutions and administer reforms, but there are untold numbers who must be rehabilitated before they can participate in and share the benefits. This, briefly, is the province of Social Welfare—a program of indeterminate scope which overlaps the boundaries of more clear-cut divisions of administration. Dr. Perez de Miret spoke to us about old people, beggars, prostitutes, criminals, addicts, orphans, disease, total illiteracy, ignorance of basic facts of health and bodily care, victims of chronic unemployment, the mentally ill, children who have never worn clothes, unmarried mothers, individuals who do not understand the concept of cooperative enterprise, and a host of other human defects which the reforms must now ameliorate.

The revolutionary government of Cuba has declared war on human degradation of all kinds. There are no beggars to be seen in Havana today. They have all been gathered up and are now engaged in building a beggars' township in a coast town with the materials all supplied by the government. Prostitution and vice once rampant in Havana's tourism have been eradicated in public places. The homes of some of Batista's henchmen have been handed over to young girls 10 to 14 years old whose mothers were prostitutes and deserted them. We visited one of these homes in Havana's suburbs. Dr. Perez de Miret reminded us that the problem of social welfare in Cuba is immense, but that in the process of rehabilitating people, the main objective is the dignity of the individual. Thus it is a government policy that nothing done on a person's behalf must leave the impression that the person is being given something for nothing out of pity or humanitarianism. The recipient must pay for this help either by work, self-help or cooperative efforts with others.

But all of this was but a preparation for the greatest of our revelations about the scope and meaning of Cuba's revolution. It soon became clear to us that we had been invited to Cuba to participate in the first celebration of the 26th of July movement in the Sierra Maestre mountains of Oriente. This celebration turned out to be an event of epic proportions which we were not in the least prepared for.

On the evening of July 25, my group was transported to the Havana railroad station dressed for an occasion which was to be "very rough." This was an understatement. [. . .] At the station in Havana the celebration had already begun although Sierra Maestre was some 600 miles away. Cubans of every class and youth delegations from all Latin America were crowding into the station dressed in straw hats, boots; carrying knapsacks and canteens, satchels and bags. There was singing of revolutionary songs and slogans, dancing and cheering. A long train was backed up into the station to receive another load of celebrants headed for Sierra. The watchword was "To Sierra with Fidel, 26 July." We learned that for four days, over a million Cubans and other Latin Americans had been moving to Oriente Province by every conceivable means. We found ourselves caught up in a veritable ground-swell of revolutionary zeal. We had begun to feel the real pulse of Cuba.

Later my group was placed on a special three coach, air-cooled, diesel-drawn train—the most modern in the Cuban railroad system. This special coach was at the disposal of the international press on hand to report on the Sierra Maestre celebration, Latin American youth delegates from other countries, visiting dignitaries, and special visitors from Europe and the United States. Francoise Sagan, the youthful authoress *(Bonjour Tristesse)* was with us. Simone de Beauvoir was reported on the way but, for some reason, didn't arrive.

Once seated on the train we were given two boxes of lunch contributed by El Jardin Dulceria-Cafeteria-Lunch and Buffet, Havana. The international composition of the passengers on my train intrigued me. All the moreso since I realized that my group was the de facto American delegation to Cuba's first celebration in what has now become a national shrine—the mountain fastness of Sierra Maestre where the revolution was born. On the train I met a Negro friend who had just returned from Africa and another friend from New York who had gone to live in Mexico some six years ago. It was all like something out of an international adventure story to meet these friends under such circumstances.

We soon found ourselves singing songs now dear to the hearts of millions of Latin American youths. As we waited for the train to leave, the Cuban Revolution was being discussed by the young intellectuals from other countries. We learned that many of the young delegates were prevented by their governments from reaching Havana. Many were held up at airports, ships and borders. A tense struggle is going on in Latin America between the pro- and anti-Castro adherents.

At 9:00 P.M., Sunday, July 25, our train pulled out of the Havana station for the long haul across central Cuba. At 10:20 we pulled into the station at the city of Matanzas. A crowd of several hundred had gathered at the tracks to greet the trains as they passed through on the way to Sierra. There is only one central railroad line in Cuba, and this railroad was in the public eye all through the four days of travel preceding July 26. Every town, hamlet and whistle stop on the central railroad turned out to greet us with an electrifying display of welcoming cheers, singing, dancing and all manner of celebration. I fell in love with Cuba, as I began to comprehend the scope of this national pilgrimage to Sierra—Cuba's Valley Forge.

One can get the scope of this celebration only by imagining about one-sixth of our U.S. population (about 30 million people) moving across the country to celebrate George Washington's army's heroic suffering at Valley Forge. The press estimates that over a million Cubans took part in this celebration one way or another. These figures have been played down in the American press, which is really unimportant to quibble about. The real pity of it all is that so few Americans were on hand to witness this unprecedented event.

After a long night of sleepless revelry, speeding across Cuba, we watched the dawn open up over the Cuban landscape on the morning of the 26th. It was clear why Columbus called this rich island the "Pearl of the Antilles" four hundred and sixty years ago. But seeing the evidences of natural wealth and the extent of rural poverty from the train window, I realized that this was natural wealth—the birthright of peasants and laborers held in escrow by a long dynasty of self-perpetuating profiteers. Finally we arrived at the last stop just this side of the foothills of the Sierra mountain range. This is a country town named Yara.

We stepped out of the air-cooled coach into the hot late morning sun onto the soft earth which seemed almost too fertile to despoil with railroad tracks. Before us stood Yara, spread out toward the green hinterland, with dirt streets, palm-thatched huts (bohios) with dirt floors and open-square apertures for windows. There was not a single evidence of a window pane anywhere but on the trains that brought us and not a single artifact of modern living in sight outside the sleek, modern diesel that had hauled us swaying and flying across Cuba. Here was primitive rural poverty whose only saving grace was the promise of reforms already in motion. Here was Cuba's "Tobacco Road" or, better, "Sugar Road," for these peasants, impoverished as they were with their stark naked children and bare feet, were not shackled with the poison of racism endemic to America's "Tobacco Roads." Here the democracy of poverty was shared by white, black and brown. Here was a meeting of far-flung worlds converged in the semi-tropic rendezvous of Yara, in Oriente Province. Here Cuban campesinos (peasants) met Americans, Europeans and Habaneros whose only knowledge of country life in Cuba came from what they read.

Cameras clicked all over the scene and movies were taken of peasants to whom the name of Francoise Sagan of the Left Bank of Paris meant nothing at all. But to whom the name of Fidel Castro was a reincarnation of Jesus Christ. This was probably the biggest event in Yara's long history since the year 1868. It was on a plantation in Yara in that year that a group of patriots declared independence from Spain. It was from Yara that a ten-year siege of guerrilla warfare was launched under the leadership of General Maximo Gomez, a mestizo, Antonio Maceo, a mulatto, and Carlos Manuel de Cespedes, a white Cuban. These men led an army of mixed bloods and Negro soldiers who eventually freed the slaves in the eastern half of Cuba. This historical fact accounts today for the predominance of Negroes in politics and social life in Cuba's Oriente. In 1875 a truce, the "Peace of Zanjon," won concessions from Spain, but an outlawed rebel army under General Calixto Garcia remained in hiding in Sierra, just as Fidel Castro did in our times. Not trusting the promises of Spain concerning agrarian reform, Maceo and Gomez went into exile.

At Yara, the delegates and the press and photographers were loaded into open-topped railroad boxcars—obviously used to haul sugarcane—and taken closer towards the mountains. There we were transferred into trucks which joined a vast multitude going up a mountain road towards Las Mercedes, in the mountain fastness of Sierra. It seemed that all Cuba had come to the mountains. A long line of trucks crawled slowly up the mountain road, bumper to bumper, while another line of vehicles was returning. The road twisted up and down, around curves, across army-built bridges, through mountain streams and passages too narrow for double traffic. The trucks jerked forward, bumping, jarring, stalling as the pitiless Cuban sun beat down on us at midday. On both sides of the road, Cubans had pitched make-shift bivouacs, set up water points, fruit vendors. People were sitting, sleeping, eating, bathing in streams, trudging on foot, bicycle or riding horses.

The army was ubiquitous controlling traffic. In the distance we could see huge banners hailing Fidel Castro and the revolution attached to the peaks of the hills. How these signs were ever fixed to these almost inaccessible heights, God only knows. [. . .] This was a moment in Cuban history that it is doubtful will ever be repeated again in this scope and pitch. [. . .] In 1959, it was the Cuban *campesinos* who were brought to Havana. In 1960 Havana went to the mountains.

Finally we reached Las Mercedes, our destination, a relatively level height where a school-city is being built bearing the name of one of the late heroes of the revolution, Camilo Cienfuegos. Countless tens of thousands had already arrived on the scene. Every walk of Cuban life was represented here—farmers, cane-cutters, labor unions, the army, children's groups in uniforms, women's groups with banners and flags. Fidel Castro was already present, occupying a newly built speaking rostrum surrounded by his leaders of government— President Dorticos and others together with several heroes of the 26th of July movement. We, the American delegation, were given passes to seats on the platform directly behind Fidel Castro and his entourage. Castro turned and personally greeted each of us as we passed to our seats. By now there were twelve of us since two had succumbed from sheer physical exhaustion during the trip by truck from the railroad cars into the mountains. [. . .] One young woman collapsed after we had reached Las Mercedes. She was put under the care of the Cuban army medics as were many other victims of sunstroke and exhaustion during the celebration.

We sat on the platform through a stirring demonstration of oratory and parades which was transmitted all over Cuba by television. I studied the faces of Cuba's leaders, many with the long hair and beards, now a symbol of participation in the overthrow of Batista. Fidel Castro spoke for an hour and a half with a hoarse throat to the rising crescendo of acclaim from thousands upon thousands spread out before him on the terrain of this mountain plain. Helicopters circled constantly overhead while cameras of every size and description clicked a pictorial record of this historic event.

I could not understand every line Castro spoke at Sierra but my Spanish was adequate enough to feel its eloquence and my senses aware enough to see that Fidel Castro is being deified by the Cuban people. Whether this is good or bad only the future will tell, but it is the will of the Cuban people as of now. For a brief ten minutes or so it rained on Fidel Castro and his cheering multitude. Immediately a raincoat was thrown over his shoulders, but he never stopped speaking. In extemporaneous oratory, I do not think Fidel Castro has many superiors today. No doubt his background as a lawyer skilled in argumentation accounts for this. He is able to prepare his listeners for the dramatic persuasion of his main propositions by the skillful use of deductive ideas with words understood by peasants. And the peasantry, en masse, beat the air above them with their wide straw hats and the mountains of Sierra echoed with the clamor of wild acclaim.

When Castro finished his speech, he was hustled off the platform surrounded by a solid phalanx of peasant soldiers who bristled with protective authority. These soldiers had the looks of men who would have died on the spot to protect their leader. Castro passed within two feet of me and I looked into the face of the hero. It was strangely sober as if with the melancholy of responsibilities. Minutes before his face shone as he stood in the spotlight of personal acclaim from those who danced in the sunlight of liberation. But when he turned away [his face] bore the heavy shadows of statesmanship. This was startling. For that fleeting moment, I must confess that I felt a pang of apprehension mixed with compassion for Fidel Castro, the compassion one feels for those who carry heavy burdens. I wondered what he was thinking at that moment as he turned away from his people, from the warmth of personal communion with them to face the hard, impersonal realities of his place in history and world politics.

That night in Sierra, the National Theater of Cuba staged a cultural program—two cantatas, "Cantata Por la Paz" and "Cantata a de Santiago," and a ballet, "El Milagro de Anaquille," based on Negro dance-forms. "Cantata a de Santiago" was written in New York in 1958 by Myriam Acevedo and revised by Pablo Armando Fernandez, two Cuban poets and leading figures in the new cultural movement in Havana. [. . .] Some 600 performers were flown from Havana to perform under the stars, before a peasant audience which had never witnessed such a thing. Before the performance there had been a grand display of varicolored fireworks.

After the performance the celebration was over. We slept on the ground that night and the harshness of Sierra became a rugged physical reality. There was no water to be had and little food. Complaints became numerous now, for the glamour and adventure of the Sierra event had grown thin and the physical ordeal involved in getting there began to tell on us. The next morning we pulled our tired bodies up and began the journey back to Yara and thence to Havana.

The mountain road was again choked up with vehicular congestion and foot-sore marchers trudging back toward the different cities and towns of Cuba from whence they came to hear and see Fidel Castro. The departure from Las Mercedes was like a disorganized evacuation. Hunger and thirst had lowered our morale and the sun beat down on us with more intense cruelty. To stand upright in the densely packed truck under such conditions took our last reserves of fortitude. We later boarded our train that waited in Yara, a dirty, sweaty, hungry, thirsty, worn-out delegation of Americans.

We were a little ashamed of ourselves when we were comfortably back on our train. Ashamed that we had complained so much about conditions in the mountains. But deep within ourselves, we knew that we had had a rare experience. As the train pulled out from Yara the true dimensions of Cuba's revolution formed in our minds through our afterthoughts about Sierra.

Back in Havana, we resumed our round of interviews and meetings with Cuban leaders. The celebration at Sierra Maestre had served to bring us more into key with Cuban aspirations. We had seen the face of Cuba—the beauty of its Afro-Indian-Spanish contours. We could now seek out more facts because we were in closer rapport. There was no need to feel self-conscious about being Americans. All Cubans took great pains to explain "We are not against the American people. We are against the American government's foreign policy towards our revolution."

This is basically true about Cuban attitudes for it is against Cuban interests to hate the American people. Cubans want Americans to come to Cuba to understand what they are trying to achieve. I pondered continuously on the international implications of Cuba today. To smear the Cuban revolution with the charge of "communism" is to do the Western Hemisphere a great disservice. There is nothing communistic about Cuba but the Cuban Communist Party which is permitted the right to function aboveground. But the Cuban revolution is, in reality, a middle-class-led revolution against foreign economic control. The leaders of this revolution had to carry out agrarian reforms in order to win the support of the numerically dominant class—the peasant.

Land reform in Cuba cannot help but run into conflict with American financial interests. Nationalization of foreign-owned industries was a necessity in face of economic realities. It is too late in history for a Cuban bourgeoisie to establish itself along the lines of classic capitalistic enterprise. History demands that a nation's resources be put at the service of the masses. In this sense, the Cuban revolution is a new kind of revolution, unique in world history. [It] does not aid or abet Communism in the western hemisphere. On the contrary, the Cuban revolution actually proves that Communism, as an international philosophy in politics, is obsolete and superfluous. The Cuban revolution is an un-Marxian revolution and was carried out by non-Marxists. A Marxist revolution is not intended to make individual landowners out of landless peasants as the Cuban reforms have done. Moscow, I am sure, understands this perfectly. The realities of the Cuban revolution are more of a threat to Russia's Communist philosophy than [. . .] to the American way of life—which is why Moscow leaped into the fray to "defend" Cuba.

Consider Moscow's actions and the pronouncements of the Cuban Communist Party in its recent Havana convention. The Cuban Communists demanded by resolution that Cuba be now transformed into a "socialist" nation—which means the Cuban revolution did not go far enough to suit the Marxists. To Communists, "socialism" means collectivization of all agriculture and the complete eradication of private enterprise. This is not what the Cuban revolution has done. [. . .] Moscow must seek to influence [Cuba], for the Cuban experience puts the spotlight of critical attention on many of Russia's internal economic and social practices.

If American foreign policy was directed by truly sophisticated individuals, this fact would be understood and Cuba would not have been driven into the Communist trade camp. But in America, those who scream "Communism" the loudest actually know or understand the least about Communist theory and practice. As a result, one must walk about the beautiful city of Havana today and regret that the relations between Cuba and the U.S. are charged with conflict and misunderstanding.

My last night in Havana was spent with Calvert Casey, drama critic of *Revolución,* the newspaper of Castro's 26th of July movement. We walked about the section of Old Havana where there are churches, monasteries, homes and hotels dating back to the sixteenth century. On a warm night, history hangs over the old Spanish architecture of the city like a romantic shroud. Not even the revolutionary spirit felt in Havana seems to have disturbed the tranquil repose of traditions. Here are churches so old that bushes grow in the crevices of ledges high above cobbled streets. Here are streets so narrow that it is a marvel that modern buses can pass through them. Yet they do and it is possible for a passenger to literally step from a bus into his doorway with two strides.

I sat in a bar with Casey this last night in Havana and the journalist talked about the future of Cuba's revolution in a setting that was the actuality of Havana's past, preserved in all its faithfulness. I could hear the gulf-waves crashing against the sea-wall a hundred or so yards away. In my imagination, I conjured up a vision of men from old Spanish galleons stepping ashore and unknowingly shaping a course of historical events leading to the emergence of Fidel Castro. The New World was born in a terrible agony of plunder, murder, slavery, adventure, war, lust and glory. Three races of mankind [. . .] have paid a price for the making of this New World that is so exorbitant and cruel that history must make amends. The "Pearl of the Antilles" [. . .] is just now ready to make good on its promise of the good life to those men whom fate cast willy-nilly on its shores. If this promise is negated then civilization in the western hemisphere will become a hoax against history and a fraud in the annals of mankind.

I left Havana the next morning. At nine-thirty my plane passed over the city and headed north over the Gulf. It is not easy to take leave of a city like Havana. I had heard for years that it was a gay city, full of color and hospitality. This was probably true but I found another dimension never described in the travelogues. Havana is beautiful, it is hospitable, but today its gaiety is a revolutionary coming of age—the maturity of true nationhood. As it passed under me out of sight I wished it well.

CHAPTER THREE

Race and Bohemianism in Greenwich Village

(*The Crisis,* January 1960)

The summer of 1959 in Greenwich Village, New York City, came as usual to a feverish close in late September. Soon the chilly drafts would rustle through the jigsaw puzzle of Village streets and there would be an end to the art shows, the grand promenading in Washington Square Park, and the jam of week-end tourists seeking thrills. Actually, most local residents, unless engaged in tourist-catering businesses, were glad the summer was over. For if there is anyone a Villager detests more than landlords and high rents, he is the tourist. Villagers have a provincial, chauvinist attitude toward their community, which seems anomalous in cosmopolitan New York. But this is the result of a long history of inbred community pride. This is why its citizens welcome the end of summer, for they can again have the Village to themselves.

But when the summer of 1959 ended, Villagers were left with an awareness of a problem which they had either ignored or minimized. This was the problem of Village race relations.

Although I had been living in the Village for more than five years, the racial situation did not become tense until circa 1955. What started it was the influx of members of the "New Bohemia." And much to the surprise of old-time Villagers was the influx of many Negroes from Harlem, who were only twenty minutes and a subway fare from the heart of the Village. There were also many young Jews from the Bronx, Brooklyn, and the lower East Side. These young people were fleeing their ghettos both geographically and psychologically. Culturally, the Negro's contribution was both "racial" and linguistic. Post-war Bohemia became known as the "beat generation," whose lingo was made up of choice phrases and words originally coined by Harlem "hipsters" (people in the know). Although most Villagers did not know the origin of "beat" (which was Harlemese for "exhausted" or "broke"), and cared less, they quickly identified "beat" with those manifestations of Village life which met with their disapproval.

VILLAGE MIGRANTS

The new Bohemians, who often centered their lives around the coffee shops, went in for ornamental fads and odd dress. Some even went bare-footed; others dressed in capes and sandals; and some of the Negroes went in for earrings, in one lobe, and exotic African neck jewelry. The lure of Village bohemianism and unconventionality spread throughout the country to attract smalltown rebels from Arkansas, rural Southerners from Tennessee and Mississippi, Protestant truants from middleclass families in Michigan and Wisconsin, the sons and daughters of orthodox Jews from the Bronx and elsewhere, and workingclass people from Manhattan's Harlem. The "New Bohemia," therefore, soon approximated America's mythical "melting pot." But it was the Negro ingredient in the pot that soon put the Village's traditional racial liberalism to the test.

The Village has always prided itself on being a leader in American liberal traditions in art, science, literature, and the theater. But there is another side to Village life—the sordid and the disreputable. There are clip joints, "kibbets," gangsterism, and the dope traffic; there are also "queers," "dikes," and vagrants. There is likewise the "free-love" legend which many Villagers claim is really a fiction created for publicity purposes. Although the Village attitude toward bizarre behavior is summed up in the phrase *Each to his own,* it soon became evident that the increase in interracial sex was pricking the hidden nerves of prejudice.

As I frequented the many Village hangouts, I soon became aware of a quiet, brooding tension under the surface. Interracial sex, one cause which had all the flavor of a fad, was in full bloom in the summer of '59 in Washington Square Park. Many white girls, it seems, thought it *chic* to date Negro men. They wanted the thrill, *Boule-Miche* style, as in Paris, of a Negro lover before returning to the conventional parental hearth. Negro girls likewise became a new adventure for many white men. There were even some white girls who specialized in Chinese men. Such amorous activities across racial lines were regarded as rebellion against conventional middleclass habits.

NEGROES IN VILLAGE

This aspect of the "New Bohemia" made even the old-timers sit up and take notice. The earlier Village *habitués,* those of the time of O'Neill and Floyd Dell and Edna St. Vincent Millay, though rebels in both art and life, were more or less conventional in their racial attitudes and practices. Histories of the Village seldom mention Negroes as playing a conspicuous role in the bohemian and art life of the community. Claude McKay was probably the best known Negro writer in the Village life of the early twenties. It must be emphasized that there is a sharp distinction between Village family life and Village bohemian society. The solid citizens, many of whom are Irish and Italian, have strong family ties and are anti-bohemian and much of their anti-Negro feeling is really anti-bohemianism, since an increasing number of Negroes are identified with the Beatniks. But in the old days, New York's version of Paris' Left Bank, since it contained few Negro artists, really had no racial problem.

In the old days Negroes were concentrated around MacDougal, Bleecker, and Minetta Streets. It was harassment by the whites that started the trek to Fifty-Third Street, San Juan Hill, the upper Nineties west of Central Park, and finally to Harlem. Much of the story may be found in, I believe it is called, *The Autobiography of a Cop,* the experiences of a policeman who pounded his Village beat from 1912 to 1920.

The Negro trek south, however, did not strike old Villagers as the return of the native. It was regarded by many as an unwarranted invasion. Many Village Negroes, like myself, feared an increase in racial tension, and possibly open clashes between whites and Negroes. As early as the '40's there had been "hoodlum" attacks on racially mixed groups. Old-timers usually protested against them, and the liberals asserted the right of a man to pick his associates.

RECENT NEGRO INFLUX

I was sitting one evening in a coffee shop called Pandora's Box. One can sit in such *bistros* for hours over a good cup of coffee listening to good music, playing chess, reading books, flirting with the girls, or just conversing. On this occasion, a white acquaintance of mine—a man with a broad knowledge of Village life— sat at my table and drew me out of my book. After a short exchange of views on the latest Village "trends," he blurted out the question I had been expecting:

"Tell me, Cruse, why are so many Negroes coming to Greenwich Village?"

I looked at him for a moment while I searched for an answer. It was a question which I had sensed on the tip of many a Village tongue, in the quizzical glance of many a Village pedestrian. But I was nonplussed because the question was now verbalized—and it had come from an authentic Village bohemian. I tentatively countered with:

"Why do you ask?"

"Ohoh . . . eh . . . because never in all my years down here have I seen so many Negroes. Tell me, is there an organized Harlem movement directing Negroes to come down here to test out the Village's racial attitudes?"

"Well, I seriously doubt that. Negroes, like everybody else, are influenced by their environment and the trends of the times and some of them are coming here for new experiences. Remember that Negroes are as diversified as the whites. Many of them, like the white kids, are fed up with conventional pre-war ideas. Americanism to them means insipid conformism . . ."

My acquaintance raised his eyebrows. "Tony," that is what I shall call him, is well-known in Village circles. He has an ascetic, Christ-like appearance—long, mixed-grey, flowing hair and beard; pale blue, sympathetic eyes. His uncut hair and beard are his badges of nonconformity and he represents the waning tradition of old bohemia. "Tony" makes his living by selling esoteric magazines on art and literature, wit and humor, the theater, etc., published in New York, Paris, and London. These he sells mainly to tourists and he calls it "disseminating culture to those poor Americans who are so unfortunate that they do not live in Greenwich Village." I never learned where "Tony" lived or whether he even had a permanent address (many bohemians didn't). Actually, "Tony" was a period piece in a gallery of Village "characters" of bygone days.

"I guess you're right about Negroes," he said. "When I think back to the twenties I remember that we Village bohemians used to visit up in Harlem because it was then a fashionable thing to do. And there were also Negro bohemians up there."

"Oh, yes, yes," I replied. "What you call 'Negro bohemia' was then called the 'Harlem Renaissance.'"

"Yes, yes," said "Tony." "I remember that Carl Van Vechten used to say that."

PRESENT-DAY REBELS

What is new in the Village is that present-day white rebels have taken over much of the psychology and the outlook of the Harlem "hipster." The Negro bohemian rebels against convention mainly because of prejudice and racial discrimination; the whites, because of what they regard as the spiritual impoverishment of American society. This is probably why the new Village bohemian seldom draws the color line. It is the interracialism of these two groups that has aroused the resentment of many Villagers and conventional people.

I once tried to get a Village newspaper to carry a series of articles on the history of the Negro in Greenwich Village. I had shown that Negroes had been in the Village ever since it was the "bouwerie" and a part of Nieuw Amsterdam. I showed that several Negroes even had owned large tracts of Village land. But the editor was cool to my articles and did not publish them. [The] purpose of my articles was to educate Villagers to the fact that Negroes had always been an integral part of Village life, and that newcomers were not setting a precedent by moving into what many local citizens regarded as a "lily-white" community. Village racial tension continued to mount, since people lacked the facts; but it did not flare into violence until the summer of '59 when *The New York Times* startled New Yorkers with its headline: "Village Tension Upsets Residents . . . Racial Enmity a Cause."

When the Village editor who had rejected my articles appeared on a radio panel to discuss Village racial tensions, he opined, among other things, that the Negroes had incited attack by the bold flaunting of their white sweethearts. This, he said, offended many Villagers who objected to white-woman-Negro-man relationships. Although there was some truth in what he said, it was far from being the whole story. Yet his reaction to interracial sex, despite his liberalism, is typical of that of many local residents, including some bohemians, although interracialism is usually accepted or rejected in the Village on a class basis. Despite the social interracialism, there is still much racialism in housing.

The *Times* also pointed out that Village tension had its anti-Semitic as well as its anti-Negro tinge. Hoodlum elements were reported as being opposed to the influx of "A-trainers" and their "Bronx bagel babies." The Negroes were called *A-trainers* because they rode the Independent Subway "A" train into the

Village; the girls, "bagel babies" in reference to a type of doughnut favored by Jews. The inference was that all white girls seen with Negro males were Jews, which is, of course, not true. Yet the *Times* made no reference to another Village practice—the increasing number of Negro girls being dated by white men. But the accent on the Negro-man-white-woman angle is strongly reminiscent of Deep South attitudes toward interracial sex.

Village attitudes toward Negroes, therefore, get tied in with conservative attitudes toward the "beat generation," bohemianism, anti-Semitism, and interracial sex. Members of the "beat generation" are for the most part youthful escapists seeking refuge in "art," jazz, poetry, esoteric literature, Zen Buddhism, and marijuana. To them the Negro is both a culture bearer and a guilt symbol.

Yet with all of its troubles, the Village has less racial tension than other parts of New York despite its diversity of peoples. And the causes of some of this tension, which I have tried to point out in this article, are really not racial at all.

CHAPTER FOUR

James Baldwin, the Theater and His Critics

(Unpublished, 1963)

The appearance of Blues for Mr. Charlie *in 1963 marked the critical turning point in Baldwin's career. In its wake, he was canonized as a "Negro spokesperson" in the midst of the ascendant civil rights movement and simultaneously criticized for allowing politics to get in the way of aesthetic concerns. In creating the work, Baldwin was actually addressing Cruse's earlier concern that the Negro theater involve itself with themes important to and drawn from Negro life. Yet Cruse found the work deeply troubling and, ultimately, an indictment of the liberal establishment's influence over Negro writers. Baldwin found himself criticized by liberals for writing a play they deemed too acerbic and by Cruse for a play that seemed too ingratiatory. These aesthetic concerns would again come to the fore in the latter part of the decade when Cruse became a sort of intellectual godfather to the burgeoning Black Arts movement based in Harlem and Newark, New Jersey.*

The reaction of the New York critics to James Baldwin's recent excursion into the theater pointed up some interesting aspects of the race question and revived the old "art vs. politics" controversy of the 1920s. These aspects relate, of course, to the American racial fundamentals, which gave rise to Mr. Baldwin and ultimately, his play, but these fundamentals were only flashed into view like a dark and obscure valley by a lightning bolt. Nothing was very much illuminated, and after the clash of critical thunder subsided, most everyone was left still groping in the dark. (No racial pun intended.) Thus it is worth taking another look at the discordant chorus of reaction to Baldwin, regardless of the fate of *Blues for Mr. Charlie,* which seems headed for an early closing.

Those who praise the play took it at its face value, which, as a work of art, is considerable. On this level, Baldwin's familiar views on the "race problem" become secondary and redundant. But for the negative critics, it was Baldwin the racial spokesman, now broadcasting from the stage that became the main point of attack. The truth of the matter is that this is precisely where the fault does lie because far too many people have been listening too closely to what Baldwin has been saying all along. Within the frame of superficial social insights, Baldwin's literary skills have seduced many people to accept as profound a message that was, from the first, rather thin, confused and impressionistic.

Baldwin has protested all along that he did not want to be classified as a "Negro writer." While *Mr. Charlie* was being written, Baldwin announced that he was not writing a "Negro play." And some liberal critics upheld him in this notion. Nonetheless, in the New York *Herald Tribune* of April 19, he altered this a bit to say he wrote the play for Negroes and whites: "It has a message for both."

In this instance, Baldwin's aims are plausible. But behind all this lies an intellectual confusion concerning the Negro's group status and group goals in America, which is the current affliction of more Negroes than just Baldwin. As long as he remained an essayist, novelist and spokesman, Baldwin's confusion and contradictions were less apparent. But the theater is an American institution, which does not truly recognize the Negro as an essential human and aesthetic element in its population. Its values are so thoroughly white Anglo-Saxon and Jewish, socially, aesthetically and class-wise, that the theater is not at all representative of the American ethnic variety. Thus, the arrival of a play about Negroes (whatever Baldwin may choose to call it) that is provocative and cannot possibly be discussed without referring to America's most pressing problem. In Baldwin's case, this is all the more so because the white liberal community has elevated Baldwin to the rank of major spokesman. Having done so, many white liberals are now disenchanted with their favorite child.

This was highlighted a few months ago when Baldwin was encircled and set upon by a coterie from the environs of *Commentary*. (This fracas took place in the "Liberalism and the Negro" issue of *Commentary*, March 1964.) Until then, Baldwin had been seen as essayist, novelist, plus spokesman. This roundtable discussion dealt with Baldwin as spokesman and critic of white liberalism, not as a writer as such. The *Commentary* group gave Baldwin a rough going for having the ungrateful temerity to be critical of white liberalism. Remembering that it was they who first acclaimed him uncritically as Negro spokesman, they now admonished, "Well, Jimmy, who else are you going to fall back on, conservatives?" But they did not seriously question Baldwin as spokesman. They were merely defending themselves. If they had been as truly critical of him in that role as some of the critics were of *Mr. Charlie,* it could have cleared the way to explore what was wrong with liberalism in general.

The race problem creates the Baldwins of America (writers or no). White liberals have gotten themselves into a sack by having sold the Baldwins a phony bill of goods about caste, class and race in America. The trouble with the Baldwins is that they all believed it and now blame the liberals because this bill of goods is hardly ever negotiable in real life. As a result, in times of crisis the liberal panaceas fail. Race relations deteriorate steadily and both the liberals and the Baldwins get frightened and panicky.

In the dramatic arts, the viewer relates to an experiential vision of real life. If there are flaws in the dramatist's vision (or in Baldwin's case, spokesmanship too), the eyes and ears will be able to detect them far more readily than in the essay or even a novel where the readers' intellectual processes are more easily beguiled by those of the author. Thus it is that the drama has revealed Baldwin's faults as a racial spokesman, despite his impassioned use of the form.

As a dramatist, Baldwin has entered a field dear to many of us Negroes as avocation, profession, medium of protest. Beyond question, the problem that arises out of Baldwin's play has its roots in the unexplored problem of the Negro artist in American culture. Baldwin, in his readiness to be race spokesman, obscures this fact and lets himself be trapped by the pundits who understand political and philosophical polemics much better than he. As a Negro artist, Baldwin could defend himself by contrasting his own role, in this instance, with that of the white artist in America, especially on Broadway. The white artist also has his problems in American culture, but the problem of "art vs. politics" is all the more burdensome for the Negro artist because it derives from the special and unique position of the Negro in American culture. What must the Negro artist be? Must he be a "pure" artist, above caste, class and race, or a spokesman who uses his craft as a medium of protest?

Many voices in the intellectual community tell the Negro artist to be "above race" but then refuse to accept him seriously if he is not a spokesman or refuse him precisely because he is one. If the artist in white skin has a problem in relating his creative impulses to American realities, he still has the option of either escaping or obscuring reality (and very often being paid handsomely to do so). But Negro artists are simply not needed in this role. A Negro artist who assumes the role of spokesman also faces many risks to his own art if he lasts long enough. These include a slovenly abuse of form in the interests of message. And even the message itself can get garbled after a while. This is the current plight of James Baldwin. The significance of his message has begun to pale in inverse ratio to the increase of his polemical passion.

In the six major New York dailies, the critics were about equally divided on the merits and demerits of Baldwin's play. It is notable that the most "liberal" of them all—the *New York Post*'s Richard Watts—was the least excited about *Mr. Charlie*. The most negative reviews were McClain and Charman of the *Journal-American* and the *Daily News* respectively. But neither was as unfavorable nor as revealing as the *Village Voice*'s Michael Smith. The *World-Telegram*'s review can be discounted because Leonard Harris reacted as if he was supposed to be positive because he was reviewing James Baldwin. The *New York Times* and *Herald-Tribune* went overboard with praise, limited only by reservations about Baldwin's lack of good form.

Michael Smith wrote that Baldwin's Blues is not Mr. Charlie's, but his own. He intimated that it is unfortunate that James Baldwin has become a spokesman for the American Negro, and even worse that he has written a bad play to compound the first mistake. But was the play bad because Baldwin's spokesmanship got in the way of art? No, says Smith; it is Baldwin's spokesmanship that is questionable. Thus, the play does not "enable us to distinguish the features of our distress more clearly." Richard Watts tended to agree: "Baldwin is essentially a novelist, even more a polemicist, and his narrative has moments of confusion and hysteria." Watts' and Smith's observations lead us to the heart of Baldwin's problem as spokesman. But is *Mr. Charlie* really a "summons to arms in this generation's burning cause" as Howard Taubman of the *Times* sees it?

This writer sees the play as a throwback to the social realism format of the 1930s. But no one in the play is summoned to arms except a white Southerner, Lyle Britten, whom the author takes great pains to characterize as a man more to be pitied than to be shot. One of Baldwin's problems is that he is so appalled by the fact that many whites have no guilty feelings about their racism. "Terrible things have happened to white people as a result of our (Negroes') history," he said to Norman Podhoretz during the *Commentary* discussion. No doubt,

Baldwin's treatment of Lyle Britten is an indication that he now knows collective guilt is a manifestation of some white liberals but it is certainly not typically American. And Britten is an ordinary Southern man. But why is Baldwin so noble and generous with this character? Why is one led to feel more pity for "Mr. Charlie" than for his victim? Who is the real protagonist of the drama— Mr. Charlie or young Henry, the victim? Why the totally incongruous way the young rebel Henry chose to die? The play seems really to be about a young man sacrificed, with extended and appropriate rituals, on the altar of racial fate, unwilling or unable to escape, while Mr. Charlie was merely carrying out the will of the gods. "This nigger has to die—it is written."

But young Henry did not die as he had lived, in reckless disregard for the mores and racial etiquette of Mississippi. He did not attempt to take Mr. Charlie along with him into eternity. The pattern of provocation which young Henry had previously established makes it unacceptable that this perceptive, wayward and rebellious individual could suddenly reverse his line of development and avow that he did not know what he was doing in Plaguetown, Mississippi, that he was, suddenly, unable to understand what had brought him and Lyle Britten at each other's throats.

All in all, young Henry's actions lead to the conclusion that the victim got exactly what he asked for. This sentiment is the crux of the drama, not the impassioned rhetoric of his girlfriend, Juanita, or his father, Meridian Henry. Yet it is precisely these monologues and sermons that lend eloquence to poor dramatic form, anti-realism and illogical characterization. Still, it is not acceptable to say that Reverend Meridian Henry's sermon, which hooked the audience with its moral eloquence, did any earthly justice to his dead son. "What a light, my Lord, is needed to conquer the mighty darkness. This darkness rules in us, and grows in black and white alike. I have turned my face against the darkness, I will not let it conquer me, even though it will, I know, one day destroy this body." In this rendering, murderer and victim alike are equally guilty in the sight of God. The large doses of eloquence in *Blues for Mr. Charlie* hardly conceal Baldwin's confusion and hysteria. Despite who Baldwin is and what he says, this play cannot stand on its own artistic merits. It is a question of Baldwin's spokesmanship after all. He said the play has a message for both Negroes and whites—what is that message?

The message of this play is one of racial doom in America if the cruel and ignominious end of young Henry is taken symbolically. It is a doom that nothing but religiously inspired pleas to the immanence of God can save us from. Failing the intervention of God's will to set men's hearts right (both black and white), then men in these times do not have the innate abilities to set a multiracial society on the path towards rational existence and reorganization. This is what Baldwin says and this is certainly no call to arms either of the shooting kind or of the intellectual kind. Like Martin Luther King, Baldwin does not believe in arms since he gave young Henry a pistol which he wouldn't let him use in self-defense. Baldwin sees no way out for the Negro in America, hence the unavoidable confusion in the presentation of social values and ideas that characterizes much of his work. This lack of clear vision also accounts for the Baldwin hysteria. But why is this a characteristic of Baldwin?

Blues belongs to the American cult of racial obscurantism bred by white liberalism itself. The black community certainly has conditioned the Baldwins in many ways, but since they cannot seek their fortunes, literary or otherwise, in this black community, they pursue that elsewhere. This is demanded by the American system. But who in the white world receives them but liberals (or leftists)? Even though the Baldwins may secretly suspect liberal motives, they still play the game the liberal way according to liberal etiquette. They do not practice self-censorship to the extent that left-wing radical Negro intellectuals do, but they know that it is the better part of valor to tell only half-truths about the Negro in America. They will attempt to make it appear that every other Negro conforms, or must conform or wants to conform to white liberal values about race. But it is only when the Baldwins themselves begin to have gnawing doubts about the efficacy of liberal panaceas that they really show their confusion. To break with the liberals leaves them without a leg to stand on— they have depended upon the liberals too long. Consequently, the race crisis becomes cause for hysteria, garbled messages and the polemics of racial confusion.

It is a mistake to believe that Baldwin hates liberals. This is a gross misreading of Baldwin. Richard Watts, for example, spoke of Mr. Baldwin's suspicion of white liberals. This is nothing more than a lovers' quarrel because Baldwin cannot do without the liberals. He is angry with them because they have deceived him, but he clearly does not hate them because his Southern liberal character, Parnell, is a man of honorable intent, one who deceives no one. Baldwin has so little if any resentment against Parnell that he stereotypes him out of all native resemblance to a real Mississippi liberal. Parnell is a Southern liberal as created by Baldwin for northern audiences and in order to simplify his own frantic problems of character, which are considerable.

In the South come good times and bad, progress or reaction, racist upswings or eras of racial goodwill—the Negro will always know exactly where he stands. Not so in the North. In the North, the liberals will hoodwink the Negro with promises about "full integration into the mainstream of American life," which means, in effect, assimilation into the culture whose dominant core group remains steadfastly white Anglo-Saxon and Protestant. These WASPs have never assimilated anyone but North Europeans. Ethnically, America has never been an open society and has never been a "melting pot" for the races. No amount of integrationist pressure and protests will ever make America an open society to such an extent that the communal or group life of the American Negro ceases to be the fundamental reality of Negro social experience. This is a fact, which the Baldwins cannot face. It is a result of a gross misreading of the meaning of the American experience further confounded by white liberal myths about social equality and the great American dream.

It is the reality of the segregated black community that worries the Baldwins wherever they may go—Paris, Istanbul or to cocktail parties of the liberal-creative intellectuals of New York. The persistence of the black community is the symbol of racial segregation and the origins of all the psychic hurts and repressions of those who can manage to escape the ghetto. For Baldwin, America will not be a fit place to live until his Harlem ghetto is eradicated through integration. Whether he really believes this or not, he must say it because this is what white liberalism has surmised as the ideal. The trick is that white liberals never meant to integrate all Negroes—only a handful of deserving ones.

If Baldwin could see through the liberals around *Commentary* and comprehend that these Jewish liberals don't believe in integration and assimilation for themselves and don't really need it to survive and live the good life in America, it might help him to clear up some of his confusions about race in America. He would understand that America is divided into three great communal groups: white Protestant, white Catholic and white Jewish. None really care too much about integrating and assimilation with the other. There exists no neutral group outside of these three subcultures for Negroes (or Indians, or Puerto Ricans) to integrate into, and the white Protestant group with whom the bulk of Negroes share the same religion maintain a centuries-old closed-door policy. As for the Catholics and Jews, even switching religions does not change the status quo ante. Thus, when the Baldwins break with the white liberals, there is only one place to go and that is back home. There the Baldwins will discover that it is the Negro's communal life that needs to be put in order, revamped and rehabilitated.

This, of course, refers especially to the northern Negro ghetto which Baldwin knows much better than he knows the Southern interracial realities. There is much in *Mr. Charlie* that is suggestive of an allegorical morality play. There is no argument here since the writer has the right to choose his own form.

But it is high time that Baldwin made up his mind whether or not he wants to be a "Negro writer."

He is confusing more issues than he is clarifying about Negroes with this sophomoric line. But here we are dealing not only with Baldwin's alienation from liberalism, but also his prior alienation from the black world, which is often revealed in his lack of true historical focus even on the black community which bred him. There is a striking discrepancy between what Baldwin writes and speaks about and what Baldwin investigates intellectually. For example, it was exasperating to read the interview with him in the *Herald-Tribune* and find him garbling Harlem theatrical and cultural history. Everything that Baldwin said was happening in Harlem (when he was growing up in the 1930's) actually happened in the 1920's and even earlier. It was in the 1920's that whites "discovered" Negro musicians, actors and dancers and Bill Robinson and Louis Armstrong were well known to whites long before Baldwin says they were. The Lafayette Players were organized around 1910, and that this pioneer Negro stock company existed after the 1920s is very doubtful. Baldwin is obviously confusing the Lafayette theater vaudeville shows that were popular in Harlem in the 1930's with a theater group whose popular heyday was during the years of World War I.

And even when speaking of the contemporary theater, Baldwin's off-the-cuff observations are much too superficial and thoughtless. "There is not a large Negro audience for Broadway plays," he says. This may be true, but Baldwin ought to give more reasons than the high cost of tickets. For a Negro writer who could go so far as to admit that he once despised Negroes, "possibly because they failed to produce [a] Rembrandt," as Baldwin did in *Notes of a Native Son,* one would expect a more substantial remark. The Negro audience *is* growing and it is a middle-class audience well known for its conspicuous consumption. What has Baldwin to say about this middle class—a very crucial and unexplored element in the interracial picture? What is the relationship of this class to the theater—a middle-class institution? It would be more relevant to investigate why the Negro has not produced an Ibsen rather than a Rembrandt.

Russia never produced a Rembrandt either, but they produced a Russian theater and some other things. Moreover, for Baldwin to add that he does not believe there is a Negro theater in the U.S. and that such a development would not, in his opinion, be worthwhile shows that he is out of touch with much of black thinking today. Many of us emphatically do not agree with that statement. The dismal plight of the Negro in theater today is precisely because we have no theater of our own. It is all a part of the integration hang-up and the liberal integrationist legacy as reflected in Baldwin.

We can agree, on the other hand, with Baldwin's sentiment that the Broadway theater is a desert. His contribution is, by contrast, often forceful and impassioned. The white writers continue to contribute to the drying up process of the theater. But then there is all the more reason to demand of Baldwin more profound and sharper application of his mind to a debate which fires the emotions of so many while enlightening so few.

CHAPTER FIVE

Letter to the
Amsterdam News

April 19, 1956

In April 1956, the Amsterdam News *ran a series of articles on the failure of Nat King Cole to address blatant discrimination and segregation of audiences for whom he performed. Harold Cruse's letter to Nora Holt, the entertainment columnist for Harlem's Negro weekly, appeared on April 19, and contained several themes that would be central to* The Crisis of the Negro Intellectual *eleven years later. Always critical of the relationship between Afro-American artists and the liberal white entertainment establishment, Cruse, like his predecessors in the Harlem Renaissance, believed art to be of critical importance to the black freedom struggle. The letter updates themes discussed a quarter century earlier in Langston Hughes's noted essay "The Negro Artist and the Racial Mountain." In Cruse's view, the fact that black artists and entertainers often relied on a largely white audience for their survival made it nearly impossible for any authentic—and therefore controversial—examination of the black condition to take place in these forums. This was no abstract concern for Cruse since he describes himself as "a practicing dramatist, writer and novelist who has up to now been unsuccessful in getting published or produced."*

This was going to be a letter to the *Amsterdam News* Editor giving my two cents worth on the King Cole affair, but after reading your column, I thought it more worthwhile to comment on the questions you have raised because I think it has indirect bearing on the implications of the King Cole business.

I am going to take this opportunity to be quite frank and long-winded because we are dealing with a big subject. [. . .] It must be necessarily long because the problem has many ramifications which unfortunately we American Negroes refuse to discuss publicly and honestly. These questions have long bothered me since I am a practicing dramatist, writer and novelist who has up to now been unsuccessful in getting published or produced. Please accept what I will say here more as a personal answer to your questions.

When you speak of the (Negro) public and the cultural arts, it is my belief that Negroes do not support operas, musicals, plays, symphonic concerts, art exhibits, etc., because the majority of Negroes don't really believe such cultural expressions really represent them. Thus only a handful of highly conscious Negroes will go out of their way to attend operas, plays, musicals, concerts, exhibits, whether such vehicles are Negro, interracial, or not. I must be honest and say that I believe the Negro public is right and justified in its attitude, while at the same time the Negro public is not [to be] absolved of its basic responsibility in these cultural matters.

One can talk about democracy, equal rights, integration, and the rights of Negroes to free expression and participation in the cultural fields, and the Negroes' right to opportunities to train and achieve professional status in any and all branches of the cultural fields, but what are the objective facts? The cultural arts have been a means for a certain limited number of Negroes to attain stardom, influence, affluence, money and status by catering to the tastes and demands of the American majority. This majority is *white*. It is this majority that pays off. This lays the basis for a kind of professional separation of these stars from the Negro public and most Negroes can look at them as individual Negroes who are "making it" in high places. And what is this but the Negro version of the great American Creed of "Individualism"? We are all trying to "make it." Never mind how. [. . .] Art in America is one road to mink coats and Cadillac cars, the home in the country, trips to Las Vegas and the Bahamas or a sojourn in Paris. Socially, it affords racial integration on high levels, marrying white mates, hobnobbing with scions and debutantes and heirs and heiresses.

Which means further separation from the Negro public. Now one can have their own personal opinions on these matters, pro or con, but the fact remains: What has all this to do with the lives, outlooks, and experiences of ordinary Negroes who must ultimately make up the public you speak of? Again I say, I must go along with the public, the Negro public, in this instance. For if the Negro has a responsibility to his Negro stars in the cultural fields, it is also true that the Negro stars have a responsibility to the Negro public which in practically all instances the Negro stars have not carried out. Most of them don't really give a damn about the Negro public anyhow! Many Negroes look upon Negro stars from a distance separated by a wide social gulf and many Negroes accept this as normal. Why question it? They're making it! Who wouldn't do the same thing if they got the break? But is this correct?

I once sat in on a conversation in Greenwich Village where some Negroes were discussing Eartha Kitt's disparaging remarks about Negroes when she was in Chicago. Some Negroes condemned her, but some said, "So what? She's making it! It wasn't easy for her to come up. [. . .]" The point is [that as long as our values reflect the American creed of individualism, of "making it," the Negro public cannot see that these artists have any community responsibility]. If you can't make it, shame on you! [. . .] In a situation like this one cannot expect idealism from either star or public.

It has long been known that many individual Negro stars have long harbored an independent, callous and contemptuous attitude towards the Negro public and they will justify it. One could attribute this to all kinds of motives. I suspect not a little feeling of guilt plays a part here. In other instances, it is a question of racial values, skin color, social status, educational achievements and all that. It crops up in the instance of [Nat] King Cole on social and political questions where he can blithely and blindly disavow his responsibilities in the Negroes' fight against Jimcrow. Let's remember, however, that what King Cole said in his defense [was] mild. He had his reasons and he thinks he's right. Haven't Negro stars always done the same thing in different forms? Many a star's career was launched in night clubs and places where the Negro public was openly barred, some of them right in Harlem. [T]imes have changed; the public—Negro and white—is changing, but the change has not been so revolutionary that individual Negro stars and the Negro public are going to see their respective responsibilities and start living up to them unless these responsibilities are pointed out to them consistently, day by day, week by week, year by year. [. . .] So far, we haven't done this. We Negroes are very adept at ducking issues and responsibilities. However, we'll scream to high heaven and the Supreme Court about our rights. However, let us not be deceived—we American Negroes are caught in the middle in the cultural question and we've reached a dead end. In colloquial parlance, we are badly "hung-up." This question of the Negro in culture cannot be solved by any Supreme Court decision, Act of Congress, or any sweet words or good intentions of Caucasian and/or Jewish liberals in New York City, the cultural capital of the U. S. A. This problem can only be solved by Negro initiative if it is to be solved at all. My experiences as a Negro writer in theatrical, publishing and producing circles have proven to me the seriousness of our position. The state of affairs is incredible and shocking. I would not be so pessimistic as to say it is hopeless, but it is almost so. Only a complete overhauling of the American Negro's attitude towards himself can reverse this trend into a cultural blind alley. The whole cultural apparatus as it involves Negroes is shot through with dishonesty. [. . .] Negroes who are making "progress" in cultural arts [are] bending over backwards to satisfy "white" standards. All this is covered up with claims that "integration" will solve all! It won't be as simple as all that. I have been advised by certain people in the know [that] it would be a waste of time for me to present playscripts to certain producers and agencies. They are just not interested in Negro material, good, bad or indifferent. Negro themes just aren't considered profitable. These same producers, of course, actually lose thousands upon thousands of dollars every season on worthless plays that any amateur could have told them wasn't worth it.

[. . .] From around 1950-51 to the present, I have turned out three plays, one musical drama, one musical comedy, some short stories and radio scripts, many articles. I have even attempted to start a magazine. I have been through the mill, I have made the rounds trying to get agencies and individuals interested in my work. My experiences would fill a good-sized book. I used to get bitter and hopeless, but I don't anymore because in the process I have learned what we Negroes are really up against. To understand the problem is the first step towards trying to solve it. I have learned much. I have had many reject[ions] and many encouraging letters from white agencies. [. . .] This doesn't bother me. What bothers me is not the white man's lack of interest and concern about the Negroes' participation in the cultural fields on all levels, [but] the Negroes' attitude toward his participation. In this respect, I cannot help but arrive at the conclusion that in art and culture, the Negro is his own worst enemy. [. . .]

We can all talk about art and culture, and rattle off names from Ira Aldridge to Sammy Davis, Jr. We can point to past successes and past lean years. We can talk about our rights in culture, what we have in the way of Negro talent, and what we are not allowed to achieve, "solely because of race." But is it only because of race? [. . .] It is not. [R]ather it is because of a *lack of race,* or, to put it another way, we do not strive for a racially conscious art. Today [the Negro artist is] too busy trying to represent everything in art but himself and his own racial background. One does not have to look very far to see why with all this off-Broadway theater activity in New York City, the Negro play (unless it is a revival) is still a rarity. Why, for instance, is there no Negro theater [. . .] operating the year around as for example the Circle In the Square operates in the Village? Don't we have the talent? I'll tell you why. There is no Negro theater because most Negroes in theater *don't want it.* This is the sad truth. I couldn't believe this when I was first told this by another Negro playwright . It didn't make sense, but then after some observation it did begin to make sense. [The] vogue today among many Negro actors and writers [is] the old dodge about the "universality of the human race" or [that] we "can't self-segregate ourselves." It is more necessary today for [Negro] actors to "prove something" by playing Shakespeare, Ibsen and Shaw. [. . .] The "integrated cast" or the "interracial" theatre is all the style today. Cultural integration is on the march, but to where? [T]oward a few more token jobs for some Negro actor who can pass for white, Indian, Samoan, and maybe an Eskimo. Every once in a while a Negro singer will be allowed to sing a lead role in *Lucia di Lammemoor* or some other European leftover from the Roccoco period, and that will be hailed as "progress." And a lot of Negroes around will be naïve enough to believe it because every little advance will allow somebody to slip through and "make it"! And that is really the big aim in life and art! The white folks have got this Negro progress deal down pat. All they have to do is throw us a "token of integrationism" and we all clap [as if] the millennium [. . .]is just around the corner. Well, something will be around the corner one of these days, and it won't be the millennium. It'll be something else. It'll be that thing we've been trying to duck all these years in the arts—that "do it yourself bugbear!" Oh, it'll be hard enough to have to face it. We'll have to change our ways and all that. We Negroes don't have, never had too much money (except for a few minks, fishtails, and the lush life and liquor bills) to spend on art and culture. The Negro business man, we know, doesn't give a damn about art, especially Negro art, and the Negro artist is becoming a business man, selling art to the white folks at bargain prices, considering the market value. All this will change [. . .]when American [social] realities hit us. When this integration mania runs its course and we wake up to find "there ain't no such thing."

Let us explore some more. How long and how loud have we complained of things like *Porgy and Bess?* We complain and criticize, but what have we done [. . .] with our [own] music? What have we done with our dance? Our own idiom? Our poetry? Our religious traditions? Our folk culture? We condemn white folks for taking it over and misrepresenting it and us and making fortunes for themselves, while we turn our backs on it because we are ashamed of it. We speak of European Opera. What about American Opera? Any musicologist will tell us that all great classical opera is more or less based on a nation's folk music. We are the inheritors of the American folk tradition, but we don't use it; we shrink from [it]. That's old fashioned, "too Southern," "unsophisticated," "smacks too much of that slavery and chain gangs." We want to escape that past, none of that "old nigger stuff" for us. It's degrading. We'll learn to become musical masters of the European classical tradition and sing Mozart [. . .] and German Lieder. And since the good white folks must have that good old "Southern Negro spiritual," we'll toss in a couple for after all it is good press. But we leave it right there . . . it isn't worthwhile to try to outdo George Gershwin.

In the theater we sit around hoping and waiting that some white writer (they can write better than Negroes, and know more about Negroes than Negroes) and some white producer and director will decide to cook up a Broadway vehicle for us; or perhaps throw us a sop in something "interracial." A couple of windfalls like this and "we're on our way" [to "making it"]. We hope it runs at least a year and usually it doesn't. When it runs its course and closes, the question is always brought up as to why Negroes did not support the vehicle in any appreciable numbers. True, it's a legitimate question, but the real question to be asked is why in all these years have Negro [actors] refused to come back to their own people when they're not working on Broadway or in Hollywood and help raise the cultural level and participation of Negroes by establishing cultural institutions like theaters, dramatic workshops, acting schools [or] writing schools. [. . .] We are not so tied up in our own careers that we can't do these things. What do we yell for more educational opportunities for Negroes for anyhow? To raise a yearly crop of intellectuals to spend the rest of their years seeking patronage from these Caucasians and Jews, begging the white folks to "give us all a break?" I cannot accept it as true that Negroes with all [our] gift[s] and talent [. . .] can't make our own mark in the cultural fields with the firm support of the public. If it is true that we can't then we are lost because it is also true that the white folks are not going to do it for us. They just don't have to do it! I am not a follower of this logic that the Supreme Court or anybody else is going to absolve Negroes of their racial responsibilities.

In closing, here are a few more facts. A couple of years ago, a rather successful Negro play closed on Broadway because the star of the show refused to go on the road. Here is another example of what I mean. It wasn't the public that didn't support the show, it was the *star,* the Negro star, that refused to support the show when it meant at least a year of regular salaries for several people. You see, there was nothing racial in this star's attitude, she was only out for herself, like practically every Negro star who has come along. In their attitude, the public be damned unless it pays, and who pays? It's the white folks [. . .] and that's who they spend their time catering to. [In my view,] Negroes owe these people no allegiance. [. . .]

[Not too long ago, a Negro actor] was given access to a church in which to do plays. This star had the church and was given, to my knowledge, four plays by Negro authors, all original plays. However, between sitting out the time between Broadway jobs, talking, drinking and having a good time, not one of these plays has ever been produced over a period of over three years. Not even a reading of one of these plays was ever given in this church. Of late, I hear this [actor] has renewed talk of doing a play in this church. [. . .] It's not an original play by a Negro [. . .], but a revival of a play that was done on Broadway. You see, even Negroes themselves, in the theatre, won't do original stuff. I have found them to be just as bad in this respect as the whites who are afraid of Negro material. That is why I've changed to the [fiction genre] temporarily. In my novel, I'm writing about Negroes in the theater and what a messed-up bunch of people they are. [. . .]

p.s.

[. . .] I trust you won't find my bluntness and approach distasteful but it is the only way I know how to write or speak.

The question of the Negro in Culture needs much searching analysis. It needs books, discussions, panels, organizations. We Negroes are just not doing the job. [. . .]

CHAPTER SIX

Open Letter
to Harry Belafonte[1]

November 11, 1956
(Submitted to the *New York Post*)

Cruse uncharacteristically signed this letter anonymously—a decision likely motivated by the fact that both he and Belafonte had been affiliated with the Committee for the Negro in the Arts. The letter is indicative of themes, particularly the conflict between Afro-North Americans and Afro-Caribbeans, which he would explore more fully in The Crisis of the Negro Intellectual *ten years later.*

So Harry Belafonte, you're a man driven by his conscience. Well, that's good you should be, but don't let your conscience mislead you into making false judgments on whose "community is more related"—the community in the British West Indies or the community here. The American Negro community is not responsible for what you think about the West Indies and cares less. But as one American Negro, I do care mightily about for whom you presume to speak: yourself or the West Indian community here or abroad. I have always found most West Indians a mite too insufferable on this question of being "Negro" or not being "American" when living here in the midst of American prosperity which is not forthcoming from the Islands. Also I find that when you talk about Nat Cole and what his principles are, I get the feeling of a pygmy taking potshots at a giant in the entertainment field.

You should know by this time that in the U.S. the American Negro has a white majority over ten times his number sitting on his neck; it is not similar to the West Indies where the master race and the King and Queen whom they seem to worship down there for some reason I don't quite get are several thousand miles away exploiting those islands from afar. That being the case, it is about time they ceased coming here seeking prosperity and bringing their superiority complexes with them.

Further, many Negro performers, including Lena Horne and others in the "glamour set," made their early marks singing before Jim Crow audiences, often right in the center of black Harlem, and didn't raise a peep when they should have known better, but didn't really care. It has been going on for decades and so it is indecent for upstarts like yourself to attempt any self-glorification at Nat Cole's expense. After all, Cole didn't come up through the left-wing movement like you did where everybody got hepped up on "civil rights" and then proceeded to go out and mess up Negro politics. We don't need more Powells, we need less, so stick to your folk singing, Belafonte, that's your best bet. [. . .]

Many of us remember the Committee for the Negro in the Arts with which you were connected in Harlem some years ago. Well, Harlem is a "related community" but the CNA didn't seem to be able to click with them. I wonder why? I suspect that in those years, you and some others in that most undemocratic group allowed flattery to go to your heads causing you to forget what your mission was as artists. Personally, I found you and most of the others up there a bunch of snobs. If you have changed, that is most welcome. However, you and them should have known the meaning of being "human beings" as well as artists when it really counted community-wise in the fields of Negro art and Negro culture instead of using the organization to feather your own nests while taking dictation from downtown left-wings on what was good for Negroes uptown.

Signed: A Reader

From
The Crisis of the
Negro Intellectual
(1967)

CHAPTER SEVEN

Individualism
and the "Open Society"

As the opening essay of The Crisis of the Negro Intellectual, *"Individualism and the Open Society is the most succinct rendering of Cruse's case for a pluralist conception of Black life in America. The statement that "the individual Negro has, proportionately, very few rights indeed because his ethnic group . . . has very little political, economic or social power . . . to wield" is key to the succeeding pages of analysis. Borrowing from Milton Gordon and C. Wright Mills, Cruse presents his case for the political necessity of "group" identity and makes the opening statement in an extended prosecution of the NAACP—as well as the Communist left—for their failure to recognize the "bloc" dynamic in Negro life.*

In 1940, as one of my first acts in the pursuit of becoming a more "social" being, I joined a YMCA amateur drama group in Harlem. I wanted to learn about theater so I became a stage technician—meaning a handyman for all backstage chores. But the first thing about this drama group that stuck me as highly curious was the fact that all the members were overwhelmingly in favor of doing white plays with Negro casts. I wondered why and very naïvely expressed my sentiments about it. The replies that I got clearly indicated that these amateur actors were not very favorable to the play about Negro life, although they would not plainly say so. Despite the fact that this question of identity was first presented to me within the context of the program of a small, insignificant amateur drama group, its implications ranged far beyond. A theater group, no matter how small, must have an audience. What did the audience at the Harlem YMCA really think about the group's productions?

Although I continued to work with this group, my preoccupation with its aesthetic values inevitably led me toward a consideration of other, related, social issues peculiar to Harlem. Thus began my first steps toward a long process of social enlightenment. Life was quite complicated and there were no simple answers for anything.

Harlem in 1940 was just beginning to emerge from the depths of the Great Depression and it seethed with the currents of many conflicting beliefs and ideologies. It was the year in which Richard Wright reached the high point of his literary fame, with *Native Son,* and was often seen in Harlem at lectures. The American Negro Theater, a professional experimental group, was preparing to make its 1941 debut as a permanent Harlem institution. The Federal Theater Project had been abolished in 1939, and the echoes of that disaster were still being heard in Harlem's cultural circles. Everything in Harlem seemed to be in a state of flux for reasons I was not then able to fully appreciate. But soon came the war and I was caught up in the army for four-and-a-half years. I returned with a radically altered vision to find that although Harlem had the same old problems, it had a new community consciousness. Hence, I could see these old problems from a new point of view. Indeed, what I have learned about Harlem since 1946 is pretty much summed up in this book.

∽

I have attempted to define what a considerable body of Negroes have thought and expressed on a less analytic and articulate level. I do not claim to represent the thinking of *all* the people in America who are called Negroes, for Negroes are certainly divided into classes—a fact white liberals and radicals often overlook when they speak of "the Negro." There is, however, a broad strain of Negro social opinion in America that is strikingly cogent and cuts through class lines. This social outlook cannot be and never has been encompassed by the program of an organization such as the NAACP, whose implied definition of racial integration offers no answers to the questions that agitate the collective minds of those Negroes who reject such a philosophy. And yet, since it could never be said that such Negroes do not want social progress, what are they looking for that NAACP does not offer?

To put the question in another way, and in better focus—although until recent years the NAACP has had the prestige of being the major civil rights organization—its membership, usually hovering somewhere between three hundred and fifty thousand and four hundred thousand—it can hardly be said to reflect the pervasive sentiment of an ethnic group as large and as hardpressed as the American Negro. In other words, there is a definite strain of thought within the Negro group that encompasses all the ingredients of "nationality" and strikes few sympathetic chords with the NAACP.

Historically, this "rejected strain," as Theodore Draper describes it, emerged simultaneously with its opposite—the racial integration strain—although the word "integration" was not then in the Negro vocabulary as synonym for civil rights or freedom. The prototype leader of the latter strain was Frederick Douglass, the great Negro Abolitionist, and there is almost a direct line of development from him to the NAACP and the modern civil rights movement. However, the rejected, or nationality strain that exists today can be traced back to certain Negro spokesmen who were Douglass' contemporaries but who are now barely remembered—Martin R. Delany, Edward Blyden, Alexander Crummell, Henry M. Turner and George Washington Williams. Douglass, Booker T. Washington, Marcus Garvey and W. E. B. DuBois, on the other hand, are well known to the average Negro as historical personalities.

It is important to note that just prior to the Civil War there was conflict among Negroes over what would be the best course of action for the soon-to-be emancipated slaves. Should they return to Africa or emigrate to Latin America; or should they remain and struggle for racial equality in the United States (or seek to accomplish both at the same time)? As one historian has described this conflict:

> Some Negroes in America showed an interest in Africa before the 1860's—usually in the face of the criticism of the black abolitionists such as Frederick Douglass who considered the African dream a dangerous diversification of energies which were needed in the fight for emancipation and civil rights at home.[1]

This historian goes on to point out that "one of the major pre–Civil War Negro-American exponents of the 'Back-to-Africa' dream [was] Martin R. Delany,

Harvard-trained physician and the first Negro to be commissioned with field rank by President Lincoln. . . . He visited Liberia in July, 1859, and saw in the proposed Liberian College 'a grand stride in the march of African Regeneration and Negro Nationality.'"[2] It was also in 1859 that Delany originated and used the phrase "Africa for the Africans." However, even most contemporary Black Nationalists believe that Marcus Garvey of the 1920's invented that slogan.

Thus it can be seen that the present-day conflict within the Negro ethnic group, between integrationist and separatists tendencies, has its origins in the historical arguments between personalities such as Frederick Douglass and as Martin R. Delany.[*] Although the peculiar social conditions and race relations in America have made it possible for the Frederick Douglass trend to be the more articulate and dominant up to now, this has not always been so; and it does not mean, moreover, that the opposite strain has become nonexistent. On the contrary, the emergence of the Malcolm X brand of nationalism proves its persistence, despite the fact that both strains have undergone considerable change and qualification. In fact, with W. E. B. DuBois they nearly merged into new synthesis, for DuBois, in addition to being a founder of the NAACP integrationist trend, was also a leading exponent of the Pan-Africanism that had is origins with Martin R. Delany.

∾

Throughout my adult life I have observed that the ideas of one particular stratum of Negroes on such questions as race color, politics, economics, art, Africa, minorities or interracial relations are pretty uniform. These ideas are expressed in many different ways but, because of the fact that the American Negro exists under the dominating persuasion of the Great American Ideal, the philosophy of these Negroes has not been allowed the dignity of acceptance as an ethnic

---

[*] Martin Robison Delany, born May 6, 1812, Charleston, Virginia, died January 1885. Delany should be considered the historical prototype of the "Afro-American Nationalist." As co-editor with Frederick Douglass of the leading Abolitionist organ *The North Star,* founded in 1847, Delany's presence reflected the nationalist element of the embryonic Nationality vs. Integrationist conflict within the Abolitionist movement (which also had its white faction). For a short biographical sketch of Delany see Jesse Fauset's "Rank Imposes Obligations," *Crisis* magazine, November 1926, p. 9. Important works by Delany are: *The Condition, Elevation, Emigration of Colored People of the United States, Politically Considered,* published by the author in Philadelphia in 1852; and *The Official Report of the Niger Valley Exploring Party,* New York: T. Hamilton, 1861.

conception of reality. Nonetheless, this stratum persists in its own inarticulate way as the residuum of what might be called the Afro-American ethnic group consciousness in a society whose legal Constitution recognizes the rights, privileges and aspirations of the individual, but whose political institutions recognize the reality of ethnic groups only during election contests. Every four years the great fiction of the assimilated American (white and/or Protestant) ideal is put aside to deal with the pluralistic reality of the hyphenated-American vote, of which the largest is the Negro-American. But since the Supreme Court decision of 1954 on public school integration, the Negro-American has been catapulted into the role of being the mover and shaker of modern America while putting the Great American Ideal to the most crucial test of its last hundred years.

And what precisely is this Great American Ideal? The superficial answer is that, in practice, it is the living expression of that body of concepts sanctified in the American Constitution. For the Negro, the Fourteenth and Fifteenth Amendments are of special relevance. But this is true because these Amendments, especially, have an historical relationship to the way in which the Negro has influenced the evolution of the American Ideal. They will have pertinency just as long as the Negro's lot falls short of the egalitarian ideal as set down. But does not the fact that a new Civil Rights Act of 1964 was required in pursuance of the enforcement of these Amendments, indicate that something more is implied than what is stated in them? Is it true that what this Negro stratum of which I speak wants from America is merely this enforcement? Or does the American default on these Amendments indicate that there is something conceptually or legally deficient about the scope of the Constitution itself? Does it indicate perhaps that the real scope of social implications of the Negro's demands on American society today is not fully spelled out or conceptualized by the Negro himself—or at least that body of Negroes who are today most vocal on the civil rights front?

Whatever the case, it has to be noted that the most vocal opponents of the Civil Rights Act of 1964 *cite* the American Constitution and object to measures aimed at enforcing the Fourteenth and Fifteenth Amendments as violations of the rights of individuals and private property—privileges which are guaranteed by the same Constitution. This emotional and legal conflict over the interpretation of the Constitution, in the slow and painfully bitter struggle towards the enforcement of constitutional guarantees of racial equality, points up a very real dilemma inherent in the Negro's position in America.

On the face of it, this dilemma rests on the fact that America, which idealizes the rights of the individual above everything else, is in reality, a nation dominated by the social power of groups, classes, in-groups and cliques—both ethnic and religious. The individual in America has few rights that are not backed up by the political, economic and social power of one group or another. Hence, the individual Negro has, proportionately, very few rights indeed because his ethnic group (whether or not he actually identifies with it) has very little political, economic or social power (beyond moral grounds) to wield. Thus it can be seen that those Negroes, and there are very many of them, who have accepted the full essence of the Great American Ideal of individualism are in serious trouble trying to function in America.

Very understandably, these people want to be full-fledged Americans, without regard to race, creed, or color. They do not stop to realize that this social animal is a figment of the American imagination and has never really existed except in rare instances. They cite the American Constitution as the legal and moral authority in their quest for fully integrated status (whichever interpretation out of several they lend to this idea) and find it necessary to shy away from that stratum I mentioned before, which forms the residuum of the Negro ethnic group consciousness.

However, each individual American is a member of a group. The white Anglo-Saxon Protestants, the white Catholics, and the white Jews are the three main power groups in America, under the political and economic leadership of the WASPs. The American Constitution was conceived and written by white Anglo-Saxon Protestants for a white Anglo-Saxon society. The fact that what is called American Society, or American Culture, did not subsequently develop into a nation made up totally of WASPs—because of Negro slavery and immigration—did not prevent the white Protestants from perpetuating the group attitudes that would maintain the image of the whole American nation in terms of WASP cultural tradition. These attitudes, as sociologist Milton M. Gordon points out, "all have as a central assumption the desirability of maintaining English institutions (as modified by the American Revolution), the English language, and English-oriented cultural patterns as dominant and standard in American life."[3] Naturally, the historical priorities and prerogatives established by the English settlers early in the seventeenth century have been expanded through all the succeeding generations of white Protestants into a well-entrenched social position, characterized by a predominance in economic and political power, buttressed with a strong, cohesive, group solidarity.

> Thus, what is usually referred to as "general American society" turns out in reality, insofar as communal institutions and primary group relations are concerned, to be a white Protestant social world, colored and infused with the implicit assumptions of this particular ethnic group. To be sure, it is the largest

ethnic group in the United States, and like other ethnic groups it is divided in major fashion by social class.[4]

Although the three main power groups—Protestants, Catholics and Jews—neither want nor need to become integrated with each other, the existence of a great body of homogenized, inter-assimilated white Americans is the premise for racial integration. Thus the Negro integrationist runs afoul of reality in the pursuit of an illusion, the "open society"—a false front that hides several doors to several different worlds of hyphenated-Americans. Which group or subgroup leaves its door wide open for the outsider? None, really. But Gordon does point out one subsocietal exception to this state of affairs between groups which, for our purposes, it is important to note very attentively: "The only substantial exception to this picture of ethnic separation is the compartment marked intellectuals and artists."[5]

Gordon goes on to explain this stratum, ". . . suffice it here to point out that in the situation of men and women coming together because of an overriding common interest in ideas, the creative arts, and mutual professional concerns, we find the classic sociological enemy of ethnic parochialism."[6] In other words, in the detached social world of the intellectuals, a considerable amount of racial integration and ethnic intermingling does take place on a social level. While the Negro intellectual is not fully integrated into the intellectual class stratum, he is, in the main, socially detached from his own Negro ethnic world. Gordon points out that there is evidence that the "outflow of intellectuals from the religio-ethnic groups of America, their subsequent estrangement from the life of these groups, and the resultant block in communication between the ethnic subsociety and the intellectual [might] have dysfunctional consequences."[7]

In the face of these sociological findings, then, how do Negro intellectuals measure up to the complex problem of being spokesmen on behalf of their ethnic group, the Negro masses? This has to be examined on two levels: First, as creative artists, how can their creative output be assessed? Second, as Negro spokesmen, to what extent do their analyses of the Negro situation get to the bottom of things? Also, is there any correlation between these two intellectual levels of performance, any value judgments to be derived?

For several years the chief spokesman for the Negro among the intellectual class was James Baldwin, who, it might be said, has signalized a new level of involvement. Following Baldwin there have been other literary voices, such as John O. Killens, the late Lorraine Hansberry, Ossie Davis, Paule Marshall and LeRoi Jones. However, if one closely examines the ideas, the social status, the literary content or even the class background of these writers and intellectuals, it is found that they are not at all in agreement on what general course the Negro should follow towards racial equality.

Thus, today, the Negro civil rights-integration movement calls into play two aspects of Negro reality which now demand closer examination and analysis than heretofore—the residual stratum of Negro ethnic group consciousness, of which I have spoken, and the "new" Negro intellectual class that has emerged as of the late 1950's and 1960's.

NOTES

1. George Shepperson, "Notes on Negro American Influences on the Emergence of African Nationalism," *Journal of African History*, I, No. 2. 1960, p. 301.
2. Ibid., p. 301.
3. Milton M. Gordon, *Assimilation in American Life* (New York: Oxford University Press, 1964), p. 88.
4. Ibid., p. 221.
5. Ibid., p. 111.
6. Ibid., p. 58.
7. Ibid., p. 256.

CHAPTER EIGHT

Cultural Leadership
and Cultural Democracy

Racial democracy is, at the same time, cultural democracy; and the question of cultural democracy in America is posed in a way never before seen or considered in other societies. This uniqueness results historically from the manner in which American cultural developments have been influenced by the Negro presence. Since a cultural philosophy has been cultivated to deny this truth, it remains for the Negro intellectual to create his own philosophy and to bring the facts of cultural history in focus with the cultural practices of the present. In advanced societies it is not the race politicians or the "rights" leaders who create the new ideas and the new images of life and man. That role belongs to the artists and the intellectuals of each generation. Let the race politicians, if they will, create political, economic or organizational forms of leadership; but it is the artists and the creative minds who will, and must, furnish the all important content. And in this role, they must not be subordinated to the whims and desires of politicians, race leaders and civil rights entrepreneurs whether they come from the Left, Right, or Center, or whether they are peaceful, reform, violent, nonviolent or laissez-faire. Which means to say, in advanced societies the cultural front is a special one that requires special techniques not perceived, understood, or appreciated by political philistines. There are those among the latter who give lip-service to the idea that Culture and Art belong to the People, but what they actually give to the people (not to speak of what is given to Negroes as people) is not worthy of examination. It is the Negro creative intellectual who must take seriously the idea that culture and art belong to the people—with all the revolutionary implications of that idea.

To bring this idea into proper focus, and into the context of our peculiar American cultural ideology, let us quote from Gilbert Seldes' book, *The Public Arts,* written in 1956:

> "This country, with its institutions, belongs to the people who inhabit it," said Abraham Lincoln, and as he was then facing the possible dissolution of the United States, he added, "Whenever they (the people) shall grow weary of the existing government, they can exercise their Constitutional right of amending it or their revolutionary right to dismember or overthrow it."

> I am suggesting that the cultural institutions of a country also belong to its inhabitants, and, not having the courage of Lincoln's radicalism, I do not insist upon the revolutionary right of the people to destroy whatever wearies them. Moderately, I propose the idea that the people have valid rights over those cultural institutions which can be properly called "the public arts."[1]

Seldes had come a long way from 1924 when he wrote *The Seven Lively Arts.* He pointed out, in 1956, that a revolution had taken place in American cultural arts communication, which had transformed what he called in the 1920's the "seven lively arts," into what are now the "public arts": "For convenience, the beginning of that revolution can be placed in the late summer of 1929, when millions of Americans, with more money to spend on recreation than they had ever had before, spent nothing because they were staying home to be entertained by the Amos 'n' Andy radio program."[2]

The fact, of course, that "Amos 'n' Andy" was a modernized version of the old-time minstrel show—in which whites blackened their faces in order to imitate the original plantation minstrels created by Negroes—probably did not strike Seldes as being highly significant in a cultural way because of "content." But the fact that the program was an imitation Negro comic show *is* significant. The Negro-white cultural symbolism involved here was expressed and given significance by Gilbert Seldes himself, during the 1920's when his critiques of

American art forms damned the Negro with faint praise, condemning him forever to the back alleys of American culture. Seldes claimed then that Negro music and musicians could not hope to rise to "classic" stature. He implied also that Negro theater ought not to be looked upon as art in the sense that the devotees of Western culture think of art. "The one claim never made for the Negro shows is that they are artistic," Seldes wrote. He was then talking about such hit shows as Sissle and Blake's *Shuffle Along:*

> Set beside them [Negro shows], then, a professedly artistic revue, the *Pinwheel* [a white show], compounded of native and exotic effects. It had two or three interesting or exciting numbers; but the whole effect was one of dreariness. The pall of art was upon it; it died nightly. And *Shuffle Along, without art,* but with tremendous vitality, not only lived through the night, but dragged provincial New Yorkers to a midnight show as well.[3]

Yet, according to Seldes, Negro shows were not art. And what, pray tell, *is* art? The peculiar and perverse tradition of cultural criticism, practiced by Gilbert Seldes and others, has severely distorted native American artistic standards by over-glorifying obsolete European standards. Seldes debased Negro creative artists by refusing to accept their native originality as truly American. He rejected what was truly American because it was not European, but Afro-American. Thus by downgrading Negro musical originality, he helped to undermine the only artistic base in the American culture in which the Negro could hold his own as an original artist. And, from this base, he could eventually, by dint of creative discipline, raise his own level of sophistication and finesse in all other American art forms. Thus, in the 1920's, Seldes' criticisms encouraged undemocratic ethnic tendencies in American culture. Yet contradictorily, in 1956 Gilbert Seldes wants the "public arts" of America democratized by returning them to the people. But which people? Seldes, of course, knows that the "seven lively arts" did not belong to the people in the 1920's. Because if they had, America would not have witnessed the un-cultural spectacle of Hemingway, Harold Stearns, Sinclair Lewis, T.S. Eliot, Ezra Pound—the lost generation refugees— hotfooting it to Paris and Madrid to escape American cultural suffocation. While all of these white intellectuals were escaping because they could not be real artists in America, the Negroes were trying to create new art in their own native American way. And, as things have turned out "culturally" in America, there is now *only one* group of American creative intellectuals who have the motivation (or at least the potential) for democratizing American culture and forcing the return of the public arts to the people. These are the new young generation of

Negro intellectuals—the cultural and ethnic progeny of those very Negroes whom Seldes critically downgraded in the 1920's as being mostly primitive and non-intellectual as creative artists. These young people, however, will have to go far beyond Seldes' proposed "moderation" in techniques and will have to search for the "revolutionary rights" of confrontation that Seldes disavows.

This new young generation must first clear the way to cultural revolution by a critical assault on the methods and ideology of the old-guard Negro intellectual elite. The failures and ideological shortcomings of this group have meant that no new directions, or insights have been imparted to the Negro masses. This absence of positive orientation has created a cultural void that has spawned all the present-day tendencies towards nihilism and anarchism, evident in the ideology of the young. This new generation of Negro poets, artists, writers, critics and playwrights bursts onto the scene; fed and inspired by the currents flowing out of movements at home and abroad, they are full of zeal but have no well-charted direction. They encounter the established old guard (even some lingering representatives of the 1920's) and the results are confusion and a clash of aims. The old guard attempts to absorb some of the new guard. This process has been seen at work in the Harlem Writers Guild, the Artists for Freedom group, *Freedomways* and *Liberator* magazine and in the recent proliferation of Negro Writers' Conferences. The young wave attempts to criticize *and* emulate the old guard at one and the same time, which creates more ideological confusion. The young wave cannot completely break from the old order of things cultural, because the old guard stands pat and blocks the path to new cultural frontiers. This state of interference has existed rather constantly since 1961. Out of this process a number of provocative issues have emerged and been debated, but nothing resembling a real critique has come out of it. The old guard gives no leadership, clarifies nothing and confuses everything.

How would one define cultural leadership? How would it be differentiated qualitatively from ordinary civil rights leadership, or the overworked "civil writism" of the old guard, or the emulation of the new? This has to be clarified because American Negroes are, after all, Americans who pattern their social reasoning on white American standards of social logic. White Anglo-Saxon Protestants are fundamentally anti-theoretical, anti-aesthetic, anti-cultural, anti-intellectual. They often try hard not to be that way, but have a deep-seated suspicion of art, culture and intellect nonetheless. They prefer the practical, by which they mean the application of practical values in the pursuit of materialistic ends. They actually look upon the enjoyment of art and culture as a materialistic end, especially if it is "entertaining." But they are not overly concerned about the cultivation of creativity. Creative values are usually subordinated to materialist values. This outlook permeates everything in the United States, including the outlook of American Negroes. The philosophy of the civil rights movement is predominantly materialistic, aiming at the achievement of a bigger share of American materialistic abundance. But whereas most American whites see the enjoyment of art and culture as one of the acceptable ends of materialistic achievement, Negroes (who might imitate these values, socially) rarely participate as cultural or artistic personalities for any purpose other than materialistic ends. In either case there is no creative cultural philosophy involved.

The civil rights movement cannot really give cultural leadership in any effective way—it is too suffused with the compulsion to legitimize its social aims with American standards. The leaders of the civil rights movement, along with all the "civil writers," subordinate themselves to the very cultural values of the white world that are used either to negate, or deny the Negro cultural equality, and to exploit his cultural ingredients and use them *against* him. This is one of the great traps of racial integrationism—one must accept all the values (positive or negative) of the dominant society into which one struggles to integrate. Let us examine two very prominent cultural questions out of the American twentieth-century past and see how they were handled. Both of these are issues of the 1920's that have become institutionalized in today's Americana. One is exemplified by the folk-opera *Porgy and Bess,* a cultural product, the other by Duke Ellington, a cultural personality.

In May, 1959, following the successful opening of *A Raisin in the Sun,* its author Lorraine Hansberry debated Otto Preminger on a television program in Chicago, over what she labeled the deplorable "stereotypes" of *Porgy and Bess.* The film version of the folk-opera, directed by Preminger, had just been released and it starred none other than Sidney Poitier, who also headlined Miss Hansberry's play on Broadway. This was, of course, not the first time *Porgy and Bess* had been criticized by Negroes. Ever since its premiere in 1935, it has been under attack from certain Negro quarters because it reveals southern Negroes in an unfavorable light. Hence Miss Hansberry's criticisms were nothing very new or original. What *was* new, however, were the times and the circumstances. Miss Hansberry objected to *Porgy* because stereotypes "constitute a bad art" when "the artist hasn't tried hard enough to understand his characters." She claimed that although Gershwin had written a great musical score, he had fallen for what she called the exotic in American culture: "We, over a period of time, have apparently decided that within American life we have one great repository where we're going to focus and imagine sensuality and exaggerated sensuality, all very removed and earthy things—and this great image is the American Negro."

When Preminger asked Miss Hansberry if she suspected the motives of those who had written and produced *Porgy,* she replied: "We cannot afford the luxuries of mistakes of other peoples. So it isn't a matter of being hostile to you, but on the other hand it's also a matter of never ceasing to try to get you to understand that your mistakes can be painful, even those which come from excellent intentions. We've had great wounds from great intentions."[4]

During this debate there was also injected a discussion of *Carmen Jones*—a white-created, Negro version of the Bizet opera, *Carmen*. Miss Hansberry did not like *Carmen Jones* either; but oddly enough (and also characteristically), she weakened her argument on the subject of artistic integrity by wanting to know why no whites had been cast in this caricature of *Carmen*, as if to imply that interracial casting would have made it more acceptable as art. Behind this query there lurked, of course, the whole muddled question of integration in the arts. Also implicit was the Negro integrationist's main peeve in the theater—the "all-Negro play" (or musical), which they deplore as a symbol of segregation, and the "all-white play," which it is their bounden duty to "integrate" even if the author never had Negroes in mind. Needless to point out, the film *Porgy and Bess* had its Broadway and neighborhood run, and hundreds of working-class Negroes (whom Miss Hansberry claimed she wrote about in *Raisin*), lined up at the box offices to see this colorful film "stereotype" of their people.

This whole episode revealed some glaring facts to substantiate my claim that the Negro creative intellectual does not even approach possession of a positive literary and cultural critique—either of his own art, or that other art created for him by whites. In the first place, Lorraine Hansberry revealed that she knew little about the history of this folk-opera, or how or why it was written. She was only concerned with the fact that it was a stereotype. This already precluded the possibility of Miss Hansberry or anyone rendering the kind of critique *Porgy and Bess* deserves from the Negro point of view. Hence, the whole debate was worthless and a waste of time except from the point of view of making some more noisy, but superficial, integrationist propaganda.

The real cultural issues surrounding *Porgy and Bess*, as it relates to the American Negro presence, have never been confronted by the Negro intelligentsia—inside or outside the theater. The two most obvious points a Negro critic should make are: 1.) that a folk-opera of this genre *should have been written* by Negroes themselves and has not; 2.) that such a folk-opera, even if it *had been written* by Negroes, would never have been supported, glorified and acclaimed, as *Porgy* has, by the white cultural elite of America.

Lorraine Hansberry, taking to the television rostrum on art and culture *à la Negre*, was like a solitary defender, armed with a dull sword, rushing out on a charger to meet a regiment. But once having met an opposing general she immediately capitulates—"My intentions are not really hostile but you all have wounded *us*."

For Miss Hansberry to have criticized *Porgy* merely on content was, of course, her unmitigated privilege; but on this basis, her own play was wide open for some criticism on art and the image of the American Negro, which it never got. To criticize any play today involving Negroes, purely on content, is not enough. Most Negro criticism of *Porgy* has been of middle-class origin, although the Negro middle class has never been at all sympathetic to the realities of southern Negro folk characteristics in any way, shape or form. Hence, a generically class-oriented non-identification was inherent in Miss Hansberry's views.[5]

Porgy and Bess has successfully weathered all such criticism on its content and has been enshrined in America's rather empty cultural hall of fame as the great American musical classic. It has been shipped all around the world and proudly displayed as America's greatest artistic achievement. How can one really attack America's "greatest artistic achievement," especially when it is about Negroes? *Porgy* is surely the most contradictory cultural symbol ever created in the Western world.

To attack it, one must see it in terms of something more than mere content. It must be criticized from the Negro point of view as the most perfect symbol of the Negro creative artist's cultural denial, degradation, exclusion, exploitation and acceptance of white paternalism. *Porgy and Bess* exemplifies this peculiarly American cultural pathology, most vividly, most historically, and most completely. It combines the problems of Negro theater, music, acting, writing, and even dancing, all in one artistic package, for the Negro has expressed whatever creative originality he can lay claim to, in each of these aspects of art. However, Negroes had no part in writing, directing, producing, or staging this folk-opera about Negroes (unless it was in a strictly subordinate role). In fact, the first recording of *Porgy* used the voices of Lawrence Tibbett and other white singers, because it was not at first believed that Negroes were "good" enough. As a symbol of that deeply-ingrained, American cultural paternalism practiced on Negroes ever since the first Southern white man blacked his face, the folk-opera *Porgy and Bess* should be forever banned by all Negro performers in the United States. No Negro singer, actor, or performer should ever submit to a role in this vehicle again. If white producers want to stage this folk-opera it should be performed by white performers made up in blackface, because it is distorted imitation all the way through. Musically, it is a rather pedestrian blend of imitation-Puccini and imitation-South Carolina-Negro folk music that Gershwin culled.[*] In theme, it presents the "simple black people" just the way white liberal

---

[*]   Seldes said, "It seemed to me that the style of the opera had been imposed on the materials, it did not grow out of them." *The Seven Lively Arts,* p. 94. See also Hall Johnson's critique of *Porgy and Bess* in *Opportunity,* January, 1936, pp. 24-28. Probably the best professional criticism on record.

paternalists love to see them. The fact that such Negro types *did* exist is beside the point. Culturally, it is a product of American developments that were intended to shunt Negroes off into a tight box of subcultural, artistic dependence, stunted growth, caricature, aesthetic self-mimicry imposed by others, and creative insolvency.

But the superficial Negro creative intelligentsia, who have become so removed from their meaningful traditions, cannot see things this way, so blindly obsessed are they with the modern mania for instant integration. They do not understand the cultural history of America and where they fit in that historical scheme. They understand next to nothing about the 1920's and how the rather fluid, contending cultural trends among blacks and whites were frozen in that decade, once white control of cultural and creative power patterns was established to the supreme detriment of blacks. They are not aware that the white critics of that time were saying that Negro creative artists were, for the most part, primitives; and that Gilbert Seldes, for example, asserted that Negro musicians and composers were creatively and artistically backward. They are not aware that for critics like Seldes, the Negroes were the anti-intellectual, uninhibited, unsophisticated, intuitive children of jazz music who functioned with aesthetic "emotions" rather than with the disciplined "mind" of white jazzmen. For such critics, the real artists of Negro folk expression were the George Gershwins, the Paul Whitemans and the Cole Porters. Seldes asserted in 1924:

> Nowhere is the failure of the Negro to exploit his gifts more obvious than in the use he had made of the jazz orchestra; for although nearly every Negro jazz band is better than nearly every white band, no Negro band has yet come up to the level of the best white ones, and the leader of the best of all, by a little joke, is called [Paul] Whiteman.[6]

This was a personal opinion, but whether true or false, it typified the white cultural attitudes toward all forms and practices of Negro art: Compared to the Western intellectual standards of art and culture, the Negro does not measure up. Thus every Negro artist, writer, dramatist, poet, composer, musician, *et al.,* comes under the guillotine of this cultural judgment. What this judgment really means is that the Negro is artistically, creatively, and culturally inferior; and therefore, all the established social power wielded by the white cultural elite will be used to keep the Negro creative artist in his place. But the historical catch in all this is that the white Protestant Anglo-Saxon in America has nothing in his native American tradition that is aesthetically and culturally original, except that which derives from the Negro presence.

Seldes' mixed feelings and critical ambivalence concerning Negro music stemmed from his awareness that jazz would have to become America's national music, or at least form its basic ingredients. This grievously worried many white critics then, and it explains why they still maintain the artistic superiority of the European symphonic music tradition, refuting that jazz is the basis of the American classical music tradition. From these attitudes on the cultural arts, based on racial values, whites have cultivated their own literary and cultural critique. But it has been a critique predicated on the cultural ideals of a group whose English–North European antecedents have been too culturally ego-ridden, unoriginal, ultra-conservative and desiccated to generate a flourishing national culture. Hence historically, there has been on the cultural front in America a tense ideological war for ethnic identity and ascendancy. This competition has taken on strange and unique patterns. Often it is between WASPs and Jews, but more often than not, it is a collaboration between WASPs and Jews, on high levels, against the Negro. Since it is less possible for the Negro to "pass" for a WASP, than for a member of any other ethnic group, it is the Negro minority who is the most vulnerable and defenseless on the cultural front. In this war of identity over cultural arts standards, the Negro functions under a double or triple jeopardy: Without a literary and cultural critique of his own, the Negro cannot fight for and maintain a position in the cultural world.

Thus the Hansberry attack on *Porgy and Bess* was almost totally meaningless. Even a total Negro boycott of this film which (theoretically) should have been called, could not have been—for the same reason that Negro actors and performers, led by Sidney Poitier, did not refuse to act in this film in the first place. If the Negro creative intellectuals actually had any real aesthetic standards of their own, Hollywood could not have made this film at all. Since the 1957 boycott by the Montgomery Negroes, showing what kind of sacrifices are necessary when it comes to a principle, every Negro—high or low, rich or poor—has the moral obligation at all times to give up immediate comforts and privileges for long-range objectives.

The *Porgy and Bess* controversy had another important angle. In December, 1955, the State Department sent a company to perform it in the Soviet Union. The folk-opera was well received by the Russians and given a tumultuous ovation. Truman Capote, the American novelist and playwright, reported on this cultural exchange in his book *The Muses Are Heard.* One of the Leningrad critics said, in part, of *Porgy and Bess:* "We are not used to the naturalistic details in the dance, to the excessive jazz sound of the symphony orchestra, etc. Nevertheless the performance broadens our concept of the art of contemporary

America, and familiarizes us with thus far unknown facets of the musical and theatrical life of the United States."[7]

Of course, this is an enthusiastic overstatement of the facts of life, inasmuch as the opera was written in the 1930's, based on a novel written in 1925. But the fact that the Russians praised the work revealed the awkward, false, and highly irrelevant position of the American Communist leftwing on the Negro in culture. From the leftwing's cultural thesis on art, we get the aesthetics of Soviet socialist realism that was imposed on left-wing Negro writers. This thesis agrees with those non-Left Negroes who call the folk-opera a stereotype. But, if Soviet-loving Paul Robeson, for example, ever publicly set the Russians right on how to assess this work of art, I am ignorant of when or how.[8] The Russian reaction proved that it is impossible to attack *Porgy and Bess* on content alone, for the Russians could not possibly have grasped the real and actual "facets of the musical and theatrical life of the United States" simply by seeing this work performed in Leningrad.

~

In 1965, Duke Ellington, America's greatest exponent of orchestrated jazz music and compositions, was turned down for the Pulitzer Prize citation for "long-term achievement" in American music. In *The New York Times* story, the Pulitzer Prize advisory board gave no reason for refusing the citation to Ellington. For just about forty years, he has been, by general popular and professional acclaim, the foremost jazz orchestra leader and composer in America. This turn-down indicates that the same old, ethnic-group war for cultural supremacy in American music is still being waged.[*] Ellington was quoted as saying: "Fate's being kind to me. Fate doesn't want me to be too famous too young."[9]

Ellington could be denied this kind of recognition only because of the undemocratic way the cultural machine in America is run. Here was an affront to the entire musical and cultural heritage of every Negro in America. If the Negro creative intellectuals were really educating their people—every jazz musician, singer, and actor would have understood the meaning of this contemptuous attitude. They would have walked off their jobs and demonstrated collectively in a march down Broadway. Every movie house in Negro neighborhoods would have been boycotted, in a sympathy strike against the

---

[*]   Seldes, in 1957, still did not consider Ellington's impact on American music comparable to Whiteman's, *et. al.*

racist views that have for decades permeated American culture, poisoned its creative bloodstreams, corrupted its ideology, and retarded the national potential. But the incident passed with only a momentary response to its cultural implications, so blind, benumbed, amoral, crass and corrupted have we become, so aesthetically untutored are our collective sensibilities. The Negro creative intellectuals, the literary and cultural civil righters, supposedly understand and appreciate jazz music. But even LeRoi Jones, whose *Blues People* is an important critical landmark in the analysis and interpretation of jazz in terms of a social art, almost completely passed over the 1920's. He did not deal at all with those first attacks on Negro jazz and the "damning-with-faint-press" criticisms of Seldes and others. Jones deals adequately with the evolution of jazz styles (*i.e.* the *content* of jazz and blues modes of expression), but not enough with the social structure (the nature of the cultural apparatus to which Negro jazz and its artists are subordinated). Afro-American folk music became the aesthetic ingredient, the cultural material, the wealth exploited by white American cultural imperialism. This kind of appropriation can be explained only by an analysis of the cultural apparatus in all its economic, class, political and institutional ramifications. Without it, one cannot explain how or why an Ellington does not achieve his due recognition today, while the Gershwin-type musicians achieved status and recognition in the 1920's for music that they literally stole outright from Harlem nightclubs. The impact of Negro jazz was powerful enough to arouse the concern of white critics about the idiomatic direction of American music. But it was a concern that critics like Seldes could not afford to extend to its logical conclusion. The critics would talk all around this question while evading it, as Seldes did, when he wrote: "Of the music itself—of jazz and the use of spirituals and the whole question of our national music—this is not the place to write."[10]

This same attitude crops out in the 1965 Pulitzer Prize issue; one could almost paraphrase: "Of the music itself—of jazz and the use of spirituals and the whole question of [Duke Ellington]—this is not the [time to give prizes]."

Negro creative intellectuals, however, are neither equipped nor willing to contribute cultural leadership on a question like this. They are most adept when it comes to sentimentalizing in public about their preoccupation with indigenous qualities of the "Folk." But somewhere deep in their consciousness is the same attitude, borrowed from whites, that jazz music does not edify but merely entertains. A jazz artist is, therefore, merely an entertainer who, in certain cases, makes a lot of money—or at least a lot more than the average Negro earns. Such artists are successful, at least in quasi-middle-class terms. Therefore, in their practical minds, jazz entertainment is rated according to what degree its Negro practitioners earn money enough to achieve middle-class status. When this earning power reaches a level that permits one to purchase a Life Membership in the NAACP, an entertainer has "arrived." Sammy Davis, Jr. even went one better, for he was recently elected Chairman of the Association's Life-Membership Drive. This is an entertainer who has *truly* arrived! *The New York Times* described the occasion this way: "This is the serious side of the entertainer, a man whose public image is that of a perpetual-motion, rapid-fire showbusiness factotum."[11]

Every NAACP bigwig feels exactly the same way about entertainers of color: Just as long as they do not stereotype the Negro and offend middle-class sensibilities in such vehicles as *Porgy and Bess,* they are appreciated, but not taken too seriously. Thus the real impact of the Negro entertainer on race politics in American culture does not penetrate the minds of these colored, middle-class philistines.

These people do not want to comprehend the fact that the role of the Negro, as entertainer, has not changed since the 1920's. In 1967 the Negro entertainer is still being used, manipulated, and exploited by whites (predominantly Jewish whites). Negro entertainment talent is more original than that of any other ethnic group, more creative ("soulful" as they say), spontaneous, colorful, and also more plentiful. It is so plentiful, that in the marketplace of popular culture, white brokers and controllers buy Negro entertainment cheaply (sometimes for nothing) and sell it high—as in the case of Sammy Davis. But there is only *one* Sammy Davis. In the shadows, a multitude of lesser colored lights are plugging away, hoping against hope to make the Big Time, for the white culture brokers only permit a few to break through—thus creating an artificial scarcity of a cultural product. This system was established by the wily Broadway entrepreneurs in the 1920's. Negro entertainment posed such an ominous threat to the white cultural ego, the staid Western standards of art, cultural values and aesthetic integrity, that the entire source had to be stringently controlled.

Forty years after the 1920 era, Duke Ellington has outplayed, outcreated and outlasted all the Benny Goodmans and Paul Whitemans—yet the situation has not changed very much. A Sammy Davis goes on Broadway in a musical, *Golden Boy,* which was fashioned as a theatrical vehicle using the same cultural rule of thumb as *Porgy and Bess,* with a few minor variations. The story was not originally about Negro life, but was adapted. The creative functions—writing, composing and lyric versifying—were all done by whites. The music was purely routine. Although it is well known that it is a rare white composer, indeed, who can write Negro music, the Broadway entrepreneurs did not employ any of the several gifted Negro composers available who have never been commissioned to write music for the theater. Yet the public, Negro and white, are propagandized to believe that *Golden Boy* was a landmark in theatrical and symbolic racial democracy, simply because it was "integrated" on stage. This is tantamount to saying that if *Porgy and Bess* were to be staged with an integrated cast, that would make it more acceptable to the audience as an achievement in democratic casting. But all of this amounts to nothing but a dishonest illusion. Theatrical practices in America that exclude the participation of Negro creative artists—the writer, dramatist, poet, composer, designer, *et al.*—are not democratic practices at all. No amount of integrated casting can cover up this fact.

But the Negro creative intellectuals cannot exert themselves to deal with the *roots* of these problems, because they permit too many of the surface issues to pass without dealing with *them*. The question of Ellington and the Pulitzer Prize is a surface issue. The prize itself is not really important, but what lies behind the denial of the prize, *is:* a whole history of organized duplicity and exploitation of the Negro jazz artist—the complicated tie-in between booking agencies, the musicians' unions, the recording companies, the music publishers, the managers, the agents, the theater owners, the nightclub owners, the crooks, shysters, and racketeers. The Negro creative intellectuals have to look into the question of how it is possible for a Negro jazz musician to walk the streets of large cities, jobless and starving, while a record that he cut with a music company is selling well, both in the United States and in Europe. They have to examine why a Negro jazz musician can be forced to pay dues to unions that get him no work, and that operate with the same discriminatory practices as clubs, halls and theaters. The impact of the cultural tradition of Afro-American folk music demands that the racially-corrupt practices of the music-publishing field be investigated.

The Negro creative intellectuals must also take action against the film-producing conspiracy in the United States, where a "one-star" system has been manufactured around Sidney Poitier. He is supposed to represent the cultural presence, the aspirations, and the social psychology of the largest minority in the United States, a minority whose population is considerably larger than many independent nations in the world. The Negro creative intellectuals cannot make peace with a cultural apparatus that will not take *Invisible Man,* or any other representative novel, and film it. Whether such works are good, bad or excellent is academic, in view of the millions of dollars wasted annually in filming trash for the movie market. There are those who will object to this criticism of the cultural apparatus—allegedly in the interests of a cultural laissez-faire policy. However, any advanced nation that has allowed its inner cultural expressions to be so debased and corrupted, deserves nothing less than governmental investigation, correction and control.

But the Negro intelligentsia cannot give cultural leadership on these questions because they have sold out their own birthright for an illusion called Racial Integration. Having given up their strict claim to an ethnic identity in politics, economics and culture, they haven't a leg to stand on. They can make no legitimate claims for their group integrity in cultural affairs. They take the *illusion* of the integrated world of the creative intellectuals as the social *reality*, and do not know how to function within its cultural apparatus.

What lurks behind the disabilities and inhibitions of the Negro creative intellectuals is the handicap of the black bourgeoisie. Unless this class is brought into the cultural situation and forced to carry out its responsibilities on a community, organizational, and financial level, the cultural side of the black revolution will be retarded. The snail's pace of bourgeois civil rights reform, and white power-structure manipulation, will combine to stall it indefinitely. The problem of cultural leadership, then, is not only a problem of the faulty orientation of the Negro creative intellectuals; it is also a problem of the reeducation of the black bourgeoisie, especially its new, younger strata.

NOTES

1. *The Public Arts* (New York: Simon & Schuster, 1956), p. 207.
2. Ibid., p. 1.
3. *The Seven Lively Arts,*[sic] op. cit., p. 147.
4. *Variety,* May 27, 1959, p. 16.
5. See also, "Why Negroes Don't Like Porgy and Bess," *Ebony,* October, 1959, pp. 50-54.
6. *The Seven Lively Arts,* p. 100.
7. New York: Random House, 1956, p. 180.
8. See "Porgy and Bess Wins Ovation in Moscow," *Daily Worker,* January 12, 1956, p. 2. See also, David Platt, "Letters from Prague Reveal Divided Opinions on Porgy and Bess," *Daily Worker,* March 22, 1956, p. 6.
9. *The New York Times,* May 5, 1965, p. 49.
10. *The Seven Lively Arts,* op. cit., p. 150.
11. April 13, 1966, p. 24.

CHAPTER NINE

Negroes and Jews— The Two Nationalisms and the Bloc(ked) Plurality

Few subjects in American social politics have elicited as much hand-wringing, invective, lament, critique, and fury as the moribund "Black-Jewish alliance." Historians have charged that the "golden age" of Black-Jewish relations (roughly 1909 to 1939) was characterized by a humanitarian impulse that led disproportionate numbers of Jews to participate in the civil rights struggles of Blacks (including the founding of the NAACP). Contending voices have argued that altruism was not the sole adhesive holding together the fabled alliance, that Jewish Americans reaped a social windfall from the advances of blacks—gaining what one historian has called "civil rights by remote control." Cruse's withering assessment notwithstanding, James Baldwin's essay "Negroes Are Anti-Semitic Because They Are Anti-White" makes a similar point. The Watersheds of the Bakke case, the Ocean Hill-Brownsville conflict, and Andrew Young's dismissal as U.S. ambassador to Israel brought the subject into full view. In recent years the internecine riots between Blacks and Jews in Crown Heights, Brooklyn, and the appearance of demagogic figures shouting racist and/or anti-Semitic platitudes have only increased the relevance of Cruse's analysis. Irrespective of the particulars of his ideas, the analytical dissection of this topic in many ways has its roots in the questions Cruse raised in the following essay.

≈

Throughout this critique we have referred repeatedly to Jews and Negro-Jewish relations. If this shocks or offends certain readers, they might note that the Jewish press deals with these interminority group imperatives much more often than the diffident Negro press would ever dare to. For example, *Commentary*, the leading organ of Jewish intellectualism, hardly skips an issue in which Negroes and/or Negro-Jewish relations are not analyzed at length. This magazine is a true reflection of what the inner Jewish world really thinks about the Negro problem. Like the pre-Hitler German Jews who were "more German than the Germans," some assimilated American Jews become more American than the WASPs in their response to Negro uprisings, and more conservative than the editorial board of *The National Review*.

For many years, certain Negro intellectuals have been unable to face the Jews realistically. Among the many myths life and history have imposed on Negroes (such as that of Lincoln's "freeing" the slaves) is the myth that the Negro's best friend is the Jew. Far more accurately, certain Jews have been the best friends of certain Negroes—which, in any case, is nothing very unusual. This idea of Jewish friendship seems to have been born and given currency in the twentieth century. There is little evidence that the Jewish group was much interested in the Negro's plight for "social uplift" reasons prior to the age of Booker T. Washington and the NAACP era that followed. But this is not to say that Jews were not acutely aware of the Negro's existence. How aware certain Jews were, is revealed in a very unlikely source—the autobiographical notes of the great Russian writer, Feodor M. Dostoevski. Writing about the Jewish question in Russia, in the year 1877, he said:

> But let them be morally purer that all the peoples of the world, nevertheless I have just read in the March issue of the *Messenger of Europe* a news item to the effect that in America, in the Southern States, they have already leaped *en masse* upon the millions of liberated Negroes, and have already taken a grip upon them in their, the Jews' own way, by means of their semipaternal "gold pursuit" and by taking advantage of the inexperience and vices of the exploited tribe. Imagine, when I read this, I immediately recalled that the same thing came to

my mind five years ago, specifically, that the Negroes have now been liberated from the slave owners, but that they will not last because the Jews, of whom there are so many in the world, will jump at this new little victim.[1]

It is known that during the last phases of the Civil War, Union Army generals in the South had serious difficulties suppressing the business activities of Jewish traders from the North who followed closely in the wake of the invading Union troops. The American frontier, both South and West, of course presented an open market readily available for any enterprising tradesman seeking a new stake in the world. But it was from the Jewish shopkeeper and trader that the Southern Negro got his latent anti-Semitism. Down through the years, Negroes learned to differentiate between whites and Jewish whites in trade, by the designation "Jew Store," as opposed to other kinds of stores. In one of his superb stories, Richard Wright told of certain taboo subjects that a Negro was not allowed to discuss with a Southern white man. One of these was the presence of the Jew who prospered in the South, despite anti-Semitism. W. J. Cash wrote: "The South had relatively few Jews—certainly not enough to constitute a Jewish Problem. . . . But fears and hates often clothe themselves in old forms. . . . And in addition there was the consideration I have already suggested: the Jew, with his universal refusal to be assimilated is everywhere the eternal Alien."[2]

An "alien" yes, but one who knew how to manage, prosper and be self-sufficient. American Jews had long learned how to get along with American white Christians and the latter's "Negro problem"; they learned what they as a *group* must, and must not, do about this situation. Considering the hazards involved, one cannot blame the Jews for their nineteenth-century neutrality on the race question. Thus it was that the oldest Jewish fraternal organization in America, the Germanic B'nai B'rith, established in 1843, never involved itself even in the moral crusade of the Abolitionists. As a body, American Jewry took no action, either pro or con, on the slavery issue, even while the Christian churches were rent by warring factions over the issue.

As regards the slavery issue, American Jews *as individuals* were no different from other individual American whites: They were pro-slavery, anti-slavery, slave-owners, slave-traders, pro-Union, pro-Confederate, war profiteers, army officers, soldiers, spies, statesmen, opportunistic politicians or indifferent victims of intersectional strife of the Civil War. There were Abolitionists such as Rabbi David Einhorn of Baltimore, and pro-slavery Confederate statesmen such as the scholarly and brilliant Judah P. Benjamin, the Secretary of State from Louisiana: "It was not, however, as Jews, but only as individuals, that the men who have been referred to espoused the pro-slavery cause; the Jewish community, as such, took no stand."[3]

But it was the Civil War itself that inspired the first notable anti-Semitic manifestation from the North, and it came from the high command of the Union Army. The collapse of its armies in the Tennessee-Mississippi districts had opened a breach in the Confederacy's economic fortress, paving the way for widespread speculation and thievery in cotton and other Southern products badly needed in the North. "Bribery and corruption in every branch of the [Union] service" was rampant, and "in the midst of this nightmare of profiteering . . . the most sweeping anti-Jewish regulation in all American history was issued. It was wired from General Grant's headquarters in Holly Springs, Mississippi, on December 17, 1862."

The order read: "General Order Number 11—'The Jews, as a class violating every regulation of trade established by the Treasury Department and also departmental orders, are hereby expelled from the department within twenty-four hours from the receipt of this order.'"[4]

This order, signed by U. S. Grant, created a major scandal for the War Department in Washington. Jews protested, bringing the American Jewish question into focus in such a way as to give American anti-Semitism the political tone it was to assume into the twentieth century. In 1877, anti-Semitic social discrimination created another cause célèbre when Joseph Seligman, the immigrant German-Jewish banker, was denied accommodations at a certain fashionable Northern WASP hotel. This incident, among others of less notoriety, alerted such Jewish groups as B'nai B'rith to the fact that the status of American Jewry was then less than secure. It was said that Seligman arrived penniless in the United States, yet he made such a name for himself as a financial wizard in the field of international banking that the same General Grant who issued General Order Number 11, offered Seligman the post of Secretary of the Treasury during Grant's tenure as President. The American national group problem was a long way from being cogently defined and American jimcrowism, as opposed to anti-Semitism, was even farther away from any compensatory amends from the power structure.

But the deepening anti-Semitic trends of those years were to culminate tragically before subsiding into the American mood of what is called "tolerance," when Leo M. Frank was lynched in Georgia in 1915 (the only recorded lynching of a Jew). On the basis of racist passions, Frank was judged guilty of the 1913 murder of a young white girl long before he was brought to trial. Legally, his guilt was never proven, and he is the only Southern white man ever prosecuted and judged guilty on the testimony of a Negro (who was also circumstantially implicated in the crime). Frank was a young married college graduate, the manager of a manufacturing establishment in Georgia, and incidentally the president of his local branch of B'nai B'rith. His death [sentence] was instrumental in the creation of the Anti-Defamation League in 1913.

This is some of the historical background, indefinite as it is, that led many Negro intellectuals to believe there was something of a special quality about Jewish friendship for the Negro, that Jewish liberalism was different from white liberalism proper. Thus it must have been quite a shock to certain Negroes when Norman Podhoretz, the editor of *Commentary*, made public his considerable phobias toward the Negro, in his article "My Negro Problem and Ours."[5] Lorraine Hansberry, one of the most convinced exponents of Negro-Jewish unity, retorted indignantly that Podhoretz had to "hold his nose" when contemplating Negroes at close range. But after all, Podhoretz only expressed honestly what many other Jews who had intimate dealings with Negroes, had intimated in random conversations.

What lay behind Podhoretz's avowals, however, was the fact that the Jewish community was in the process of reevaluating the position of Jews in American society. A new Jewish image was in the throes of formation, calling for a studied shift from the former stock appraisals of Negro-Jewish relations. For example, on the evening of November 17, 1965, an influential rabbi—Arthur Hertzberg of Englewood, New Jersey—speaking at the Zionist Theodore Herzl Institute, stated that American Jews were no longer among the "have-nots" but associated with the "haves." He stated that this required the Jewish community to reassess its entire relationship with American society, and also with the Negro civil rights movement. He declared that he was happy to be in the presence of such "positive Jews" as those associated with the Theodore Herzl Institute, who were unlike certain other kinds of Jews who go "crawling on their bellies to Rome." In other words, the rabbi was saying that today American Jews are a power in this land and should act accordingly. Behind this power, of course, is the State of Israel, which immeasurably enhances the new status of American Jewry as a "have" group.

To solve Hertzberg's equation the American Negro must seriously reassess *his* relationships with American Jews. Such reassessment should have taken place immediately after the establishment of Israel in 1948. For the emergence of Israel as a world-power-in-minuscule meant that the Jewish question in America was no longer purely a domestic minority problem growing out of the old immigrant status tradition. A great proportion of American Jews began to function in America as an organic part of a distant nation-state. This power, in fact, was exerted beforehand, in the very formation of this state. During the 1948 presidential election, Senator McGrath, chairman of the Democratic National

Committee, had to warn his colleagues "that our failure to go along with the Zionists [on Palestine] might lose the states of New York, Pennsylvania and California. . . ."[6] It was established that "the United States was primarily responsible for the creation of a Jewish State in the heart of the Arab world, but Soviet support made it possible."[7] This fact attests to Zionist power in the United States. But the United Nations partition of Palestine did violence to the Charter's promise of "respect for the principle of equal rights and self-determination of peoples," and made the Charter "look like unblushing hypocrisy."[8]

Neither the Negro movement as a whole, nor the Negro creative intellectuals as a class stratum, has ever taken a forthright position on either the international implications of Israel vis-à-vis black Africa or the domestic implication of Jews vis-à-vis the Negro movement. Negroes have either been uncritically pro-Jewish or critically tongue-tied on both matters. Such ambivalence toward Jews stems partly from the fact that Negro intellectuals and critics allow them to deal with the Negro issue on *their own* terms from *their* position of social power. That is why the *Commentary* magazine round-table discussion in the winter of 1964, featuring James Baldwin, was such a disastrous failure in terms of clarification of issues. When Norman Podhoretz put the following question to Baldwin, the latter could not answer it, as he had neither the insight nor the knowledge to do so: "Mr. Baldwin, is it conceivable to you that the Negroes will within the next five or ten or twenty years take their rightful place as one of the *competing groups in the American pluralistic pattern* [italics added]? Or is something more radical—or perhaps less radical—more likely to happen the way things are going now?"

Nothing that Baldwin has ever written indicates that he could deal, even superficially, with the implications of that question. Yet it was the most important question asked during the whole discussion, and Baldwin (along with Kenneth Clark) had to sidestep it, either from lack of knowledge or conviction. Podhoretz, of course, was merely voicing *Commentary*'s contemporary understanding of an old question. For years American Jewry has been much concerned with the implications of cultural pluralism. Jewish intellectuals have written extensively about it,[9] inasmuch as official Zionist policy has always been that of anti-assimilationist, pro-Jewish group solidarity.

The problem here is that Baldwin, strictly speaking, is not a pluralist. In fact, Baldwin does not know what he stands for, sociologically. Thus it was unfair to the public, as well as ludicrous and embarrassing, to see Baldwin floundering and frantic under the pointed questioning of Jewish experts. They, at least, even if uncertain as to where they are headed in Negro-Jewish affairs, *do know exactly what they want in America.*

It would not be correct to call Baldwin a Jew-lover, inasmuch as Baldwin simply loves everybody, even those he feels are against him. More exactly, he fits the category of apologist for the Jews, true to the tradition of Negro expreachers well-versed in Hebrew biblical lore and all that deep-river-waters-of-Jordan history. But the most critical problem for the Negro today in Negro-Jewish affairs is posed not by the apologist, but by the professional pro-Semite. Political Negro-Jewish interracialism has cropped out in all its peculiar preciousness on the American cultural front. Many of our creative intellectuals have been caught up in the rather exclusive, and often intolerant, interethnic social orbit, especially in the civil rights movement.

American Negroes (as distinct from West Indians) do not come out of the European tradition, know very little about it, and care less. I am speaking of the masses here, not the colored elite of various "sets." Hence, what European Jews suffered in Europe has very little bearing on the American experience (excepting that many of the Jewish intellectuals here tend to adopt as their own, the martyr's mantle of those who were nailed to the German Iron Cross). One cannot deny the horror of the European Jewish holocaust, but for all practical purposes (political, economic and cultural) as far as Negroes are concerned, *Jews have not suffered in the United States.* They have, in fact, done exceptionally well on every level of endeavor, from a nationalist premise or on an assimilated status. They have mastered the fine art of playing both ends against the "middle" of group status. But the fact remains that the European experience shows that when it comes to playing the role of the Chosen People in history, the danger is that *two* can play this game as well as one. When that happens, woe be to the side that is short on numbers. The European experience also shows that European imperialism was not exclusively a Christian affair: Witness the international machinations that brought about the State of Israel.

Thus no matter how many organizations are at work today, watching the ideological weathervanes for traces of anti-Semitism, the average Negro is not going to buy the propaganda that Negroes and Jews are "brother-sufferers" in the same boat. As a matter of fact, most Negroes and Jews in America are quite justifiably either embarrassed or resentful over this kind of talk. However, merely to point this out is not enough, and the whole question of Negro-Jewish relations needs to be seriously examined. The misinterpretations and misinformation involved give off very ominous overtones, and presage some very nasty group clashes when and if the racial question really explodes in America. The truth is— and has always been—that if anyone in America wants to find Anti-Negroism, Anti-Semitism, Anti-Catholicism or Anti-foreignism, one need go no farther than precisely these same Negroes, Jews, Catholics and foreigners; there, you will find black against black, Jew against Jew, Catholic against Catholic, foreigner against foreigner—plus all four ethnic categories against each other—and the WASPs against the whole lot. These are the ingredients that never blended within the American melting pot. And it is time for intelligent American opinion to recognize that the country is *not* homogeneous, and that consequently, the group question has been misinterpreted and mishandled for many decades. Hence, today, a fateful triangular tension among national groups is coming to the fore, packed with the high explosives of ethnic, racial and religious conflicts. This triangle, comprising Anglo-Saxons, Negroes and Jews, cuts across class lines and has deep ramifications on the economic, political and cultural fronts. For deep within the social consciousness of these groups lie three nationalist ideologies— Anglo-Saxon nationalism,* black nationalism and Jewish nationalism (Zionism). The first is both overt and covert, especially in the South; the second is openly avowed and vocal, but poorly organized and even more poorly directed; the third is the most highly organized of all—the most sophisticated, scholarly and intellectual, with the most highly refined propaganda techniques—and hence the most successful of the three. A study of Jewish Zionist organizational and propaganda techniques reveals that influential Zionist thought sees Anglo-Saxon nationalism in the United States as its main potential political threat. Zionist thought also correctly sees the Negro civil rights drive for social equality and racial integration as a possible indirect threat to Jewish status, in the event that Negroes drive Anglo-Saxon nationalists into the radical rightist political camp. Hence, Jewish trends that are pro-Zionist and anti-Jewish-integration-assimilation, are forced to take a pro-Negro integration position and an anti-black nationalist position. *Thus, pro-Zionist influences within Negro civil rights organizations are strategically aiding and abetting Negro integration (assimilation), albeit Zionists, themselves, do not believe in integration (assimilation) for Jews.* This nationalist triangle is further complicated by the fact that not all Anglo-Saxons (especially the Northern liberal variety), nor all Negroes, nor all Jews, are nationalists or Zionists. Some Jews, however, are assimilationists, as are some Negroes: Witness the jesting "ethnic" idea behind the bit of dialogue in *Brustein's Window* to the effect that Brustein was an "assimilationist Jew." But this line had serious "folksy" intent, as far as the playwright's ethnic sentiments went. Lorraine Hansberry had not simply married a man who "just happened to be of Jewish antecedents" as the liberal-humanist-moralists would have it; she had "assimilated" into white Jewish cultural life.

---

*   Often called Christian nationalism.

Other Negro intellectuals who reflect this white-Negro-Jewish ideological muddle are LeRoi Jones and James Baldwin. The latter, of course, has given us his allegedly "angry" view on whites and white Jews in his essays. LeRoi Jones, however, is a rather special type. He is a writer who cannot so easily be categorized as a Negro intellectual, completely lacking a critique. This is because Jones is of a younger trend and therefore more amenable to new styles of thought on cultural problems. As I have pointed out, when Jones was involved in the On Guard for Freedom Committee in 1961, he had a hard time understanding why the mass of Harlem Negroes should be anti-white. His close friend, musician Archie Shepp, took the same position. At an On Guard meeting Shepp took the floor and argued against the economics and the politics of nationalism, in connection with a proposal that On Guard set up a movement in Harlem to foster self-help economic cooperatives among ghetto Negroes. Shepp proposed instead that On Guard stage a black demonstration on a corner of the richest section of New York's Park Avenue (note the protest mentality). Yet note the direction that Jones and Shepp shortly took.

By 1964-65, both Jones and Shepp were staging bitter anti-white diatribes downtown, in places like the Village Vanguard. Why? What did it prove? Why did Jones and Shepp object to anti-white nationalism in Harlem, only to assume it in Greenwich Village as *individuals?* It was because Jones and Shepp are artists who function in cultural and artistic spheres without being motivated by a serious, well-thought-out literary and cultural critique on the white society they are attacking. They would be hard put to explain their contradictory behavior on this score; but what they were in fact expressing in the Village was a *cultural nationalism* which has not been analyzed in terms of its political, communal and cultural categories. In other words, because Jones and Shepp wanted nothing to do with political or communal nationalism in *Harlem,* they rejected it, despite the fact that their own *cultural* nationalism had not yet matured ideologically. Harlem nationalists, themselves, have had no program for the political and communal realities of the Harlem ghetto, hence, they had no understanding of the cultural nationalism that would later emerge from Jones and Shepp. Organizationally and ideologically, there could be no meeting of the minds on these levels, hence Jones and Shepp had to reject a nationalism to which they could not relate. Yet when they began to express their own anti-whiteness—their cultural nationalism—in 1965, they were not only anti-white, but specifically critical of *Jewish* whites. But their attitude toward Jews was like the reverse side of James Baldwin's superficialities on Negro-Jewish relations. Baldwin refuses to "hate" Jews on ethical grounds; both Jones and Shepp refused to "love" Jews on some other ethical grounds, which were never explored. Hence neither position is predicated on any meaningful inquiry into the real social status of Jews as compared to that of Negroes, in order to determine the very real inequality therein.

At the Village Vanguard, when Jones and Shepp were reminded of the six million Jews exterminated by Hitler, Jones replied to Larry Rivers, "You're like the others [whites], except for the cover story." Shepp added: "I'm sick of you cats talking about the six million Jews. I'm talking about the five to eight million Africans killed in the Congo. King Leopold is his name."

When a white woman expressed the view that Jones and Shepp should be thankful for the aid and assistance given by whites (and Jews) to the civil rights causes in the South, Shepp replied: "I give no civil service charity for going to Mississippi to 'assuage their consciences.'"[10]

In discussing the Mississippi murder and martyrdom of Andrew Goodman and Michael H. Schwerner, both Jews, Shepp observed that the first victim, James E. Chaney, a Negro, had been beaten into an unrecognizable state, while even in death the white lynchers had "embraced" their fellow whites by treating them "less harshly." There are profound moral and ethical problems involved here, but the question is—How far into the historical roots of these moral issues are Jones and Shepp willing to go? How far afield from New York City, where free speech is permitted all factions from Freedom Riders to Fascists, will Negro intellectuals go to search out the economic, cultural, political and imperialistic strands and bind them together into a meaningful critique? If they reject Schwerner and Goodman today, they must reject John Brown(*ism*) of yesterday and expunge his name from Negro history, along with the Abolitionists as the precursors of paternalistic freedom assistance for blacks. But the Robesons, the Apthekers, the Shirley Graham DuBoises, *et al.*, would not like that. To tie in the slaughter of Jews in Germany and the slaughter of Africans in the Congo, one must look into the question of Zionism and the role it has played in Europe, especially in Germany and Russia, but also in the Israel of today.*

The truth is that Jones and Shepp are confused on the Jews. Jones called the slain Goodman and Schwerner "artifacts" and "paintings on the wall." But Shepp said, relentingly, to Larry Rivers, "I consider you a friend, an enemy." There was laughter from the audience, but Shepp insisted: "I spoke the truth. I

---

* Edmond de Rothschild, the early founding father of Zionist colonization, was one of the big financial backers of Cecil J. Rhodes' African explorations in the 1870's and 1880's, when the British capitalist and explorer founded the DeBeer's Mining Company and established monopoly over the Kimberley diamond production enterprises.

mean *both* things." Of course he did, because he is mixed up emotionally about Jews (and all whites), but about Jews, especially.

Can one accept and reject Jews at one and the same time? In terms of Africa today, can an Afro-American accept American Jews and the fact of Israel together, when to most Jews in America a refusal to accept Israel's reality is an affront to all Jews? Can one fight neo-colonialism in Africa today without fighting Israel? These are tough questions because the headquarters of some big trusts who are still extracting millions upon millions in profit from African copper, gold and diamonds, have connections in Israel.* Such questions as these can be raised and lightly touched on in Greenwich Village jazz salons, but they cannot be explored or settled there. They are much too big and supercharged with political dynamite.

It has become almost axiomatic that one can determine just which political, economic, cultural, or civil rights "bag" any Negro intellectual is in, by whether or not he is willing to criticize American Jews publicly. If he is wary, he is either ignorant of the facts of life in multi-group America, or else organizationally involved with a Jewish and/or Zionist influence, as is prevalent in certain civil rights groups.

When James Baldwin writes about Jews *in* Harlem he does not know with whom and what he is dealing. He thinks that he is dealing with Negro-Jewish relations on a strictly moralistic level. In recognizing the fact that there is much overt and covert anti-Semitism among Negroes, he lumps all of this into an international-moral question concerning Jewish martyrdom on the European scene. Hence, he concludes that "both the Negro and the Jew are helpless; the pressure of living is too immediate and incessant to allow time for understanding." Baldwin pinpoints the essential, historical bias:

> The Negro's outlets are desperately constricted. . . . Here the Jew is caught in the American crossfire. The Negro facing a Jew, hates, at bottom, not his Jewishness but the color of his skin. It is not the Jewish tradition by which he has been betrayed but the tradition of his native land. But just as a society must have a scapegoat, so hatred must have a symbol. Georgia has the Negro and Harlem has the Jew.[11]

---

* Today, Israel ranks second to Belgium in the export of finished diamonds, although Israel mines no diamonds in the Negev. Her diamond exports increased from five million dollars in 1950 to one hundred and thirty million in 1965. This raises the question of Israel's relationships with the great mining interests in South Africa involving the Oppenheimer empire—the DeBeer's Mining Syndicate, the Anglo-American Copper trust, etc.

Just before this, Baldwin talks about his "Jewish friends in high school" who were not like those "other Jews" that other Negroes hated, or pretended to hate "because the nation does." These Jewish friends, said Baldwin, "had no intention of exploiting me, we did not hate each other." However, Baldwin points out that those Jews in Harlem who *are* exploiting are small tradesmen, rent collectors, real estate agents, and pawnbrokers, who "operate in accordance with the American business tradition. . . ." In other words, Jews don't exploit because of hate; it is rather that Negroes *hate* to be exploited. This disturbs Baldwin who feels that it is wrong and pointless for Negroes to react this way, for such criticism of Jews on this score is to Baldwin, the rebel, equivalent to anti-Semitism. Even if Harlem Negroes simply said they hated to be exploited by whites and never mentioned the word "Jew," Baldwin would still consider that anti-Semitism by implication. Presumably, Baldwin is suggesting that Negroes in Harlem should simply accept exploitation and say nothing at all, because, after all, exploitation is "in accordance with the American business tradition." What all this really means, again, is that Baldwin wants to avoid dealing with the facts of Harlem as they *exist.*

This essay on "The Harlem Ghetto" was really a chic piece of magazine journalism that rehashed all the time-worn superficialities of Harlem "local color" and decrepitude. It has been done before, and it was merely the added flavor of Baldwin's personal reminiscences that made an essay out of glorified journalese. However, the great flaw in Baldwin's approach to Harlem (and its Jews and its business traditions) is that he wants this blight totally obliterated. Yet he overlooks the fact that the same "American business tradition" from which exploitation flows will not let Harlem be erased so easily from the American scene. No one ever willingly allowed a gold mine to be blown up, so Harlem is going to remain with its Negroes, its Jews and its businesses. Somewhere along the line Negroes and Jews in Harlem are fated to confront the issues of economic and social imbalance between them.

James Baldwin looks at the Jewish question with the eyes of a rather innocent and provincial intellectual. Bending over backward to avoid criticism of Jews while pretending to be angry with whites, he overlooks the fact that if *American* Jews are "caught in the American crossfire" they are also very much in control of the situation and have their enemies well "cased" from all directions. Baldwin's unfortunate mismatch with Jewish intellectuals on *Commentary* magazine showed that Jews also have Baldwin well "cased"— only he does not know it. Baldwin has not learned that Jews themselves are divided on many issues and that some Jews are more "crossfired" than others—especially those who are neither Zionists nor pro-Zionists. But among American Jews, who is who?*

To probe this important dichotomy one must first have some understanding of the relationship of American Jews to Israel. It has been described in the following way: "They [Jews] are not one and the same, in fact, they are bewilderingly different. I mean the Jews of the world and the Jewish leaders of Israel. But a sort of courtship goes on between them, a half sincere courtship, because both parties are married to somebody else. Yet they woo each other, the Jews, Israel; and Israel, the Jews."[12]

Since 1948, the relationship of American Jews to Israel has taken on a very special significance in terms of Negro-Jewish relations. As said before, these relations now become colored by the incipient clash of two ideologies—Black Nationalism and Zionism. These nationalisms, totally dissimilar in most respects, share one essential motivation: a yearning for national redemption through regaining a "homeland" that was lost. Both Zionism and Black Nationalism have undergone historical conditionings peculiar to themselves, and have never, to my knowledge, confronted each other on any domestic or international issue. *But today things are different, and Black Nationalism, Zionism, African affairs, and Negro civil rights organizations are intimately interlocked on the political, cultural, economic and international fronts, whether Negro intellectuals care to acknowledge it or not.* Today it is no longer possible for Negro intellectuals to deal with the Jewish question in America purely on a basis of brotherhood, compassion, morality, and other subjective responses which rule out objective criticism and positive appraisals. Taking a critical approach to the Jewish question does not preface a call to arms against Jews, so much as ensure a critical reexamination of how the national group question is handled in the United States.

Basically, all groups strive for survival and identity but certain groups cannot be allowed to survive at the expense of other groups. Hence, when American Negroes talk about survival, Negro intellectuals had better begin to study some of the necessary survival techniques, both organizational and propagandistic. Much more important than developing a critique on Jews, is the challenge of learning the methods and techniques that the Zionists have developed in the art of survival against all kinds of odds. Despite the fact, as Baldwin says, that "Jews

---

*   The American Council for Judaism, an anti-Zionist organization, reported in a news-letter, "Education in Judaism," dated April 4, 1965: "The Zionist movement, subservient to Israeli national interests, plays an important ideological role in American Jewish religious education; and most parents are unaware and uninterested."

are helpless," their helplessness has the enduring quality of a "lost battalion," which despite losses and desertions, manages to live off the land and survive. One of the key contributions to this art of survival has been the Jewish intellectuals' open support, in large numbers, of the Jewish nationalist-Zionist cause. Very few of the Negro intellectuals, from the 1920's down to James Baldwin, have supported any such movement among Negroes.

The movement among modern European Jews to regain Palestine as the base of a Jewish nation, was founded not by a politician or a religious leader, but a Hungarian Jewish playwright named Theodore Herzl (1860-1904), a "cultural nationalist." It is this that really lent the Zionist movement its inner strength— it had intellectuals as propagandists.* Unfortunately, Negro nationalist movements have *never* understood the significance of this. At the time Malcolm X was murdered, the young nationalists were still caught up in a highly unsophisticated and debilitating wrangle directed against writers and intellectuals, as such. The Zionists, conversely, during a period when the European Jews were really and truly helpless against the German genocidal assault, were able to launch a uniquely successful movement in America for the aid of those European Jews, garnering the support of: thirty-three United States Senators; one hundred and nine House Representatives; fourteen reigning State Governors; the same number of outstanding Ambassadors and members of Roosevelt's Cabinet; fifty-five justices and judges of various Supreme and District Courts; sixty mayors of leading American cities; four hundred rabbis in all the centers of American Jewry and almost twice as many Catholic and Protestant priests and ministers; a score of American Army generals, colonels and Navy admirals; scores of national leaders in high government posts; five hundred university professors and presidents, and an equal number of playwrights, poets, editors, novelists, star actors, singers, dancers and showmen.

These estimates, taken from Ben Hecht's book, are cited here to show that the ability to corral such broad support for Jewish causes does not exactly corroborate the "helplessness" in America to which Baldwin refers.

Ben Hecht was no mere respectable Zionist, but a functioning propagandist for the most extreme group—the Irgun Zvai Leumi—the young fighters who

---

* Interestingly enough, Martin R. Delany, one of the first nineteenth-century Negro leaders to express the idea of Africa-for-the-Africans, was a social critic and novelist as well as a physician. His novel, *Blake—Or the Huts of America,* was published in several installments in the 1859 *Anglo-African Magazine.*

   Theodore Herzl's Zionism represents the political phase which comes after the original economic colonization of the Jewish capitalists-founders of Zionism, such as Edmond de Rothschild.

scandalized the Weizmann–Ben Gurion Zionists by taking up arms against the British. Hecht was a successful Hollywood writer, well known in both the early Chicago and Greenwich Village bohemian circles of the 1920's. He was a close friend of Maxwell Bodenheim, *et al.*, but his cultural background did not prevent Hecht and others like him from siding with a dissident-extremist faction within respectable Zionism when that movement was struck by the crisis of world war and Jewish extermination. Hecht revealed the fateful nature of this Zionist split when he wrote:

> I list the number of our notables [listed above] not to show how powerful we were, *but how powerful was the opposition of Jewish Agency and Zionist organizations.* For the opposition of Jewish Authority won the day. Although we could break the conspiracy of silence in large meeting halls and in coast-to-coast newspapers and magazines, we could not grab the ear of government. *The slick and respectable Jewish organizations of the United States kept this ear plugged* [all italics added].[13]

The Irgun Zvai Leumi faction had accused the ruling Weizmann–Ben Gurion groups of pursuing policies that were tantamount to abandoning European Jews to their fate. Thus Hecht involved himself in campaign committees "for a Jewish Army in Palestine to help fight the Germans, for a Free Palestine, for the smuggling of German-doomed Jews into British-closed Palestine, etc. . . ." Prominent in these committees were such notables as Kurt Weill, Arthur Szyk the artist, Billy Rose the producer and Leonard Lyons, *The New York Post* columnist. Involved also was S. N. Behrman, a prominent Broadway playwright on the one hand, and a political admirer of Chaim Weizmann. (Behrman later wrote a biography, *Chaim Weizmann—the Builder of Zion.*) The fate of European Jews and Zionist ideology bound the Jewish intelligentsia together—at home and abroad. Hecht wrote of Ferenc Molnar, the prominent Hungarian-Jewish playwright who was rescued from Hungary along with other Jewish artists and intellectuals, largely through the efforts of Hecht's anti-respectable Zionist faction: "I was in especial public disfavor at the time for some anti-British, anti-Roosevelt and anti-Jewish Agency outcries I had helped loose in the press." During this time Hecht dropped by the home of Leonard Lyons where a party was in progress:

> Some sixty literary, theatrical, and financial luminaries sat at a dozen tables. . . .
> The guests were mostly Jews and Jewesses, with a few British—all Top Drawer.

One figure stood at the end of the room and walked slowly and a little dramatically toward me. It was Molnar.

He took my hand, bowed over it, kissed it as if I were a dowager, and said, "Thank you."

Thus Ferenc Molnar, who found it difficult to be a Jew; but having to be one, he ran up his colors under the enemy's nose—and saluted a comrade.[14]

What was demonstrated here was not mere "helplessness," Mr. Baldwin: This was also *power*—power refractorily subverted in the factionalism of partisan politics, as is often the case—but power nevertheless. The affair of the seventy thousand Rumanian Jews was another enlightening case in point in Zionist power politics. During the war, the Rumanian government had made an offer to the American and British governments to allow seventy thousand Jews to leave Rumania at the cost of fifty dollars a head for transportation. The American State Department had received the offer and pigeonholed it. Hecht and the Irgun went to work to expose the story—against the wishes of the official Zionists in New York. Hecht ran an advertisement in the New York papers announcing: "For sale, 70,000 Jews at $50 Apiece—Guaranteed Human Beings." Hecht wrote:

> On the appearance of this news advertising copy, Rabbi Stephen Wise, Zionist chieftain in New York and guiding light for the city's Jewish respectables, issued the following statement. The date was February 23, 1943. "The American Jewish Congress, dealing with the matter in conjunction with recognized Jewish organizations, wishes to state that no confirmation has been received regarding this alleged offer of the Rumanian Government to allow seventy thousand Jews to leave Rumania. Therefore no collection of funds would seem justified."

Hecht continued:

> The Jewish Agency in London also denied the Rumanian offer. This denial was cabled to American newspapers, and carried by them. And reading it, American Jews felt grateful to the Jewish Agency for removing the ugly Rumanian problem from their consciences.

Hecht explained that this Zionist policy derived from the fact that Jewish leaders such as Weizmann, Ben Gurion and Sharett "had limited their dream of Zion to a British-Jewish suburb" in the Middle East. Thus there was really no place in their Zionist scheme for very many poor Jews from the ghettoes of Europe. Hecht condemned these leading Zionists:

> These organizations, these philanthropists, these timorous Jewish lodge members in Zion, London and America—these Zionist leaders who let their six million kinsmen burn, choke, hang, without protest, with indifference, and even with a glint of anti-Semitic cunning in their political plannings—I sum up against them. These factotums, these policy-makers . . . who hung onto their jobs, who lorded it over their real estate holdings in Palestine, who obeyed the British demand that no ruckus be raised about Europe's Jews being murdered . . . I haul into the prisoner's dock of this book.[15]

The above is intended to elucidate certain truths about American Jews and Negro-Jewish relations for Negro intellectuals such as James Baldwin. The relationships between groups in America, and on the international plane, are actuated by the power principle, not by morality and compassion for the underdog classes. However, when Baldwin discussed Negro problems with the Jewish intellectuals on *Commentary* magazine in the winter of 1964, he did not, and could not, ask a more pertinent question: Where do you Jewish intellectuals of *Commentary* stand on the question of international Zionism? For without prefatory clarification on this issue, no Negro or Jew is prepared to discuss, in any serious way, any alleged approaches to better Negro-Jewish relations at home or abroad. In the April 30, 1954, issue of the *Jewish Press*, an article on the Black Muslims compares them with American Nazis like Lincoln Rockwell.[16] For Jews of this newspaper's persuasion, Muslims are racists and extremists. They conveniently forget, of course, that the Irgun Zvai Leumi and the Stern Gang (the Lehi) in pre-1948 Israel were called the same things—"Jewish racists and extremists." Yet it was these very people who truly forged Israel by forcing the British Army to vacate the territory. When Winston Churchill came to the United States after the war and met secretly with producer Billy Rose and Bernard Baruch, an American elder statesman and an obvious pro-Zionist,* Churchill admitted to both of them:

> If you were interested in the establishment of an Israeli Nation, you were involved with the right people. It was the Irgun that made the English quit

---

* Said Hecht, "Another Zionist Pied Piper was Louis Brandeis, to become Supreme Court Justice in Washington." (See *Perfidy*, p. 11.) Felix Frankfurter, Supreme Court Jurist, has Zionist connections. (N.B.)

Palestine. They did it by raising so much hell that we had to put eighty thousand soldiers into Palestine to cope with the situation. The military costs were too high for our economy. And it was the Irgun that ran them up.[17]

The Irgun, of course, was cast in a position where the use of arms was feasible, and as Palestine was an occupied war zone, armed terror was the order of the day. Peoples and nations have a habit of thoroughly hating everyone's nationalism but their own, and Jewish nationalists are no exception. Eventually, terroristic tactics will be used in Harlem against white-owned businesses by a nationalist faction, and the Jews will certainly call it anti-Semitism. Naturally Baldwin will not like to see this, but the Jewish writers on the newspaper *Jewish Press* do not even agree with Baldwin that Jewish exploitation in Harlem is a natural result—"in accordance with the American business tradition." They rationalize this exploitation by claiming that if it were not for the Jews there would be no businesses at all in Harlem to provide jobs for Negroes. Notice the arrogance here, boldly printed in the *Jewish Press*. Even if this were true, it is a good thing that Negroes do not read Jewish magazines and newspapers regularly, because such a statement would have certainly worsened already inflamed Negro-Jewish relations. What the *Jewish Press* said, however, does not tell the whole story of white-owned businesses in Harlem. There was a time, not too many years ago, when these Jewish-owned businesses *would not hire Negro help at all.* They did not do so, in fact, until forced to—*not* by the NAACP or the Urban League—but by the Black Nationalist organizations during the 1930's and early 1940's. Baldwin, however, in his Harlem ghetto essay does not even touch on such crucial and fundamental truths of Harlem history. If the Baldwins had historical perspective they would be better writers. If they knew and searched for facts, they would be better spokesmen. If they were more like Jewish intellectuals and creative artists, they would not be as afraid of becoming propagandists for their own kind in politics and culture as they are about writing "Everybody's Protest Novel"—only to wind up writing bad protest plays. If Negro intellectuals could become more objective and less subjective about the Negro-Jewish "thing," they might become more perceptive about the prevalent Jewish intellectual and literary mystique that has developed in America.[18]

What was the meaning of Nathan Glazer's article, "Negroes and Jews: The New Challenge to Pluralism"?[19] Glazer quoted Baldwin's observations on Jewish business in Harlem. Is the Negro—*i.e.,* are the Negro masses—really a challenge to pluralism, when real, true democratic pluralism has never been achieved? Is Nathan Glazer simply confusing the needs of the Negro masses with the aims of its spokesmen? In effect, Glazer admits that these leadership aims do not square with the facts of group life in America. Yet he upholds these aims as being not unrealizable. Whether or not Nathan Glazer is Zionist, pro-Zionist or anti-Zionist, the fact remains that pro-Zionist policies in civil rights organizations are pro-integrationist for Negroes and anti-assimilationist for Jews. Frankly, Jews can take integration, or leave it. Accordingly, Glazer recognizes that "the Negro now demands entry into a world, a society that does not exist, except in ideology. In that world there is only one American community, and in that world, heritage, ethnicity, religion, race are only incidental and accidental personal characteristics."

Glazer admits that such a world is mere illusion, yet against all manifest obstacles, he provides of its birth: "There may be many reasons for such a world to come into existence—among them the fact that it may be necessary in order to provide full equality for the Negroes. But if we do move in this direction, we will have to create communities very different from the kinds in which most of us who have already arrived—Protestants, Catholics, Jews—now live."

As a Jew, Nathan Glazer could be said to be most magnanimously free with other people's ethnicity. On the other hand, if things do not work out just right, Negro integrationists will be driven (as they already are) into a desperate blind alley with such an approach. So it remains to be asked: Just what is behind Nathan Glazer's fervent insistence that Negroes be integrated as fast as possible, and by any means? There is much evidence that today Negroes truly have a Jewish problem, and the Jew is not just a hatred symbol. There are far too many Jews from Jewish organizations into whose privy councils Negroes are not admitted, who nevertheless are involved in every civil rights and American-African organization, creating policy and otherwise analyzing the Negro from all possible angles. No matter what motivates such activity, the Negro in America will never achieve any kind of equality until more Negro intellectuals are equipped with the latest research and propaganda techniques to move into control and guidance of every branch of the Negro movement. Knowledge is power. The path to more knowledge for the Negro intellectual is through cultural nationalism—an ideology that has made Jewish intellectuals into a social force to be reckoned with in America.

NOTES

1. *The Diary of a Writer* (New York: George Braziller, 1954), p. 642.
2. *The Mind of the South* (New York: Doubleday, reprint 1941), p. 334.
3. Max J. Kohler, "The Jews and the American Anti-Slavery Movement," *Publication of the American Jewish Historical Society,* New York (1896), No. 5, p. 145.
4. Bertram W. Korn, *American Jewry and the Civil War* (Philadelphia: Jewish Publication Society of America, 1951), p. 122.

5. *Commentary,* February, 1963, pp. 93-101.

6. Chesly Manly, *The UN Record* (Chicago: Henry Regnery Co., 1955), p. 51.

7. Ibid., p. 50.

8. Ibid.

9. See bibliography of Milton M. Gordon's *Assimilation in American Life,* op. cit.

10. *The New York Times,* February 10, 1965, p. 47.

11. "The Harlem Ghetto," *Notes of a Native Son* (Boston: Beacon Press, 1957), pp. 71-72.

12. Ben Hecht, *Perfidy* (An account of the birth of Israel), [New York: Julian Messner, 1961], p. 7. Reprinted with permission of Julian Messner, Division of Simon & Schuster, Inc., from *Perfidy* by Ben Hecht. Copyright ©1961 by Ben Hecht.

13. *Perfidy,* op. cit., p. 189.

14. Ibid., pp. 86-87.

15. Ibid., pp. 191-193.

16. David Gilbert and Jack Brown, "The Black Muslims," *Jewish Press,* April 23, 30; May 7, 1965.

17. Hecht, op. cit., p. 40.

18. See Irving Malin, "Jews and Americans," *Crosscurrents,* 1965.

19. *Commentary,* December, 1964, pp. 29-34.

PART THREE

Black Power Era

CHAPTER TEN

On Explaining
20th Century Negro History

(*Negro Digest,* July 1967)

"The Negro Movement, in all of its aspects we know today, are nothing but a continuation of those early trends . . . Anyone who does not understand this cannot grasp what is wrong with the Movement today."

The article on A. Philip Randolph, "Portrait of an Afro-American Radical," by John Henrik Clarke (*Negro Digest,* March 1967) raises serious questions about the way our history is treated in the popular press. Although Mr. Clarke's purpose in writing this piece was, ostensibly, to present a brief sketch of what went into the making of an "Afro-American Radical," it so happens that "radicals" such as Mr. Randolph do not make history solely according to the dictates of their own personal designs. Such leaders are also shaped, molded, and propelled by social forces outside of and beyond themselves. Hence, it is impossible to get an understanding of a "radical" forty-odd years after his beginnings by telling *only* what he accomplished. We have a right to also know some of his failures, and at least a hint of what outside trends and forces during his career made for both his successes and his failures. Mr. Clarke failed to do this although he could very well have.

A. Philip Randolph is one of the more outstanding leaders in the *20th century history* of the American Negro. This is emphasized in order to *separate* the 19th from the 20th century. This is done because the most serious weakness in the outlook of the Negro civil rights movement in all its factions is that most of the *new* leaders and ideologists have very little understanding of the Negro movement's 20th century beginnings, and the mixture of ingredients that went into those beginnings. This ignorance of the 20th century is most glaring in the so-called "militant," "nationalist," "Black Power" wing of the Negro movement. Once the effectiveness of militant "direct action" techniques is blunted by racial realities in America, the militants are in serious trouble. They are forced to retrench behind slogans like "Black Power," etc., and to formulate "new" programs for "action." There is very little understanding here that, as leaders and "activists," this new militant breed of the 1960's is nothing but a continuation or repetition of similar trends, issues, slogans and "programs" brought to life from 1900 to the 1920's, the very period which produced a man like A. Philip Randolph.

Our movements for "freedom," "equality," "liberation," "emigration," "separation," "integration," and even "migration" from one state to another section are *20th century movements.* They have only the most tenuous "historical" connections with the 19th century trends of Frederick Douglass and others. Yet there is a persistent belief in articulate Negro circles that our present day movements are traceable back to pre–Civil War slavery, emancipation, Reconstruction, etc. But this is true only in a historical "Romantic" sense. We honor a Frederick Douglass in this historical sense, but all that Douglass stood for and fought for in post–Civil War Reconstruction was washed away by Southern Bourbon restoration of the 1880's and 1890's.

Douglass died in 1895 during the very decade when the United States became an openly, aggressively imperialist nation in its war against Spain in Cuba and the Philippines. When America became imperialistic in foreign policy, the relationship of the Negro to American society changed character and became something else not experienced by Frederick Douglass and the leaders of his heyday. The Negro was still committed to struggling for the same objectives as Douglass had, but under radically changed social, economic, political, and cultural conditions. It was for these reasons that the 1890's and early 1900's produced two entirely new leaders in the person of Booker T. Washington and

W. E. B. Du Bois who came into mutual conflict over "program" in a way that Douglass never had to experience with his own black contemporaries over slavery and emancipation.

Thus, the 20th century produced the movements, the leaders, the trends, the ideas, the conflicts which formed the historical and organizational beginnings to which our current 1960 movements are heirs. From 1895 to 1915 we had Washington's Tuskeegee movement; in 1905, we had Du Bois's Niagara movement which helped establish the NAACP in 1909. In 1911, the Urban League was formed and, a few years later, began the greatest mass migration in American history of the Negro out of the South into the North.

In the meantime, the American Socialist Party had attracted a corps of Negro intellectuals of whom A. Philip Randolph was one of the most outstanding. The Messenger magazine which he edited, along with Chandler Owen, was a black socialist organ which grew out of the Hotel Messenger which Randolph had founded in 1917. In 1919, the American Communist movement was established following the Russian Revolution of 1917. As a result, certain Negro Socialists associated with Randolph on his Messenger broke with the Socialists to become Communists. Randolph, however, remained a Socialist and became an anti-Communist. Thus, there developed a bitter political feud between Randolph and certain of his former Socialist colleagues in the Communist Party, which lasted from the 1920's into the 1940's, and beyond.

A. Philip Randolph emerged as a Socialist leader just prior to the time Marcus Garvey established his nationalistic "Back to Africa" movement in Harlem, after having failed to set it up in Jamaica, British West Indies. There developed a bitter feud not only between Randolph's Messenger group and the Garveyites, but also a fight between the Garveyites and the very same ex-colleagues of Randolph's who had become Communists. There was also a violent polemical conflict between Marcus Garvey and Du Bois's NAACP. At the same time, the young writers on Randolph's Messenger were criticizing W. E. B. Du Bois as an "old leader" from the "old school" who no longer spoke for the "New Negro." This was the same thing Du Bois had told Booker T. Washington about 20 years earlier when he revolted against Booker T.'s conservative economic nationalism with the Niagara movement.

What was going on here in the 1920's Negro movements? It was a fateful clash between NAACP civil rightsism, Garvey nationalism, Negro Socialism, Negro Communism, plus black trade unionism, when Randolph launched his Brotherhood of Sleeping Car Porter's organizing drive in 1925. Then, to add to this wild conflict of black politics and economics, came the provocative and, as yet ill-understood, question of "cultural consciousness" of the Negro Renaissance movement which produced Langston Hughes, Paul Robeson, Claude McKay, Countee Cullen, etc., and the "Jazz Age." The "grass roots" ferment underlying all of this provocative social ferment was the mass migration into New York of southern Negroes and West Indians.

The West Indian character of the Garvey movement spawned a clash between West Indians and American Negroes over group social values, leadership priorities, and accommodation to the ways of life in American northern cities. The attacks on Garveyism emanating from Randolph's Messenger and Du Bois's NAACP took on an anti–West Indian flavor and Garvey saved his choicest blasts for Du Bois. Yet, the facts are that, behind the scenes, Garvey's most effective enemies, the ones who had him jailed, were West Indians. All of these, and more, were the basic ingredients that went into the formation of the 20th century Negro movement, we know today. *And every single one of these issues are still with us* only in a more complex and exaggerated form. What we are dealing with in today's civil rights movement are the unsolved problems *not* of the 1930's, but the 1920's.

It was against such a background that A. Philip Randolph started the Brotherhood of Sleeping Car Porters. But for Mr. Clarke to merely cite the opposition of the Pullman company against Randolph's efforts is of little crucial importance today. Everybody knows that industry management was always anti-labor, whether white or black. What is more important for us is an insight into Randolph's personal Socialist politics *before* he started organizing porters. For example, who were some of the other prominent Negro Socialists Randolph was allied with? Why were they so critical of the politics of W. E. B. Du Bois? Clarke's Freedomways magazine is a very pro-Du Bois publication, but in 1919, Randolph's Messenger said that "Du Bois's conception of politics is strictly opportunist. Within the last six years he has been Democrat, Socialist, and Republican." "He must," said the Messenger editorially, "make way for the new radicalism of the new Negro."

During the same period, several of Randolph's Socialist colleagues around the Messenger broke with the Socialist Party and joined the newly formed Communist Party movement. They became the pioneer Negro Communists of the 1920's. It is important for us to know why Randolph refused to become a Communist himself while some of his friends did. Randolph always remained an anti-Communist. At least two of Randolph's former 1920's friends are still alive, and one of them even writes for Freedomways occasionally. In view of the fact that W. E. B. Du Bois finally joined the Communist Party in 1961 (some 40 years after it was formed) and in view of the fact that Freedomways is pro-Du Bois, how can Mr. Clarke, as a Freedomways editor, call Randolph a "radical"? What was the precise difference between Du Bois's "radicalism" and Randolph's "radicalism?"

The Communists of the 1920's looked with disfavor upon Randolph's organizing of the Pullman porters into a *separate all-black union.* None of Randolph's ex–Negro Socialist friends who had become Communists supported Randolph in his efforts to organize the porters. Why did they take this attitude? During the same period, Randolph's Messenger said editorially that Negro Communists were a menace. Why did Randolph believe this? What about Randolph's relationship with the Garvey movement? It is a fact that Randolph's Messenger writers were implacable enemies of the Garvey movement. In 1923, the Messenger attacks on the Garvey movement were so bitter that W. A. Domingo, one of Randolph's ex-friends among the Negro Socialists, wrote a letter of protest accusing the Messenger of being "anti-West Indian." Domingo had quit the Messenger as a staff writer because of Randolph's handling of the Garvey question. Domingo complained:

> Who are the bitterest enemies and most persistent opponents of Garvey? Aren't they West Indians . . . ?

W. A. Domingo was anti-Garvey; Randolph was anti-Garvey; and the Communists were anti-Garvey, and Garvey was particularly anti-Communist. But what was Garvey's attitude towards Randolph's organizing of the pullman porters? This question is no longer crucial for Garveyism today since Garveyism is no longer an important force. However, it is still important relative to the Communists because the enmity between Randolph and the Communist Party has been an everlasting fact. Mr. Clarke, however, must pass over many of these facts as if they were not important, *but they are.* Not only must we review all these historical trends—Garvey Nationalism, Black Socialism, Black Communism, Black trade unionism, Black civil rightsism, etc.—we must also have some historical understanding of why all these factions were at each other's political throats. What were they really fighting over?

Consider Mr. Clarke's treatment of Randolph's role in the organizing of the National Negro Congress. Clarke gives us a long quotation from Randolph's speech at the 1936 founding convention of the NNC in which he optimistically accepted the presidency of the new organization. But Mr. Clarke has nothing to say about why Randolph quit the NNC four years later. He quit because the National Negro Congress very quickly came under the control of the Communist Party and Randolph, the "radical," did not go along with the Communist takeover. Again Randolph clashed with the Communists as he had back in the 1920's. Why this conflict?

According to one historian of this period, Randolph quit the National Negro Congress because:

> The [organization] was nothing more than an enlarged (Communist) Party cell. He knew that to continue in office would mean acceptance of a program which he could not endorse in principle; he knew, too, that it would mean serving as a stooge for Party bureaucrats. [. . .][1]

Randolph stated his own reasons for quitting the presidency of the NNC in *The New York Times* of April 29, 1940:

> The National Negro Congress should be dependent on resources supplied by the Negro people alone. The grounds for my belief is that history shows that where you get your money you also get your ideas and control.[2]

E. Franklin Frazier, writing of the National Negro Congress meeting of 1940 said:

> The large attendance of whites in 1940 was the result, it was reported, of the influence of the Communist Party . . .
>
> When one considers the diverse interests that were represented in the organizations officially affiliated with the National Negro Congress, it is obvious that its unity and solidarity rested upon a precarious basis from the beginning.[3]

These were some of the facts concerning Randolph and the National Negro Congress. Thus, for Mr. Clarke to contend that the NNC "was a forerunner of present-day civil rights groups such as the Congress of Racial Equality (CORE) and the Student Non-Violent Coordination Committee (SNCC)" is a gross distortion of historical fact. CORE started in 1942 as an independent, non-political, non-Communist affiliated civil rights group, while SNCC started in the sixties as a student-youth movement under youth leadership. The NNC was certainly not a youth group. How can a historian as experienced as Clarke make such shallow and inaccurate comparisons? The NNC was a product of the severe economic depression of the 1930's plus the CIO-Labor organizing upsurge that distinguished this period. It was a product of its times and had little in common with the issues of the 1960's except "civil rights," which has always been with us through the lean years and the fat.

Lastly comes Mr. Clarke's glowing account of Randolph's role in organizing the famous move for his "March on Washington" of 1941. The threat of this march caused President Roosevelt to issue his renowned Executive Order 8802 establishing the President's Committee on Fair Employment Practices Committee (FEPC). This order was effective in outlawing racial discrimination in war defense industries. Randolph then called off his intended march on the capitol, having achieved his aims. But here again, it is important to note that none other than the Communist Party, Randolph's antagonist since the 1920's, was in opposition to this March on Washington. In fact, both the Communist Party *and* Randolph's former organization, the National Negro Congress, were against Randolph's March on Washington movement. The reasons for this opposition were too complicated to be analyzed here, but they were based mainly on the Communist Party's enmity over Randolph's undisputed influence in the Negro community which the Communists tried mightily to undermine. The historian quoted earlier wrote, "Some of the most vitriolic attacks ever leveled by the (Communist) Party at a Negro organization were visited upon the March on Washington during this period."[4]

If it was Mr. Clarke's intent to merely write a laudatory piece on A. Philip Randolph as the "Dean of Negro Leaders," that is his privilege. Yet, Clarke is a historian and more is demanded of a historian today. Mr. Clarke, however, succeeds in lifting Randolph out of too much of the social context that is pertinent to our understanding of what made Randolph what he is and was. Randolph, as a leadership personality, was molded by a great conflict of 20th century trends that emerged between 1900 and the 1920's. It was practically these trends which created the 20th century Negro struggle in all its complexity. The Negro movement, in all of its aspects we know today, are nothing but a continuation of those earlier trends on another level. Anyone who does not understand these early trends cannot grasp what is wrong with the Negro movement today.

The Negro civil rights movement is in a serious crisis now. Therefore, it is necessary that the entire 20th century development of leadership trends must be researched, analyzed, and reevaluated from (Booker T.) Washington, to Du Bois, to Randolph, to Garvey, to Robeson, to Elijah Muhammad, down to Malcolm X, and even Adam Clayton Powell. For, without such a thorough going reevaluation and reinterpretation, all such slogans as "Black Power" remain empty talk. This should be the objective of all history writing today, especially about leaders.

Oddly enough, the editorial of Mr. Clarke's Freedomways magazine for Fall 1966 supports the "Freedom Budget," another of Randolph's achievements. It says, "The Freedom Budget proposals have the support of all the major organizations in the Negro Freedom Movement." Although A. Philip Randolph guided the preparation and publication of this budget, Freedomways does not mention him in the editorial.

NOTES

1. Wilson Record, *The Negro and the Communist Party,* p. 195.
2. Randolph, *N. Y. Times,* April 29, 1940, p.7.
3. E. Franklin Frazier, *The Negro in the United States,* p. 534.
4. Wilson Record, cited, p. 205.

CHAPTER ELEVEN

The Fire This Time?

Eldridge Cleaver: *Post-Prison Speeches and Writings*
(*New York Review of Books,* May 8, 1969)

Reviewing Eldridge Cleaver's second book, *Post-Prison Speeches and Writings*, demands a critical license like that of reviewing the aspects of a man's life that consigned him to purgatory. Moreover, the review itself can offer little promise of comfort and less in the way of advice to the man in question, whose likely response would be: "If I could live life all over again, I'd do the same thing." There is, then, but one legitimate line of investigation, since we already know why the man lived the way he did. This approach would ask two questions: "Why must he do it again in that way, if he could?" and "Is there really no other way?"[1]

But even this tack is not very promising, because it offers no easy answers to these questions which would even begin to satisfy those who adhere to any of today's "revolutionary" trends in America. For if there is anyone among them who has demonstrated the full measure of his devotion to "putting one's head on the line," it is Eldridge Cleaver. What more can one demand after that? What is there more to be said about Eldridge Cleaver, the writer-activist-revolutionary, that is legitimately critically and politically apt?

In the first place, this second book presents a peculiar problem because of the nature of its content and style. As Robert Scheer, the editor of this collection of speeches and short pieces, advises us: "This collection, then, is not a sequel to *Soul on Ice,* which was written during the leisure of Cleaver's forced confinement. In this book one finds the art of the journalist, and in that sense it is a first book. Comparisons with *Soul on Ice* will inevitably be made by reviewers, but Cleaver was not in a position to work on assembling this book. . . . It was rushed through production in order to answer the need of people to come to grips with Cleaver's political ideas. . . ." Very well, then we must deal here not with Cleaver, the literary essayist, but with Cleaver, the activist, the revolutionary, the political ideologist. Also with Cleaver, the Black Panther Party's Minister of Information and associate editor of *Ramparts* Magazine. One must deal in part with all of these facets of Eldridge Cleaver because the man defies facile classification. He did not emerge from what was considered, during periods like the 1930's, the proper path to conventional revolutionary politics. His political personality is as unprecedented as the situation of racial confrontation in which he and his ideas became famous.

~

These ideas are politically interesting, although most of them were not original with Cleaver. For example, Robert Scheer thinks that Cleaver's "assumption that black people in America form an oppressed colony . . ." was original with Cleaver, when, in fact, the idea was first expressed in the United States at least as far back as 1962 as the Afro-American's condition of "domestic colonialism." All new political ideas, however, evolve slowly, and it takes time for their full implications to be generally grasped. Cleaver did not pursue the full meaning of this black condition in the United States, but prefers to find its political elucidation in Frantz Fanon's *The Wretched of the Earth.* Cleaver writes in his chapter, "Psychology: the Black Bible":

> In the aftermath of Watts, and all the other uprisings that have set the ghettos of America ablaze, it is obvious that there is very little difference in the way oppressed people feel and react, whether they are oppressed in Algeria by the French, in Kenya by the British, in Angola by the Portuguese, or in Los Angeles by Yankee Doodle.

Fanon, however, qualifies this conclusion by stating "The Negroes who live in the United States and in Central or Latin America in fact experience the need to attach themselves to a cultural matrix. Their problem is not fundamentally different from that of the Africans." But when American Negroes and Africans first discussed this problem during the 1956 congress of the African Cultural Society, Fanon wrote of their conversations:

> But little by little the American Negroes realized that the essential problems confronting them were not the same as those that confronted the African Negroes. . . . The test cases of civil liberty whereby both whites and blacks in America try to drive back racial discrimination have very little in common in their principles and objectives with the heroic fight of the Angolan people against the detestable Portuguese colonialism.[2]

To judge from Cleaver's own articles and speeches (and Scheer's interpretation of them) it would seem that Cleaver and Fanon were not in total agreement on certain aspects of this relationship. On "political revolution," Cleaver sees in America similarities with the colonial situation; Fanon did not. On "cultural nationalism," Cleaver is more explicit. Whereas, according to Fanon, both Africans and Afro-Americans have a deep need for the creation of a "cultural matrix," Cleaver impatiently objects to any emphasis in America on the need for "cultural" programs, or what is better known today as "cultural nationalism" in the black movements. Scheer (rightly or wrongly) interprets Cleaver's views on this:

> In these first months outside [prison], Cleaver found that the black community was suffering form a surfeit of militant talk without any commensurate program of action, and was attempting to camouflage this failure by emphasizing "cultural nationalism" rather than "political revolution." He soon felt that the cultural nationalists' excessive emphasis on the roots and virtues of black culture obscured the essential fact that blacks formed an oppressed colony in the midst of white America. He frequently cited Frantz Fanon's point that black culture bore the marks of oppression and that black man could wrest his manhood from white society only through revolutionary political struggle—not through posturing, dress, or reviving African cultural roots.

~

If this is a faithful interpretation of Cleaver's views on "politics" and "culture," then we have the essential key to Cleaver's problem as a "political revolutionary." Out of prison, Cleaver faced a very complex world, in a tense and agitated human mosaic in black and white tones. For Cleaver, as he said in prison, real history, black history, "began with Malcolm X." But Malcolm X's organization, the OAAU, had died with him, and Cleaver hoped and tried to revive it. His search for an organization reminiscent of Malcolm X's movement ended when he encountered the Black Panther Party. As the Panther's Minister of Information, he started a new political career. "Without the Panthers," Scheer says, "Cleaver would undoubtedly have developed a much more personal career-oriented, literary way of life. With the Panthers, he became a disciplined political revolutionary as well as a literary polemicist, although there was hardly any time for writing."

But Cleaver never sought a "literary way of life"; in fact he deliberately did otherwise: he searched for political involvement because he held a "belief in the necessity of black political revolution . . ." In this self-assumed role, Cleaver experienced in his unique way what several other black writers discovered before him: revolutionary political activity and literary creation simply do not mix. This is why "there was hardly any time for writing."

Perhaps it is safe to assume that this was the way Cleaver wanted it. For a serious writer in prison, particularly a philosophical one, there is hardly a better place to pursue the writer's lonely commitment to literature than in isolation, free from external infringements such as the need to "earn a living." The outside world is hard on the would-be writer, especially if he is black. After enduring the arduous course of literary commitment and exile, the black writer then runs the hazards of literary success: he is then induced, if not commanded, to become a black spokesman. Then he is asked: what are his political commitments? If he is willing, he succumbs and becomes, like Cleaver, a "literary polemicist," and, ultimately, a political revolutionary. Scheer applauds this metamorphosis. He also rushed this new book into print "because the media which have made so much of his name have largely ignored his ideas."

But if Scheer is moved by the essence of Cleaver's ideas which the media ignored, he can't dismiss the media so cavalierly. For Cleaver, like many others, was first legitimized by the very mass media whose social role most of us attack as the corrupting propaganda agency of the "power structure." In this fashion are writers, revolutionary or otherwise, trapped by the system in ways many of us do not like to admit. But in viewing Cleaver's essential ideas, one is led to ask, what did the Black Panthers and the Peace and Freedom Party really think about Cleaver's political ideas which the mass media ignored?

∿

This question may not appear legitimate on first sight, but it is. It is ironic that in our society the propagandist of unpopular political ideas cannot depend on his allies to propagate his views. Neither the Old Left nor the New Left could or would publish Eldridge Cleaver widely—they have neither the resources nor the disseminating range to equal the visibility given Cleaver by the mass media. It was one sector of the "power structure" that jailed him, controlled him, negated him, and finally hounded him into exile. But it was another sector of the "power structure" that facilitated and sustained his literary and political celebrity.

We must admit that Frantz Fanon was right, for the United States is structurally unlike those societies in the Third World that spawn revolutionary anti-colonialist movements in Algeria, Kenya, Angola, and heroes like Mao Tse-Tung and Che Guevara. The wish to emulate these Third World movements in the United States is understandable, but the revolutionary leaders in the Third World would find Cleaver's access to publishing houses and television studios incomprehensible. It is with the social and political reality of the United States in mind, as well as the nature of his alliances, then we must consider Cleaver's views.

We know fairly well the ideas of the Black Panther Party's self-defense program *before* the arrival of Cleaver: land, bread, housing, education, justice, peace, the end of police brutality, freedom for black prisoners, peer jury trials, exemption of blacks from military service, to name the most important. But the appearance of Cleaver in the Black Panther ranks as a major spokesman and ideologist brought to the fore again that touchy question of the possibility and the necessity of a black nationalist–white leftist political alliance. For one thing, the jailing of one Panther leader, Huey Newton, made such an alliance a necessity if Newton was to be saved. Funds and legal aid were needed. Cleaver, however, recurrently voices the theme of black and white unity as a fundamental political necessity for the Panther movement which, as he explained to Nat Hentoff in the *Playboy* interview [. . .] was intended by him to become "*the* black national movement" of America:

> We recognize that there are a lot of white people in this country who want to see virtually a new world dawn here in America. . . .
>
> They are turning into a revolutionary force, and that's why we believe the Black Panthers can enter into a coalition with them as equal partners.

Cleaver is really bidding here for the radical white youth: "These young white people aren't hung up battling to maintain the status quo like some of the older people. . . . They're adventurous: they're willing to experiment with new forms; they're willing to confront life." This is the way Cleaver more than anyone else personifies the Malcolm X legacy. Malcolm came to disavow "black racism," as it is called. So Cleaver found a way to reconcile "political nationalism" to a black and white coalition. When the white allies arrived, Cleaver tells us, "O.K. We had asked for it, and here it was: The Peace and Freedom Party. Politics. How do we relate to it?" 1968 was not so far removed in time from the day of Malcolm X's assassination, but the young black nationalist wave had come a long way since that time on the question of coalition.

Yet we should not overlook the fact that conveniently for all concerned in the coalition, it was an election year. Moreover, the white Left has a long, honorable, and expert record in the politics of freeing people. During the 1930's it was "Free Angelo Herndon," "Free Earl Browder," etc. (Who among the young knows about Angelo Herndon today? Everything is so new, and yet so old!) The martyrs and the victims of the political persecution come and go, yet this was a black and white coalition which, for Cleaver, had possibilities that were new, but which, in reality, could not shake off old convictions concerning strategy, tactics, and methods.

∼

The white Left has an abiding belief in political power and political campaigns as a means of throwing its weight around and building strength for the near future. For the Panthers and for Cleaver, a political campaign was, no doubt, something like a giant organizational step along the road to revolution. But there was once a time in this century's history of American radicalism when no hard-line revolutionary (black or white) would have been caught dead in a political campaign for federal and state office. This was considered unadulterated cooptation. The old trade union direct-actionists, the I. W. W.'s, the anarcho-syndicalists, and the revolutionary anarchists used to look down on the old Socialist Party for indulging in such lukewarm reformist activity.

But in the search for the proper vehicle for political nationalism in 1968, Cleaver and the Panthers made a kind of historic political breakthrough: they were probably not aware that it had taken the white Left about fifty years to recognize the legitimacy of black nationalism. Said Cleaver in his *Playboy* Interview (a piece which suggests, among other things, that Cleaver and the magazine see eye to eye on the centrality of Eros denied):

> We want black people to be represented by leaders of their choice who, with the power of the masses behind them, will be able to go into the political arena, set forth the desires and needs of black people and have those desires and needs acted upon.

Whereupon Nat Hentoff replied: "But, we repeat—isn't that already happening—at least on a small scale? There's a black mayor of Cleveland, Carl Stokes, a black mayor of Gary, Richard Hatcher." In 1968, Cleaver could scoff at such mild reformism in the way the old anti-political revolutionaries scoffed at the Socialist Party's 897,011 votes in 1912 or 919,000 votes in 1920. Cleaver said:

> You're talking about black personalities, not about basic changes in the system.
> . . . We are demanding structural changes in society, and that means a real distribution of power, so that we have control over our own lives. Having a black mayor in the present situation doesn't begin to accomplish that.

Despite the fact that some sectors of the "power structure" and the mass media have now conceded that "black is in," Cleaver does not want us to be too impressed by "personalities" who just happen to be black. So convinced is he of the need for the proper separation of black issues from black personalities that he says of Adam Clayton Powell: "That's why we oppose Adam Clayton Powell. He is not militant enough and he represents the black middle class, not the masses."

Something is wrong here because Cleaver cannot deny that the black masses who vote have supported Powell at home and abroad lo these many Harlem years! And these supporters include some of the most fiery black nationalists who ever frightened white storeowners in Harlem. What is reflected here is more than just a certain political callousness, but the ambivalence of the black movement toward its black middle class, a black version of the "generation gap," as well as the agony of finding the proper vehicle for political nationalism, to which is added the present agony of the new white Left. This anti-Powellism, which Cleaver has expressed on other occasions, is not predicated on any profound concern with the requirements of long-range strategy, or on a grasp of the political realities of either Harlem or the United States. Cleaver concedes this when he says: "I'm not saying that we, the Panthers, have the answer either, but we're trying to find the way." His problem, he says, is "how to find a revolutionary mode of moving in this most complicated of all situations."

t is legitimate to say now that if Cleaver recognizes the complexity of "this most complicated of all situations," it is hoped that he sees how complicated are his own responses to this same situation. His perceptions cover a wide range of social observation, often brilliantly. But, essentially, Cleaver differs not at all from other committed American militants, for, like them, he is basically American, with the same radical hang-ups and contradictions. It is the quality of his rhetoric that is unique but, as Nat Hentoff pointed out in his interview,

Cleaver is just as much a prisoner of the reformist bind and the agony of its unfulfilled promises as anyone else who, under inexorable and excruciating pressures, must resort to revolutionary slogans and threats:

> What happens, as I've said, will depend on the continuing dynamics of the situation. What we're doing is telling the government that if it does not do its duty, then we will see to it ourselves that justice is done. . . . That will depend on what is done against us and on whether real change can be accomplished nonviolently within the system.

Which is to say that Cleaver will accept government sponsored "reforms" if they prove positive and efficacious, otherwise it's "revolution." This is the age-old American radical dilemma which admits the possibility of different rates of "social change," but which says, simultaneously, that neither method ought to be seen as contradictory or in opposition to the other. Robert Scheer states that Cleaver "thrives in chaos" and is "very much the impulsive, lusty, bohemian writer." The variety of his perceptions reveal this—they roll out of his mind and onto the paper or tapes chaotically, in an avalanche which he is hard put to constrain or keep within the political frame. Inevitably, then, after giving full play to his political imagination, wherein everything, including sex, is given a political configuration, Cleaver falls back on Karl Marx:

> Let's pay our respects to Brother Karl Marx's gigantic brain, using the fruits of his wisdom, applying them to this crumbling system, and have some socialism, moving on to the classless society.

So it all comes down to that, which is where many of us came in. Before Cleaver mentions Marx, he points out that "The basic problem in this country is political confusion." True, but does the injection of Marxian ideas into this situation help to clear up this confusion? If Cleaver thinks so, then we are entitled to ask, what does he think the American Marxists have been about all these years before Cleaver appeared? Have they been adding clarity to confusion? The answer is: not much. In addition to attaching himself to the agony of his (and our) legacy of present-day political confusion, Cleaver innocently and in desperation has attached himself to the agony of the American white Left. We know that misery loves company, this was always so; but our experience in the American morass tells us that *the will to make a revolution is not the same thing as having the means to make it.*

It is a good thing that some black nationalists have arrived at that level of political maturity which allows them to dispense with enough "black racism" to understand that "Whitey," too, is caught in a tight bind in America, right along with his "black colonial subjects." But history has at last handed the black brother a torch to light up the path out of this darkness. Although certain young diehards are using the torch for incendiary purposes, the more sophisticated are called upon to understand *their* own condition in the interests of a heightened black social awareness. Questions arise: Shall the black nationalist militants accept poverty grants in the ghettos, before or after applying the torch, or shall they opt for the revolutionary millennium, during which time someone else will take advantage of the government's grants anyway! Here is one economic source of political confusion, or vice versa. It is very, very real, and what answer can Marx or Mao give to this black political and economic dilemma?

∼

The Marxists in the coalition will not tell Cleaver this, but wherever he is, he should read Eduard Bernstein's *Evolutionary Socialism* as a brief and sober respite from the work of Fanon. This demonstration of the obsolescence of much of Marx's analysis of capitalism seems more pointed today than when it was written. In fact, even Fanon himself voiced certain reservations: ". . . Marxist analysis should always be slightly stretched every time we have to do with the colonial problem. Everything up to and including the very nature of pre-capitalist society, so well explained by Marx, must here be thought out again." Well now, Cleaver, shall we argue with Fanon, or shall we try to "think it all out again"?

If so, it means a further elaboration, or stretching, of the original Marxian "theory of knowledge" which says, in part,

> The reflection of reality in people's consciousness of class society is affected by the nature of the society. For the ultimate origin of social ideas, theories, and views, it is necessary to investigate the conditions of the material life of society, social practice in its broadest sense, which these ideas and theories, in various ways reflect.

In America those who call themselves Marxists need to investigate anew what they call "social practice in its broadest sense," which is very different from the social practice Marx was more familiar with in nineteenth century Europe. For one thing, he did not live with the American race question; this question did not complicate the realities of the class struggle in Europe. In his mind, he settled the race question for Americans when he observed that "labor in a white skin can never be free while labor in a black is branded."

This was an advanced idea in the nineteenth century and had real revolutionary connotations. But today it has become one of the more banal slogans of liberal radicalism, and has no more practical use as a political slogan than Lincoln's old adage that "this nation cannot endure half slave and half free." In the nineteenth century the capitalist North waged a punitive war on the South because slavery was uneconomical and detrimental to capitalist expansion; and American white labor has long since decided that "labor in a white skin can never be secure as long as labor in a black skin is threatening white jobs."

There are Marxist friends in Cleaver's coalition who are waiting for labor to change its mind about its class role, but the late M. L. King wrote a book, *Why We Can't Wait,* and some Marxists agreed with him. Moreover, nowhere in his book does Cleaver speak directly to white labor, but to the generality of white people. He is speaking to a condition, the national human condition which is a result of generalized racism.

~

It is this very objective American bi-racial social condition which is reflected in people's consciousness and which is, in its turn, translated into their peculiarly American "social practice." Thus radical "ideas and theories" must be both a reflection of "social practice in its broadest sense" and a theoretical interpretation of what is actually happening, including working-class racism, not what some of us *wish* were happening, such as an upsurge of labor radicalism. This very objective American reality, in fact, supersedes the advent of any nascent labor consciousness; and it may lie at the bottom of the ideological and political confusion of which Cleaver speaks.

For behind the "political confusion" which Cleaver sees as the American malaise lies a vast, ignoble legacy, a grossly distorted interpretation of the political, economic, cultural, racial, and ethnic ingredients that comprise the national development. In short, the American "political confusion" is a reflection of the confusion over "national purpose." Americans generally have no agreement on who they are, what they are, or how they got to be what they are. They do not respond to their situation out of any real sense of historical determination, because their "history," when they are aware of it, gives them no guidelines to the resolution of present difficulties.

Thus the black search for "identity" (or Fanon's "cultural matrix") only underscores the fact that *all* Americans are involved in an identity crisis. Since whites and blacks do not identify with each other, it only means that neither blacks nor whites are really identifying with the realities of the American experience which bound them together so fatefully in what is supposed to be the "cultural matrix" of a nation. Thus the implied threat of the division of the nation into "two nations black and white" is another way of saying that the American experiment in nationhood has been a historical failure of the first magnitude.

Simplistically and biologically, the black and white confrontation is called a "racial" conflict, a carry-over from black slavery. But deep down, historically and psychologically, it is a *cultural conflict* over the seeming incompatibility of "group values" and aspirations which manifest themselves in our political, economic, and cultural institutions. The implied premises of these institutions are, ultimately, the perpetuation of Anglo-Saxon Protestant supremacy, which is the white-skinned side of cultural nationalism.

For this important reason Cleaver's attack on what he perceives as black "cultural nationalism," its meaning and social role, is not only superficial, but also reveals a narrow-minded and anti-historical point of view. There are some black nationalists for whom, as Cleaver charges, "posturing, dress, or reviving African cultural roots" is the be-all and end-all of "cultural nationalism." It becomes *their* form of psychological "liberation" from the values of white culture especially when it culminates in dropping "slave names." Call it romanticism, but every movement has its share of romantics. People have called Garvey's "Back to Africa" movement "Political Nationalism," but it was also scoffed at as being "highly romantic" and "utopian."

Cleaver posits the necessity for political revolution in opposition to the search for identity implicit in black "cultural nationalism" as if to say that in America blacks and whites can collaborate in making revolution without a program that will deal with the problem of black cultural identity or cultural nationalism. The Marxists have long maintained this position, but this reviewer, while understanding the logic of this position, will continue to maintain that it is erroneous.

～

One can claim, as Cleaver's Marxist allies claim, that the American political, economic, and cultural institutions are the instruments of capitalist class rule, and that a class-struggle revolution will "democratize" these institutions in the interests of "all the people" under "working class rule." But on what kind of Western societies did Marx and Engels predicate this class analysis? On feudal and capitalist societies, in which the capitalist class, the feudal classes, the peasant classes, the serfs, the proletariat, etc., all shared in the historical evolution of the ingredients that comprised the "culture." Very often, bourgeois-capitalist unification had to contend with regional, language, or religious differences, but not with racial differences, since members of all divergent classes were whites who could lay claim to one general cultural communality—the Greco-Christian heritage.

In France, for example, the Paris cab-driver, the factory worker, the farmers in the provinces, the bourgeoisie, General de Gaulle, the Communist Party, and the students, all have the same loyalty to the glory of France, the French Revolution, Joan of Arc, and the memory of Charles Martel, who drove out the hated Arabs. In this kind of "cultural matrix," the divergent classes are bound together by the "nation" concept, and French "cultural nationalism" transcends class lines when American Coca-cola intrudes into the culinary habits of wine-drinkers.

Thus, in the politics of "class struggle," the issues of politics and economics are clearly etched in a nation like France since all the cultural factors peculiar to the evolution of French society—its literature, art, music, poetry, historiography, sociology, aesthetics, linguistics, philosophy, law, etc.—may be seen as aspects of the French tradition. What is French is a settled question in France, since every Frenchman knows his place in it, and knows how he and his country came to be what they are in modern times. Roger Garaudy wrote: "It was in Paris that young Marx became a Marxist." Marx's collaborator Engels explained why:

> France alone contains Paris, the city where civilization has attained its highest expression, where all the strands of European history converge, and from which, from time to time, electrical discharges emanate that shake the world. This city whose population combines in itself, as no other people, a passion for enjoyment and for historical initiatives; this city whose inhabitants know how to live like the most refined Epicureans of Athens, and die like the most intrepid Spartans.[3]

As a result Marx became a Francophile, claiming that for one to act and live in a revolutionary manner one had to speak French, and adding: "When all the inner requisites are fulfilled, the *day of German resurrection* will be proclaimed by the crowing of the cock of Gaul." From this Garaudy concluded that it was in Paris that Marx "perceived clearly the historical law of the class struggle and the necessity of proletarian revolution in order to achieve communism."

But after more than one hundred years, the "crowing cock of Gaul" has failed to announce the doom of French bourgeois capitalism. The Paris uprising of the summer of 1968 wasted away amid the dying murmurs of reformism. If this had to be the twentieth-century fate of Marx's beloved France, on which he placed so much historical faith as the guiding light of the world proletariat, what can one say of the United States, the colossus of monopoly capitalism, which, in order to look as far back into the Western tradition as Athens and Sparta, has to pretend not to see something much more close to home—its pilgrims, slaves, Indians, refugees; as well as a Revolutionary War and a Civil War which are still embarrassing the historians whose function it is to explain them. Moreover, there are other historians who maintain that both wars were unwise, if not unnecessary. What kind of a tradition is this that induced its inheritors to attempt either to deny, or to minimize, explain away, or else distort its historical heroism?

~

The non-white, non-European, non-Western racial elements are bound up with that tradition, and the keepers of the archives of the traditions, the molders of historical opinion, are both ashamed of and embarrassed by all of his. Hence decades of guilt, ambivalence, hatred, racial arrogance, and cultural particularism accumulate and are legitimized in all the American intellectual mythologies concerning our collective backgrounds. Among diverse American groups, especially between black and white, there does not exist the communality of cultural interests and heritage that exist in other countries. It is this lack of national cultural cohesion and sense of community that obviates class struggle on the political and economic fronts. The great Spanish scholar and socialist, Enrique Tierno Galvan, said at an International Seminar held last December at Princeton University:

> In a romantic sense, the United States has never been a nation—and never will be one. Today we are witnessing a fragmentation of nations, and by nation we mean a community that is held together by common beliefs and principles that survive historical changes.
>
> The romantic idea of "nation" is being supplanted by the more pragmatic term of "the people," that is, a society that fuses a number of different elements, even heterogeneous, in the crucible of common interests. It is precisely these common interests—not common ideals—that have provided the American people with social cohesion. These interests have crystallized into ideologies, and these ideologies have become mythicized into ideals which, however, remain within the frameworks of interests that are regarded as essential.

By "common ideals" Galvan really meant a common culture. The United States is not held together by "common ideals" but by common interests rooted in capitalist enterprise. In America, said Galvan, "Politics has also been conceived as a 'capitalist enterprise' in the sense of competition among different interests of profit-sharing and of desire for success." Hence:

The American political framework offers a unique example of the interaction of economic forces and political institutions. This is seen, for example, in lobbyism, electoral campaigns, and above all, in the prestige that wealth carries implicitly—in a political institutional character—and which is presumed in Supreme Court rulings.

Few American historians, economists, or political scientists could or would view the United States in these harshly realistic terms; thus the American people are the spiritual recipients, not of the unblemished truth of their national existence, but of what Galvan called "ideologies which have been mythicized into ideals." They become helplessly manipulated by these mythicized ideals and are, therefore, unable to face political and economic realities.

Eldridge Cleaver clearly sees the chaos of generalized "political confusion," the black and white conflict, the Vietnam War, etc., etc. He calls for "political revolution" to be carried out by manipulated people, led by militant blacks and "revolutionary" whites. But there are very few blacks and whites who are ready and committed to this leap into a revolutionary position. Americans are a pragmatic people when it comes to "political action." They have been, as Galvan said, "Very naïve, very frank, about [the] special link between politics and economics. The different waves of immigrants have fully identified themselves with this pattern of social behavior."

Left out of the mainstream of this political and economic process in America are black people, including Eldridge Cleaver, who, in the absence of American "common ideals" with which they can identify, begin to seek common ideals of their own. In doing so, they project what is, in effect, a cultural challenge to the rest of the American people. Either we as a nation create and cultivate, out of our collective past in this hemisphere, common cultural ideals which are expressed in our institutions, or our present crisis deepens and we face ultimate social disaster.

Thus in the midst of our racial and social crisis does a "cultural revolution" begin to gather momentum. The crisis in education is a cultural crisis with the students' unrest as its natural corollary. Decentralization of ghetto schools and the drive for "black studies" in the colleges and universities become the main expressions of black "cultural nationalism," but in his dismissal of cultural nationalism, Eldridge Cleaver completely misses the real meaning of all this. The black and white encounter on cultural ground demonstrates the irrelevance of much of what passes for "social science" in our academic disciplines, and the inability of most of our social scientists and planners to relate creatively to the urban crises.

∼

In the midst of this racial crisis, this deep conflict in cultural values, whites of all ages and classes sing the black people's music and dance to the black people's bodily rhythms, and there is no cultural history written and taught in the educational systems that explains why this is so, and is so American. History books by the score are turned out yearly in America, and yet they cannot truthfully reveal how the black people's presence, hovering in the background of white men's thinking and plans, shaped white men's political and economic decisions, influenced white men's military strategies, delayed or advanced westward expansion, arrested or encouraged industries, created wealth by being wealth that laid the basis for banking systems, and influenced the national character.

We are witnessing at this moment visible efforts to correct our accumulated intellectual deformations in these historical and cultural concerns, and it must be recorded that these efforts came about in response to demands of black cultural nationalism, in varying degrees of insistence. The Marxist analysis of the nineteenth century could not relate to this American social patterning by using a French model. Hence, today, the "theory of knowledge" on "social practice" must create new sociological and psychological concepts to deal with the American racial and cultural patterns of behavior. This is the crucial task of the black and white radical youth. If American complacencies are not challenged and seriously analyzed in schools and colleges, the racial crisis will not explode on the crest of "political revolution" as Cleaver sees it, but into nationwide and uncontrollable social chaos of race war and revolutionary anarchy.

"In the near future," said Galvan, "the United States of America may offer to the world two different model outlooks of life":

One, by solving the internal problems now dogging the American people. . . . These problems are, to my way of thinking, the following:
   a) The intellectual rebellion
   b) The racial disorders
   c) The latent problem of a generalized class-struggle
   d) The problem of harmonizing United States foreign policy with internal
      moral crisis.

How will the "American people" solve these outstanding problems? This is the question the old European "nations" are asking themselves. Perhaps the future role of the United States of America will consist—from the standpoint of "people"—*in the providing of new answers and cultural challenges that are the common heritage of the old European nations.* [Italics added.]

At the Princeton Congress where Señor Galvan delivered his remarks on the internal problems of the United States, Eldridge Cleaver's name was mentioned a number of times. From one of the students' representatives, Sam Brown, now of Harvard, came the criticism that the congress of intellectuals did not include representative spokesmen of the young American revolutionary wing, such as Cleaver. But whether Cleaver would have attended even if invited is doubtful. Had he attended his presence would have been electrifying, but, as his book reveals, it is doubtful that he would have added much to the analysis of other speakers. His second book powerfully documents the thoughts of a man fully engaged in the tactics of "political revolution" as he is able to define them.

∾

Much more could be said here, especially on the content of his "Stanford Speech" and his "Farewell Address," where he is at his best as a platform orator. The truth is, however, as Cleaver himself admits, his insights into "political confusion" do not go far enough. "I'm not saying that we, the Black Panthers, have the answers . . . ," he says, and we know that this is true.

The problem with Eldridge Cleaver and those of his generation who opt for "political revolution" is that a new set of social and philosophical concepts are needed to substantiate the political activism toward more and specified goals. To say that America is a racist society is not enough—there is more to it than that. If American racism created the institutions, it is now the institutions themselves which legitimize the racist behavior of those who are the products of the institutions. The problem, then, is how to deal *structurally* with these institutions—how to alter them, eradicate them, or build new and better ones? What is the method of social change to follow the demonstrations, the oratory and polemics, the jailings, the agony, and the exiles?

NOTES

1. *Studies on the Left,* Vol. II, No. 3, 1962, p. 13.
2. *The Wretched of the Earth,* p. 216.
3. This is quoted in Roger Garaudy's *Karl Marx: The Evolution of his Thought,* International Publishers, 1967.

CHAPTER TWELVE

The Integrationist Ethic as a Basis for Scholarly Endeavors

(Speech Given to Yale University Black Student Alliance, 1969)

On behalf of the Black Student Alliance of Yale, I am pleased to be called before you to discuss this very unique and very important problem: the significance of the black experience to intellectual pursuits and scholarly studies. I have been asked to concentrate on one theme, namely the failure of the integrationist ethic as a basis for scholarly studies. And from that point of departure, I will attempt to deal with this problem in a way which will be in consonance with what you call the "framework," or method of attack on this problem.

It is my belief that the integrationist ethic has subverted and blocked America's underlying tendency toward what I would call a democratic ethnic pluralism in our society. This ethic has been a historical tendency stimulated both by Anglo-Saxon political ideology, rampant industrialism, racism, and an

Americanism whose implied goal has been the nullification of all competing subcultures indigenous to North America. It is my belief that both black and white scholarly rationalizations have historically supported the integrationist ethic in pursuit of the ideal of the American creed. This approach was obviously predicated on an intellectual consensus which held that the political, economic, and cultural values of the Anglo-American tradition were sufficiently creative and viable enough to sustain the American progression to realization of its ultimate potential. But the present internal social and racial crisis we are experiencing proves beyond a doubt the failure of this integrationist ethic. As a result of this failure, at this present moment we have no viable black philosophy on which to base much-needed black studies programs.

Upon examining the black and white reactions to his failure, we find different reactions on both sides of the racial fence. You have separatist reactions coming from the black side of the equation, and you have white intellectual resistance toward acceptance and ratification of another ethic in scholarly endeavors. In response to pressures for black studies, whites often attempt to speed up piecemeal integrative processes in favor of black integrationists. Another response to demands for black studies involves questioning the validity of separatist doctrines; whites question the nihilist, irrational, or anarchistic tendencies they note in separatist doctrines and, by extension, question whether the whole approach, including a trend toward black studies, is valid. Thus, black intellectual critics of the integrationist ethic—students, writers, scholars, critics, historians, and so on—must assume an obligation to establish black studies in the curricula whose subject matter, critical thrust, and social objectives fully answer those who would question curriculum reform in the direction of black studies.

Such black studies programs must achieve or establish certain critical and/ or creative criteria which would make manifest their validity in the face of white intellectual criticisms. Needless to say, this is a big question and a complex one. I don't know how far we can go into the analysis of it today. However, from my own point of view, having thought about these perplexing questions for many years, having based my whole creative life on the examination of, and the response to, these pressures, I have something which I think is of value in lending understanding to the problem.

I believe that if it were left to the black students themselves, the black scholars, the undergraduate students, the graduate students, the writers and the critics, to create this black studies curriculum, they would employ a historical approach. I think one of the main points of departure in an approach to the content and thrust of a black studies program can begin with an analysis of black middle-class formation from generation to generation, beginning possibly after the Civil War and proceeding down to our day; this would involve a minute analysis of the class ideology noted in middle-class formation from era to era. I think an investigation into plantation life should begin to verify whether there were sharp class divisions on slave plantations between field hands and so-called "house Negroes," and to see whether the social carry-over into Reconstruction and twentieth-century developments really reflects a sharp class division, evolving out of plantation origins. All this I think could be verified as a historical basis for the beginning of a black studies curriculum.

I think an examination should be made of the extent to which the white Protestant ethic has achieved the American creed's stated aims of democratic inclusion of the Negro in American society. To what extent has the Protestant ethic aided, abetted, or checked what we would call normal middle-class development on the black side of the racial fence in American life? Was the intention of the Protestant ethic to aid and abet the development of a black middle class? Or was the racism inherent in the approach meant to deny the democratic inclusion of this black middle-class development into the American mainstream? Carrying this analysis further, how has the retardation of the black bourgeoisie historically affected the outlook of the "intellectual class" in black life? For example, how did this retardation of normal development affect W. E. B. DuBois' contention that the black race in America required the development of a kind of talented-tenth leadership stratum which would deliver the Negro mass from its degradation? I believe that a black studies curriculum should investigate DuBois' thesis of the talented-tenth and ascertain to what degree this expectation was rooted in our historical development. These questions are some important points of departure toward laying the basis of a black studies program.

I make these assertions mainly to answer certain questions about intellectual procedure in the approach to the establishment of a black studies program. From the standpoint of these historical considerations I think that by looking at the problem of developing intellectually valid black studies curricula, one can see a legitimate point of departure.

To get deeper into this problem, I think that the whole question of the demand for a black studies program falls under the heading of what we would call a movement, a tendency, an ideology of "black cultural nationalism." This phenomenon is emerging today among the young black intelligentsia, the young black students, and the young black activists. This tendency is emerging in response to the feeling that at present there is no viable intellectual approach to the problems facing both blacks and whites in American society. Though these activists have espoused cultural nationalism, it is understandable that at this moment the historical roots and implications of cultural nationalism in our society are quite unclear to some members of the younger generation.

It is my belief that cultural nationalism as an ideology, nurturing the whole desire and thrust toward a black studies program, can only be understood if it is approached, first, historically, and then, by analyzing many of the deep problems which enmesh the Negro intelligentsia today. All over the country, in different aspects of the black movement we can see a general thrashing about, a frenetic search for method, and a search for both internal and external criticism. We see splits and factions; we see movements running into dead ends and, we see the assassination of Martin Luther King and the outpouring of people's anguish, both black and white. We see all this and we have to ask, as King asked before he was assassinated, "Where do we go from here?" And how?

I have cited several historical antecedents to make it easier to understand how to deal with the current manifestations of these historical problems in the black world. These problems must be confronted; the effort to resolve them should be reflected in affirmative actions in relation to the demand for black studies. Black studies must be geared to the question of black institutional developments on all levels—political, economic, cultural, and social. I believe that the black studies program, using the thrust of cultural nationalism, might for example base one of its approaches upon the study of the development of the black church, especially from the class aspect, from the Episcopal and other "higher" denominations down to the store-front church. It might deal with institutions such as the theater. It should deal with black business trends and it must investigate, on an economic level, how the black movement is going to adjust its aims within the context of American society.

How best to respond to demands for black studies is a very complicated problem because we have two distinct trends in the black movement, even though these trends are seldom verbalized. We have implied here what is often called a "radical" or "revolutionary" thrust, and we also have what can be described as a "slow reformist" thrust. Even though this conflict is not verbally expressed in all instances, we can see, if we look closely enough, a clash of aims and methods involved in these underlying trends. We can describe this problem in terms of a conflict between "radical-revolutionary" and "reform" or "gradualist" thrusts toward the achievement of stated goals.

This conflict presents a peculiar problem in America for the simple reason that at any moment it cannot be determined precisely whether American society, as now constituted, is conducive to a revolutionary rate of social change for any kind of adjustment, be it for the black man or for the white man or for any other kind of man or class. Moreover, the implied rate of social change, as it is effected in the reactions of certain strata in our society, may lead one to accept slow reformist methods for social change. This presents a very complicated problem for all concerned, particularly for the spokesmen, the activists, and the leaders of the black movement. It also presents a difficult problem for those who want to institute black studies programs, because in either case we have to deal with a method of study which is related to the realities of the society around us; this throws everyone into a quandary—"everyone," black and white—but particularly the blacks, because the young generation today is very impatient. They do not desire slow change; they demand rapid change.

Whether we are going to have rapid change or slow change is important. Aside from that, we must determine the quality, the thrust, and the approach of any black studies program. Will its content accept—or be based on—slow gradualism? Or will the studies thrust the gears, hopefully, toward radical change? This is a problem. Those who want to institute a black studies program must take into consideration all of these realities, because hopefully the black studies program will be used to speed positive social changes in our society; I think the program has to begin with careful consideration of the necessities of the present situation and with the ultimate possibilities for change in this society.

Leaving that question for the moment and getting back to the content of the program in general, I want to reiterate that the question of deciding upon the content of the program is very difficult to resolve. But we have to begin to pinpoint this in order to give some immediate direction to these efforts.

Black cultural nationalism has to be seen as an attempt, a necessarily historical attempt, to deal with another kind of cultural nationalism that is implied in our society, namely, the cultural nationalism of the dominant white group. You might call it a kind of cultural "particularism" which is found when you examine the cultural particularism of the Anglo-Saxon group or the WASP or whatever name you want to give to this stratum. I think we find that an ideology exists which *has* to deny the validity of other kinds of cultural values that might compete with its own standards—whether in the social sciences, the arts, literature, or economic activity. We find this particularism of the Anglo-American implicit in all that is done in our society, whether it is done unconsciously or consciously.

I think that this particularism provides a clue to the problem of acceptance of the validity of the concept of black studies. It has been assumed in history that all that was required to make America attain its ideals was the confirmation and extension of an Anglo-American political and economic creed. Today we see that this creed, unfortunately, has reached the point where it is seemingly unable to deal with the crises that beset the nation.

This failure demands that *another* set of cultural and political values be extended into our society to fill the void. Black studies must make the dominant particularism, the dominant racial creed, more capable of dealing with the internal crises facing us all. I think that this awareness is something that has to be cultivated meticulously by any black student movement. There must be a quality of intellectual clarity and intellectual patience in dealing with those tendencies in the intellectual world which would resist both the institution and the thrust of such a black studies program. I think that those who would institute the black studies program must not only understand their own particular black history but must also grapple with, and understand, the dual tradition that has been nurtured in this society and that has given our society its unique character. I think the question of a black studies program is intrinsically a two-way street: a black studies program—even if it expresses black particularism—is a kind of particularism which understands its own limits and its social function. Its social function is not to replace one particularism with another particularism but to counterbalance the historical effects and exaggeration of particularism toward a more racially balanced society, a society which would include expectations regarding the democratic creed.

Previously I mentioned certain particular aspects or approaches that I feel black studies must begin with. I mentioned the church, I mentioned economic activities, I mentioned institutions such as the theater, I mentioned criticism, literature, and the allied arts, and so forth. I believe this is an adequate starting point. I have also dealt with the overall ideology and with black cultural nationalism as the main intellectual spirit behind the increasing demands for the institution of black studies programs. However, I want to extend that concept into a discussion of how the academic thrust of black studies might begin to impinge upon and to modify the broader social structure.

Such considerations are necessary because, after all, we are not going to study black history in a vacuum. We are going to study black history with an eye toward its being socially functional. We are going to have black social studies with the understanding that this is a new social method of dealing with the infirmities of our society. I believe that a black studies program must at all times keep its eye on the broader manifestations of what I would call—and I mentioned this in my book—the functioning of America's "cultural apparatus" in all of its aspects. I believe that in terms of the society at large, whatever long-range effect black studies will have on the broader realities of America must first begin in the general area of our cultural apparatus.

For example, the university is part of our cultural apparatus. These are institutions of a special kind engaged in socially useful activities. But beyond that, in the broader society, we have other impactful and meaningful manifestations and functionings of the cultural apparatus. It is in this general area that black studies must direct its initial interest and attention. Black studies must begin to deal with the effects of the communications media on the society as a whole as well as with the effects of the communications media on the black community. It must also begin to examine the role of the film and the role of the theater in black society. It must begin to deal with the impact of the music world on the cultural life of the black community. In short, black studies must initiate a critical examination of, and a critical approach into, the manifestations of these aspects of the cultural apparatus.

To take one example, consider the Negro in the theater—one of my pet subjects. The theater, if one studies it very closely, reflects in many ways all of the successes, the failures, the ups and downs, the defaults, the want of criticism, and the adaptation of the black intellectual class and the black creative class to the larger society. If one examines the position of the Negro in the theater today, he will have an example, set apart from all other institutions, of the plight of the black intellectual, the black creator, in all aspects of American culture. The theater should become one of the prime laboratories of those who are going to use cultural nationalism as a basis for the creation of a black studies program.

As an institution, the theater reflects the failure of the integrationist ethic most uniquely and most glaringly, perhaps more clearly than any other institution that we can name in the cultural sphere. A historical examination of the black experience in the American theater will show that it is a good barometer of the rise and fall, the successes and failures, of all other black institutions. At one time Negroes had a thriving theater, particularly in New York. It was an autonomous institution. It was crowded with talent, creativity, and pioneering. This happened at the same historical moment that the American or white theater was beginning to make its debut in American society as a unique American institution.

There was a time when there was almost "democratic" collaboration between black and white in the development of American theater. Somewhere down the line, around World War I and thereafter, the manifestations of what I call the white cultural particularism began to assert itself in the American theater; and mind you, this trend has reference also to the plight or the status of the white theater today. From that point on, black creativity began to wane and the black performer and creator was, little by little, pushed toward the fringes of the theater.

This development paralleled developments in other areas of black-white relations—this is why I claim that the theater should become a prime laboratory for a cultural approach to a black studies curriculum. In recent years, the Negro performer has raised the question of exclusion and discrimination in the American theater. These complaints continue unabated. Black complaints about discrimination come at a time when the American theater is in a crisis to the same degree that the nation itself is in a crisis. Therefore, at this moment, the Negro performer calling for integration echoes the contention of the black students who are questioning the integrationist ethic. Paradoxically, the Negro in the theater must—at this moment—maintain that the solution to his plight is more integration. However, he is losing sight of the fact that the theater is a sick institution and cannot accommodate the aims and desires and potentialities of the black presence in America.

This indicates, as far as I am concerned, why the black theater can and must become one of the prime exhibits here in dealing with the failure of the integrationist ethic. The Negro in the theater, as in all areas of American life, can only begin to regain or to win his rightful place within the American set-up through a retrenchment into self, a retrenchment into history. The creation of black studies must reflect his black history and an investigation into his past. These are the only ways in which the black student, the black intellectual, or the Negro of any calling or class can begin to re-examine his position in society as a whole, and then to begin to work from there toward a more equitable and democratic inclusion within American society.

CHAPTER THIRTEEN

The Little Rock National Black Political Convention

(*Black World*, October 1974)

The Black Power movement, conceived in the fading embers of the Civil Rights Movement of the 1960s, reached its social and political zenith in the 1972 Gary Convention. As a diverse—and at times nebulous—concept, "Black Power" came to be understood as a catch-all term, an ideological umbrella under which reform-oriented pluralists, revolutionary nationalists, and cultural nationalists could be grouped. Added to this equation was a critical mass of black politicians who had begun, for the first time since Reconstruction, to be elected to public office in significant numbers. Richard Hatcher of Gary, Indiana, Carl Stokes of Cleveland, Ohio, and Kenneth Gibson of Newark, New Jersey, constituted a triumvirate of black mayors elected to the helm of major American cities in the years between 1967 and 1970.

The inaugural gathering of the National Black Political Assembly in March 1972 marked the creation of an umbrella organization that echoed the efforts of the National Negro Congress of the 1930s, Kelly Miller's stillborn Negro Sandhedrin movement in the 1920s, and the Afro-American League of the nineteenth century. And following an established historical pattern, racial unity (or unanimity, as the case may be) within the NBPA quickly broke down amid the diversity of interests and ideological persuasions involved. While the 1972 gathering is credited with vastly increasing the numbers of black elected officials and marks an important, albeit brief, rapprochement between black nationalism and black electoral politics, the NBPA lost a significant degree of its influence over the next two years. It is telling that Cruse did not attend the second NBPA convention in Little Rock, Arkansas. Given his coverage of the event, and his perspective on "Black Power" as defined by Stokely Carmichael and Charles V. Hamilton, it is also clear that the ideological fault lines within the organization had become virtual chasms by the time of this essay.

∼

Some readers will recall my series of articles in *Black World* in 1971 under the title, "Black and White—Outlines of the Next Stage." Those articles were then intended as a preview of parts of a new book. Due to certain full-time administrative functions I had to assume at the University of Michigan which left little time for sustained writing and research, this book outline was shelved. Moreover, events in the general Black movement were moving so far ahead of the ideas I had worked out that the book would have been too redundant.

By 1971, these events were shaping up a recognizable political phase of new dimensions. This meant that no definitive summing up of new developments could be attempted until the new political climate of the Seventies had revealed something of its direction and potential. The Little Rock convention of March 1974 graphically illustrated the present limitations of the political thrust called the National Black Political Convention. What the Little Rock results indicate for Black Politics in the coming decades is a question that demands serious and honest appraisals.

I did not attend the Little Rock convention for the following reason: It had been my intention to assemble a University of Michigan student delegation from our Center For Afro-American and African Studies. This delegation could not be formed, however, because I could not induce political science (and other) students to engage in systematic research for historical data on Black third-party movements. It had been my plan to include such data in a position paper to be presented at Little Rock. However, the majority of Black graduate students at the University of Michigan show little or no compelling interest in

Black Politics, as such. This should be viewed as rather strange in view of the vociferous Black students' demands a couple of years back that "academic" studies be developed that were more "relevant" to the needs of the "Black community." Unfortunately, the lack of enthusiasm for performing directed research on Black Politics is one measure of the serious absence of a research-orientation characteristic in most Black Studies programs.

Since my plans for a student delegation failed, I had no desire to attend the Little Rock affair empty-handed, especially in view of the Gary convention which had left me with certain doubts. These doubts were reaffirmed by the results at Little Rock. The following ideas on Black Politics represent critical problem-areas where much research, discussion and clarification are essential.

—H. W. C.

When Mrs. Daisy Bates published her book, *The Long Shadow of Little Rock,* back in 1962, little did she, nor others whose personal lives had been dramatically and traumatically transfigured by the events she recorded, imagine where and how that "long shadow" would reach into the future and overtake the long march to the Seventies. They could not have foreseen that, in the very presence of Mrs. Bates herself, a political event would take place in Little Rock's Central High School in 1974 that would represent a craven mockery of events of the Little Rock in 1957. The National Black Political Convention in Little Rock, 1974, when seen against the school-integration events of 1957, was indeed a weak-kneed, backsliding retreat from the quality of decisive boldness and firm resolve that characterized the leadership in the school crisis. The National Black Political Convention of 1974 was a betrayal of the Black militant potential built up during the struggles of the Sixties. It was a political retreat from a field of battle on which the enemy *itself* was floundering in the Watergate disasters with its flanks openly exposed to further ambush. All in all, Little Rock, 1974, was an ironic commentary on how the Black post-Sixties have been transformed into the Black Seventies, where the hollowness of the "Black Power" slogan is revealed in all its nakedness. However, what occurred at Little Rock, 1974, was no surprise at all; it could have been prophesied with all the certainty that after midnight comes the dawn.

In Little Rock, 1957, the salient issue of the desegregation of Central High School had almost solidly unified the Black and white populations against each other. It was a cruel, strident, gut-harrowing and racially embittered confrontation. People died, some by suicide, others lost jobs, livelihood, status and settled careers (both Black and white). Still others uprooted themselves in the aftermath, sold their homes and abandoned life-long ties in the state of Arkansas. Mrs. Bates and her husband lost their newspaper publishing business—all for an all-consuming ideal. And during this entire siege of soul-rending racial and legal turmoil, nine Black high school students displayed the most incredible bravery and fortitude in pursuit of their self-chosen ideals. First, they bent, and then broke, the once-solid racial wall of Southern folkways. In 1957, it was not absolutely necessary to have agreed with the principle of "racial integration" of the schools to have appreciated the long-range importance of the events.

By 1974, "Black militancy" has long ceased to be synonymous with "racial integration" and is now wedded to the psychology of "Black separatism" of varying persuasions One must ponder the meaning of this unique Black dialectic, since it was the pro-integration forces of 1957 which made it possible to hold a "separatist" political convention in Central High School in 1974. Of course, many Black commentators pointed out in 1957 that "desegregation" did not mean "full integration," in any event. However, in 1957 the NAACP and all the pro-integration forces were both embattled and undaunted and deservedly elated over the hard and costly victory at Little Rock. Also, it is safe to say that 99 percent of all Afro-Americans felt an inner surge of pride in a number of ways. Not even the most ardent Black nationalist of the 1950's (and there were a few) could afford doubts that integrating Central High was a "victory." Even as school integration moved across the South against the hardening resistance of White Citizens Councils, and as the see-saw struggle between the Federal Courts and the States Rights defenders reopened the pages of Reconstruction, the mass of Blacks put aside their emotional doubts and accepted the ethics of integration as necessary.

At the National Black Political Convention in March 1974, Black history of the last 20 years came full circle to confront the reality of an historical constant in Black and white relations—*i.e.,* "desegregation" does not necessarily mean "full integration." Mrs. Bates was on hand with an all-Black ingathering that was supposed to symbolize the ultimate in the ideologized process of the return to "Blackness" unqualified on a new *political* level. Ironically, Mrs. Bates, who never preaches such a philosophy, was given an award for her sacrifices and achievements. But her personal history is so inextricably wedded to the memories of Central High's interracial transformation that one has to wonder whether the tears she shed were those of gratitude or profound dismay at what was happening. No doubt there were many chastened, if still unregenerate, Little Rock whites who remembered 1957 with undiminished bitterness, and who are still bemused. (*"See there, we always said that integration was a big mistake forced on them niggers. They always did want to be together. Leave it to them New York Jews, Liberals and Communists to mess things up"*... *"Uh-huh, you are right! But they did get our schoolhouse.")* Also, one wonders if Mrs. Bates still shares the view of Mrs. Alvin Todd, the mother of one of the 13 plaintiffs in the lawsuit "Oliver Brown *et al vs*. Board of Education of Topeka, Kansas" settled by the May 17, 1954 Supreme Court Decision, who said of the current generation of Black students: "They want to segregate after we worked so hard to get them the right and the opportunity to be where they are. We worked too hard, too long and gave up too much to make it the opposite of that."[1] Such sentiments, while understandable, would, of course, be wide of the mark of perceiving the meaning of the contradictory evolution of prevailing Black ideologies.

In retrospect, the Sixties had a crucial turning point, that is, in terms of ideology. That turning point was the shift to "Black Power" when the "direct action" protest activists (members of SNCC and CORE, the veterans of Freedom Rides, the disillusioned camp followers of the March on Washington of 1963, and the urban militants who had listened with rapt attention to the message of Malcolm X) realized that militant-protest integrationism had reaped the last dregs of diminishing returns. This was the turning point which led ultimately to such efforts as the National Black Political Conventions of Gary and Little Rock. The moment the slogan "Black Power" was sounded, it signaled a turning inward, a reversal of self-motivated aims in the direction of "Black Economic and Political Control" of Black communities. However, the broader implications of the slogan were elaborated upon in the book, *Black Power—The Politics of Liberation in America,* by Stokely Carmichael and Charles V. Hamilton. Mr. Hamilton is a *political scientist,* it should be noted, and Mr. Carmichael was a leading activist. One would have hoped that this rather congenial and functional marriage of "theory" and "practice," coming at a critical moment, might have revealed a strikingly new theoretical synthesis for the "politics of liberation." That the book failed to present anything so advanced was no reflection on either the zeal or intent of the authors—it was only a very real reflection of the collective state of Black consciousness in force at the "Black Power" juncture of the Sixties. And only the revolutionary vanity current during the Sixties could have induced Carmichael and Hamilton to claim that their book ". . . presents a political framework and ideology which represents the last reasonable opportunity for this society to work out its racial problems short of prolonged destructive guerilla warfare." The book, *Black Power,* was a well thought out and thoroughly documented survey of strategies for reforms. "Black Power" militancy was a call for more militant reformism.

Reformism itself was nothing to be condemned, but the most critical weakness in *Black Power* was revealed in the authors' arguments about the need for establishing "new forms," by which they meant "new political forms":

New forms may lead to a new political force. Hopefully, this force might move to create new national and local political parties—or more accurately, the first *legitimate* political parties. Some have spoken of a "third party" or a "third political force." But from the viewpoint of community needs and popular participation, no existing force or party in this country has ever been relevant. A force which is relevant would therefore be a first—something truly new.[2]

The authors left it to their audience to answer the question—relevant to what? They also failed to suggest even the outlines for a "new form." And, curiously, the authors shied away from full endorsement of a "third party" as a legitimate mold for a "new form." There is a close connection between Carmichael's and Hamilton's views and the fact that the Black political conventions at Gary and Little Rock refused to endorse the "third party" resolutions. It became clear that Carmichael and Hamilton saw the "third party" or the "third political force" idea as a political concept that has been rendered suspect by past historical usage. In their chapter, "The Myths of Coalition," the authors cite the "third party" movement of the 1890's called "Populism" under the leadership of Tom Watson. They wrote:

> Or take the case of Tom Watson. This Populist from Georgia was at one time a staunch advocate of a united front between Negro and white farmers . . .
>   . . . But this is the same Tom Watson who, only a few years later and because the political tide was flowing against such an alliance, did a complete turnabout.[3]

Thus, the authors concluded: "The history of the period tells us that whites—whether Populists, Republicans or Democrats—always had their own interest in mind. The black man was little more than a political football, to be tossed and kicked around at the convenience of others whose position was more secure."[4]

That position was symptomatic of the "Black Power" mood as first enunciated—a retreat from the "myths of coalition," an escape from the ensnaring traps of white political manipulation, a rejection of the enforced role of playing the foil for white political adventurers and strategists. Yet, in March 1974, we saw the National Black Political Convention at Little Rock summarize several days of militant deliberation on the needs of "new politics" by voting to remain tied to the conventional "lesser-evil" two-party barter-game between the Democrats and the Republicans! How is all of this dismal backtracking to be assessed?

The book by Carmichael and Hamilton accomplished one notable thing:

Unconsciously, the authors revealed in several ways exactly where the "Black Power" trend was really headed. For one thing, it was not directed toward the realization of any "new forms." In fact, *Black Power* gave a documented analysis of the anatomy of the Black political, economic and cultural dead-end to which the militant protest movement of the Sixties was headed—indeed to where, for all intents and purposes, it already had arrived. Whatever occurred after publication of *Black Power* was simply anti-climactic. The book's analysis was not of the quality that it could have lent meaningful guidance to the movements which were visibly running out of steam in the late Sixties. These movements were infused with the methodology of militant pragmatism, and rife with the competing clash of varying consensuses. There was no vocally dominant consensuses (nor could such have been expected) as to just where Black people were going, or should go. Or, to be more precise, there was no general consensus as to where the competing factions of the Black militant *élites* wanted to lead the black "masses." ([. . .] Few of the vanguard militants of the Sixties cared to admit that they were *"élites,"* self-elected to lead the "masses" to "Liberation.") However, the "masses" clearly demonstrated by their response (or lack of response) that what they appreciated the most were many of the very "Black Power" reforms so cogently analyzed and projected by Carmichael and Hamilton. Consequently, the illusion of leadership by the sloganeering *élites* foundered on the shoals of pragmatism in pursuit of "goals" which allegedly transcended "reformism," but which were not programmed because they could not be conceptualized. The Black Power theorists presented no "new forms." But it was already foreshadowed during the Sixties that the "Black Power" and other movements eventually would have to attempt to regroup around some kind of collective political banner (a third political force!) in order to be consistently attuned not only to social reality but to history.

During the Sixties there were two important attempts to establish a Black independent political party—the Afro-American Party movement in the South in 1960 and the Freedom Now Party of 1964 in the North.* Both ventures were,

---

* In 1960, the Afro-American Party, initiated by Rev. Clennon B. King, polled some 1,485-plus votes in Alabama and elsewhere. The case of Rev. King and his clash with the NAACP and the Black students of Alcorn College, Mississippi, in 1957 merits some review. King held strong views on the meaning of "integration" in the South. King stated that his Afro-American Party was launched as a "Calling to all colored people to find a solution to the racial problems." (See [the] NAACP's *Crisis* magazine, May 1957, pp. 290-1, June-July 1957, pp. 349-51, 382-3, on Clennon B. King and Alcorn College. For Comments on the Freedom Now Party, see Hanes Walton Jr., *Black Politics* . . . cited, p. 126.

of course, organizational failures, but they signaled that sooner or later, the Black movement of the Sixties would have to advance beyond the methodology of intuitive pragmatics in pursuit of "Liberation," to organizational competition in national politics. This was necessary not only to maintain some continuity and momentum, but also to sustain the hard won right to be taken seriously as a movement that had more to offer than militant protest for more militant reformism. It should be noted that Carmichael and Hamilton did not mention these Black party efforts of 1960 and 1964, one of the indications that their book was too weak in historical analysis to justify their claim that it represented a "last reasonable opportunity" to assess Black matters. The Mississippi Freedom Democratic Party (MFDP), which the authors *did* discuss, was not the only effort during the Sixties to establish "new political structures."

Seen historically, the challenge of the Seventies is that the period shapes up as a second "Post-Reconstruction," comparing the Nixon Administration's response to the Black Sixties with the responses of Hayes, Cleveland, Harrison and McKinley from 1877 to the 1890's. Rayford W. Logan observed that: "A succession of weak Presidents, between 1877 and 1901, facilitated the consolidation of white supremacy in the South, and Northern acceptance of victory of 'the Lost Cause.'"[5] Comparisons, however, are historically *relative* inasmuch as the *real* status of Blacks in the South (and North) in the Seventies is definitely not suggestive of the assaults—physical, economic and political—which terrorized Blacks into silence during the 1880's and 1890's. History repeats itself, but it never follows the previous script to the letter. This is one of the reasons why the suspicions of "third party" movements and coalitions are rather "unscientific" for a political scientist (Hamilton) and simplistically "anti-dialectical" for a Black activist who seriously flirts with Marxist dialectics (Carmichael). The politics of Populism in the 1890's were by no means as simple on the question of race as Hamilton and Carmichael make out.

[. . .] It was certainly true that the Populist "third party" movement tripped and fell over the question of Black and white alliances, to the political misfortune of Southern Blacks who supported Tom Watson. But even though the Populists were not Marxists by any means, racism was *not* the *only* factor that doomed the Populist movement. Rayford W. Logan pointed out that, ultimately, "The economic program of the Populists floundered on the shoal of Free Silver, and the racial solidarity concept was overwhelmed by a new tide of demagoguery."[6] In other words, the Populist's program had little chance against the economic alliances of powerful Northern capitalism with pro-industrialist Southern political and economic leaders in Henry W. Grady's "New South." Stokely Carmichael today claims to be a disciple of Nkrumahism, and he says:

"Nkrumahism does not and cannot negate the universal truths of Marxism-Leninism; it merely incorporates these truths."[7] Now, although Nkrumah is no longer with us to speak for himself on these matters, it is believed that the Osagyefo could have rendered a much more perceptive "Marxist-Leninist" analysis of Populism than Carmichael and Hamilton.

[. . .]

[The authors of *Black Power*] wrote about this ill-fated Populist coalition between Black and white as if Blacks themselves were not willing partners in the Populist dream, or that they were not co-opted by the "Fusion" politics of wavering white Populists who succumbed to the Democrats. Black Populists were solidly behind both Tom Watson, the independent agrarian rebel, and James B. Weaver, the two most prestigious Populists. Hanes Walton, the Black political scientist, states: "Throughout his campaign (1892) blacks supported Weaver, and when national Populism failed electorally in 1892 and again in 1896, black Populism on the state and local levels continued."[8] Hanes Walton shows that although "Black Populism died politically during the era of disfranchisement" (the 1890s), Blacks continued to be attracted to "progressive" political causes sponsored by whites. [. . .]

> Like the white progressives, numerous blacks had always believed that government should take positive action to improve society. In short, blacks too believed in progress. When Theodore Roosevelt took command of the Progressive movement of 1912, blacks joined the movement.[9]

The political history of Blacks in "Populist" or "Progressive" movements should explain why, inevitably, Blacks would throw the bulk of their support behind Franklin D. Roosevelt's New Deal of the Thirties. Historians have shown that after some 40-odd years, the Populism of the 1890's found its delayed fruition in the social reform program of the New Deal. [. . .]

During Roosevelt's New Deal, that President could claim Black people among his staunchest supporters, especially after 1936. Roosevelt's supporters made up an historic coalition of labor, farmers, Blacks, liberals, students, intellectuals, minorities, plus some Marxist factions on the Left. But interestingly enough, Carmichael and Hamilton, in their chapter on "The Myths of Coalition," do not so much as devote one paragraph to this New Deal coalition and its implications for Blacks generally. Since Carmichael and Hamilton entertained such deep doubts about the "relevancy" of Black and white coalitions, it was a critical shortcoming of their book that they airily by-passed the most eventful Black and white "coalition" of the 20th Century—the New

Deal. This is not to claim that Roosevelt's New Deal policies satisfied *all* the Black leaders; but they did satisfy the *masses* whose margins of votes kept Roosevelt in office in 1936, 1940 and 1944. What were some of the gains for the masses of Blacks that prompted Henry Lee Moon to write [the following?]:

> The gains made under Roosevelt were tangible and lasting: 66,850 new low-rent dwellings . . . hospitals, schools and recreational centers built with federal aid, the training of thousands of young Negroes in the programs of the National Youth Administration and the Civilian Conservation Corps, the aid to more than half a million Negro farmers, the opening up of new employment opportunities in government and in private industry, the stimulation of a progressive non-discriminating labor movement . . . and, perhaps most important, the appointment of a liberal Supreme Court which vindicated the Negro's basic rights and, by banning the white primary, opened the way to mass Negro voting in the South.[10]

∿

The pro's and con's of Roosevelt's New Deal accomplishments will be argued by historians and others for years to come, but, for our purposes, one historical fact about the New Deal, as Blacks are concerned, can be categorically stated: Although the roots of the New Deal social reform program can be traced back to the Populist movement of the 1890's, *it was not the same kind of coalition politics* that Carmichael and Hamilton dismissed as the Tom Watson–Populist brand of coalition in which "the black man was little more than a political football." As a political scientist, Professor Hamilton has presented us with some rather shoddy political history; as a former protest and political activist, who has of late become a rather weird ideological amalgam of "Marxist-Leninist-Nkrumahist-Pan-Africanism," Carmichael's "dialectical" grasp of political coalitions *in the United States* has diminished conversely with the enlargement of his "Back to Africa" Pan-Africanist view of international Black affairs. This was demonstrated in a speech Carmichael gave in London in 1967 on what he called "The Dialectics of Liberation."* He talked about many things, such as "Black Power," the "Third World," imperialism, Africa—in short, a typical Carmichael oration. Mostly he gave a survey-sketch of the Black condition in the United

---

*   [*Stokely Speaks—Black Power to Pan-Africanism* (Vintage Books, 1971)] pp. 77-99.

States which, in another speech he made elsewhere, he was to describe as "hopeless" and "with no future." Predictably, Carmichael was hard on American white folks, but politely critical of the British white folks (all the Caribbean-born Pan-Africanists have historically revealed a tempering of their anti-whiteness when it comes to the British). Not only did Carmichael *not* ask all of those Black West Indians why they had migrated to England (and not to Africa), he also did not tell them that *their* position in Britain's white society was as "hopeless" as the Afro-American's in America. He also did not give any fire-and-brimstone directives on how to burn down or blow-up London, or even to join hands with the Irish Republican Army when it engages in its uniquely white "anti-white imperialist" bombing crusades. Nothing demonstrates better than a Carmichael London speech that when he and Hamilton say *they* are wary of *any* kind of coalition with *any* kind of white folks, Stokely really means just what *he* says!

However, nothing that Carmichael said in his London speech on "The Dialectics of Liberation" sheds any light at all on the problems of Black political coalitions that Carmichael and Hamilton initially raised in their book. Neither an African in Accra nor a West Indian in London would ever guess from a reading of *Black Power* that both Stokely Carmichael and Charles V. Hamilton owe much of their 1960's-1970's social, political, economic, cultural and professional status to the Black achievements growing out of the New Deal and white coalition. Were it not for the Black militancy of the 1930's on the political fronts; were it not for the leadership of men like A. Philip Randolph and Adam Clayton Powell (yes, even the leadership of the NAACP), during the World War II era; were it not for the bitter struggles on the labor, civil-rights, and political, cultural and educational fronts, and the Black soldier's military ordeal in the war against Germany, *etc., etc.,* Carmichael and Hamilton would not have inherited the critical wherewithal to write *Black Power*. From the standpoint of historical "dialectics," after the Carmichael fashion, the book was weak. But without belaboring this problem of "dialectics" to the point of confusion (since the real question is whither Black politics), it is enough to point out that Marx did not reject the dialectical method because, in *his* opinion, Hegel had misapplied it; Martin Luther did not reject Christianity because of its abuse in the hands of the Roman Church; the Rev. Albert B. Cleage did not reject Christianity because it was the religion of the European slavetraders; nor did the Nation of Islam reject the Muslim faith because it is the religion of those other slave traders, the Arabs. All of these revolutionaries and reformers took over those ideas and concepts and molded them to fit their own needs and aspirations. One can well understand the misgivings of Carmichael and Hamilton regarding the value of "coalitions" as we have known them, but it is a questionable political logic that condemns unprofitable coalitions of the past, but does not offer even tentative guidelines for a new coalition concept. It appears that the real problem with Carmichael and Hamilton was that in writing *Black Power* they overlooked the fact that Black people, in general, during the Sixties, still languished under the inheritance of the Roosevelt New Deal. Not understanding this historical and political fact, most of the new generation of Black militants missed the point of the basic issues of national politics. Since the death of Roosevelt in 1945, the fundamental aim of the Republican Party strategy has been to disperse all the elements of the New Deal coalition, and to eliminate every lingering vestige of the New Deal social reforms. This is what the Nixon Administration has been all about.

Carmichael and Hamilton wrote *Black Power* in the middle of the Sixties— "The New Reconstruction"—which, similar to the first Reconstruction, was instrumental in increasing Black political involvement on the federal, state and local levels. Qualitatively, however, the resemblance ends there. The political situation which grew out of the Sixties was the kind of "Post-Reconstruction" challenge to the Seventies calling for a successful transformation from militant protest activism to militant political organization on a local and national level. In other words, once the Congressional Black Caucus (a result of the Sixties) was enthroned in Washington, D. C., the National Black Political Conventions of Gary and Little Rock became obligatory political instrumentalities. In fact, the Congressional Black Caucus, the National Black (Political) Assembly, the National Black Political Conventions, *etc.,* are the only experiments in the direction of "new forms" called for by Carmichael and Hamilton in 1967. However, the most unique of these "new forms," the National Black Political Convention, proved at Little Rock to be rather a still-born political organism incapable of generating new political ideas. This is because the participants have apparently learned little from the experience of the Sixties (not to speak of Little Rock 1957). What has happened is that the militant *protest* pragmatism of the Sixties has been transformed into militant *political* pragmatism in the Seventies.

At the Gary NBPC gathering of 1972, the most prominent pronouncement was the loudly proclaimed threat to form an "Independent Black Political Party." This was an implicit promise on the part of the prominent participants to play a "vanguard political role."* To assume that Blacks need an independent political party (or "structure" or "new form") is to assume either the need of, or an already existing, independent Black political leadership. It is also to assume that this "independent leadership" would be prepared to play a vanguard political role.

---

* The National Black Political Agenda submitted by Walter E. Fauntroy to the Platform Committee of the National Black Political Convention at Gary, Ind., March 24, 1972, stated "We are the vanguard." p.4.

There was, further, the assumption that these national conventions were already pregnant with an emergent "consensus" around which sentiments in favor of an independent Black political party could be rallied. But the Little Rock convention of March 1974 revealed the existence of no consensus strong enough to push through a resolution to form an independent Black political party. In fact, the only consensus was to hold a political convention. Now, in view of the fact that the launching of an independent Black political party was the chief motivation behind the first Gary convention of 1972, it is time to ask a number of hard questions. Do Gary and Little Rock indicate without a doubt that an independent Black party *is not really wanted?* If so, what justifiable reasons are there for holding National Black Political Conventions? One could almost swear that before the participants at these conventions were called upon to vote on any "third party" resolutions, they were first asked to read Carmichael and Hamilton on "The Myth of Coalition" in *Black Power.* And what is the meaning of the fact that, at Little Rock, where all the bold declarations of Gary 1972 regarding "vanguard politics" were repudiated, Mayor Richard G. Hatcher (of Gary!) hails the Little Rock convention as "a great success."

NOTES

1. Quoted in *U.S. News & World Report,* May 20, 1974. p. 29.
2. *Black Power. . .* p. 176.
3. Ibid. p. 68.
4. Ibid. p. 70.
5. *The Betrayal of the Negro—From Rutherford B. Hayes to Woodrow Wilson,* p. 23.
6. Logan, cited. p. 88.
7. Carmichael, *Marxism, Leninism and Nkrumahism* (Black Scholar, February 1973), p. 41.
8. Hanes Walton, *Black Politics—A Theoretical and Structural Analysis* (J. B. Lippincott, New York, 1972), p. 133.
9. Ibid.
10. [Henry Lee Moon, *Balance of Power: The Negro Vote,* Doubleday, 1948], pp. 36-37.

PART FOUR

From
Rebellion or
Revolution?
(1968)

CHAPTER FOURTEEN

Rebellion or Revolution?

I.

For the first time since the 1930's Americans of more than ordinary social insight are openly discussing the possibility of social revolution in the United States. We know that during the 1930's "revolution" implied the overthrow of capitalistic institutions—a real threat which the more enlightened wing of American bourgeois wealth successfully defeated by the implementation of the various New Deal policies. But unlike the 1930's, when it was reported that some of the idle rich were so fearful of revolution that they had their yachts readied in the harbor for a fast getaway just in case, the talk of revolution today has little to do with conflicts in labor-capital relations or the imminent collapse of the capitalist system. It has to do with the present state of American race relations which some people (hopefully or fearfully) describe as the "Negro revolution."

There is no need to mention the obvious—that the racial crisis reflects broad and profound discontent within the American Negro minority. However, when one goes so far as to say that this racial discontent contains the seeds of social revolution in America, this immediately calls up a flock of other questions concerning the present outlook of the American state of mind which, when considered side by side with the possibility of a Negro revolution, has a very sobering, if not disturbing, effect on such speculations. Without a doubt it must have been the influence of such considerations which prompted President Kennedy to counsel, some time ago, apropos of the racial question, that the revolution be a peaceful one.

Considering the social, historical and political background of twentieth-century revolutions thus far, the talk about Negro revolution also demands that all segments of the Negro movement in America be examined very closely. In doing so, we will note that none of the leadership corps of any segment, be it the NAACP-King-CORE students-Urban League-Muslims, etc., is anti-capitalist. The same can generally be said for the followers of these leadership factions. If the Negro movement, then, is revolutionary, it must be revolutionary in a sense which is uniquely different from the characteristics and aims of all other revolutions of our century.

The speculations about the Negro revolution have also inspired the usual suspicions that the integration movement is Communist-inspired. In answer to such charges one could again point to the very conservative and loyal pro-capitalist sentiments of Negro leadership. But still this would not explain very much about the Negro revolution. We know very well that Communists and other Marxist factions, such as Trotskyites, Independent Socialists, etc., are very much in support of the Negro movement in one way or another. One has only to read the Marxist-oriented press to see this. The truth is, however, that the Marxist factions are trailing very eagerly behind the Negro movement in search of issues for their programs. Marxists are no longer able, as they once were, to initiate any movements among Negroes. Moreover, what is not generally understood by those who raise the issue of Communism is that the integration movement, by its very nature, has rendered the Marxist movement superfluous and irrelevant, since Marxists qua Marxists are not needed in the integration struggle. The character of the integration struggle cuts the ground from under Marxist parties since they cannot beat the NAACP or CORE at their own game, nor can Marxist theories about revolution cope with a Negro movement that is pro-capitalist to the extent of demanding no more than an equitable share of the abundance of capitalist democracy. Yet people express the feeling that there is a revolution in the air. There is tenseness abounding as reports of racial strife become more and more a common occurrence. Instinctively we sense that America is preparing itself for great social changes of some kind and the idea of revolution is the first that comes to mind. But to conjure up the idea of Negro revolution under the present conditions in America also calls for a definition or redefinition of what one means when one says "revolution" or "revolutionary," because in highly industrialized America it is not possible to use such terms as freely as one could in describing social conditions in, let us say, Latin America and still make sense.

People who use the term "Negro revolution" loosely are unwittingly adding fuel to the flames of racial crisis which can lead to more racial chaos instead of racial solutions because such people are not helping to explain exactly what the Negro is up against in his struggle to win racial equality in America. Winning racial equality in America could very well require revolutionary methods, and very probably will; but then we will have to understand *why* a revolution and *how* the Negro could possibly make one. The why and the how are important considerations because the racial crisis does lay down an indirect challenge to the American capitalist status quo while the Negro leadership, at the very same time, seeks integration into the status quo with no professed desire to alter it. This creates for the Negro movement a highly contradictory situation which is also a dangerous one. It is dangerous because Americans, of all people in the world today, are the least amenable to, adaptable to, or desirous of any far-reaching changes in their social structures. It is also dangerous because Negro leadership has been instrumental in creating a situation which has implications far beyond its limited range of program. Taken as a whole, Negro leadership does not measure up to the demands of the racial crisis—a crisis which developed because the Negro movement has now transcended the moderate limits established by its leadership.

The Negro movement represents an *indirect* challenge to the capitalist status quo not because it is programmatically anti-capitalist, but because full integration of the Negro in all levels of American society *is not possible within the present framework of the American system*. If this sounds categorically absolute one can only say that the time has come for blunt appraisals of reality: The United States cannot and never will solve the race problem unless Americans change the economic, political, cultural, and administrative social organization of this country in various sectors. Any superoptimism concerning the race question based on a lesser assessment or hope for a neo-liberalistic American revival is heartening but hardly realistic. Is this the same thing as saying that in order to solve the racial crisis what is needed is a revolution? Again the question is: What do we mean by "revolution"?

Social change in any society can be either revolutionary or evolutionary depending on what organizational methods are pursued and who directs the organizational methods. In the United States the capitalist system in all of its major and minor levels of economic administration is owned, controlled, and directed by whites of various classes. Even white labor of the trade union type can be said to have a stake in white ownership of capital either by racial identification with the unions or with a bureaucracy with a capitalist mentality to match its capital investments. Racial discrimination growing out of the racist ideology of the dominant whites of the capital-labor alliance in America has traditionally excluded Negroes (both bourgeois and working-class) from equal participation in either the industrial or trade union fields or administration in the capital-labor alliance. Hence, if the Negro movement is revolutionary or has revolutionary potential, how can the Negro movement have the power in and of itself to enforce structural and administrative changes in this capital-labor combination in order to make room for the democratic participation of the Negro as an American equal? Essentially, this is what is implied in the word "integration" as projected by the Negro bourgeoisie—or at least that portion of the black bourgeoisie that supports integration. But since the integration program does not demand alterations in the structural forms of American society; since the white capital-labor alliance does not desire such changes and would further cement their alliance to block such changes; and since the Negro movement must have such changes in order to achieve its aims—where does this leave the Negro movement? From this analysis—which admittedly is oversimplified for the purpose of illustration—we have to conclude that the Negro movement at this moment is not a revolutionary movement because it has no present means or program to alter the structural forms of American institutions. It is pure political romanticism, at this point, to call the Negro movement the "Negro revolution." It is more properly called the "Negro rebellion" against the American racial status quo.

There is a great difference between rebellion and revolution—two conceptions which some people insist on confusing. This confusion is what led, for example, to the outcome of the situation in Monroe, North Carolina, involving Robert Williams. The American Marxists of certain tendencies—and Marxists are incurable romantics—tried to make a revolutionary out of Robert Williams, who was not a revolutionary but a rebel. The Monroe movement was but a small, local manifestation of the growing Negro rebellion which some Marxists and others mistook for the revolution in the making. One can say that the final outcome of the adventurous happenings in Monroe was unavoidable due to the tense racial situation in America. Nevertheless, this does not excuse incorrect and superficial assessments applied to the Negro movement in whole or in part. A rebellion is not a revolutionary movement unless it changes the structural arrangements of the society or else is able to project programmatic ideas toward that end. The Negro movement does not have the latter, and in America neither arms nor demonstrations nor protest marches mean very much without such ideas. The question that follows is: If indeed a revolution is required to achieve Negro aspirations of whatever class stratification in America, how is it possible to change the Negro movement from a rebellion into a revolutionary movement? Again this is predicated on whether or not social changes to come in America will be revolutionary or evolutionary. This has not yet been determined. It is a dialectical question. However, prior to making any rash, or let us say, unscientific predictions, let us get a clearer conception of the American capitalistic status quo and the American Negro's relationship to that status quo.

What all of us Americans, black and white, are facing today is a racial crisis which is composed in part of the accumulated results of white liberal lying and dishonesty about race, caste and class in this country. On the other hand, it is also due to the superficial and intellectually empty racial propaganda projected over the years by Negro middle-class moderation policies on civil rights. The liberal New York *Post* which has for years been catering to the NAACP and later to Martin Luther King, Jr., was forced to admit, through Stan Opotowsky, one of its reporters, that the class of Negroes that revolted in Birmingham and transformed King's "orderly" protest movement into a race riot had nothing to hope for, no benefits to anticipate from whatever integrated gains King's properly behaved passive protesters would achieve. The liberal New York *Post* is very late in admitting what many of us voiceless Negroes have been saying for years in criticism of white liberalism that caters to the aims and aspirations of the middle-class Negro. Belatedly the liberals have discovered a class of Negroes in Birmingham which Opotowsky described as "lost men." If these disprivileged Birmingham mavericks *are* lost then we are all lost—for the Negroes cited by Opotowsky represent the majority of American Negroes. The majority of Negroes cannot be restrained or contained within the legalistic, gradualistic, passive-moderation approach any longer. The civil rights movement has moved from NAACP protest to broad and general rebellion. It is a rebellion which cannot be put down; a rebellion which, if not handled with the highest order of internal statesmanship, will lead to racial and social chaos.

Opotowsky came to the wrong conclusion about Birmingham's "lost men." While it is true that the integration movement offers the majority of Negroes very little, it is far from proving that the majority of Negroes are lost, i.e., lost to social history and eternity. If we are that lost there is nothing left but to join the Muslims or some other like movement for repatriation or separation. On the contrary, what the Negro rebellion is proving in its own as yet inconclusive manner is that the United States, the greatest and most advanced of the capitalist nations in the Western combine, is not at all exempt or immune from the forces of social change that are sweeping the world today. Unhappily, this is a fact which American whites will find most difficult to comprehend. Americans think they are a very special and privileged people as they peer uncomprehendingly beyond their ocean beaches into a world wracked and seething with revolution, discontent, and political turmoil. Americans have been lulled into a deluded fog of complacency by America's ability to maintain long-term stability. This expertly controlled stability is why there is so much perplexity, desperation, fear, and resentment shown by whites all over the country as the Negro protest movement moves into open rebellion. These attitudes are but a reflection of the uncomfortable fact that America, at present, has no clear answers to the problems emerging out of the racial crisis. President Kennedy voiced this fact right after the Birmingham crisis when he said, "The fires of frustration and discord are burning in every city, North and South, where legal remedies are not at hand." This is the bitter truth which the NAACP et al. could not admit. For to admit there is no legal remedy for full integration means that the integrationist leadership is out on a limb.

~

We American Negroes are not a "lost" ethnic minority in America. We must admit, however, that the very widespread psychology of alienation from American civilization noted among many younger-generation Negroes could lead to the pessimistic conclusion voiced by Muslims and others that there is no hope for black people in white society. Add to this the negative attitudes of most whites, plus the incompetence and obsolescence of liberal remedies, and it is difficult for many not to believe with the Muslims that white civilization is a sinking ship. The flaw for us in the sinking ship forecast is that we are more or less doomed to sink with it. The American Negro, caught in a social situation from which he cannot readily depart, retreat, or easily advance, resembles Jean Paul Sartre's existential man who is "condemned to be free."

The American Negro must stand up and fight his way out of the social trap in which Western civilization has ensnared him. But he can no longer struggle with the old methods alone. Protest actions of whatever nature are no longer enough. The Negro must now develop and begin to use a set of new ideas. What we are up against is the fact that Western civilization is intellectually, spiritually and morally bankrupt. It is a civilization that is no longer able to originate creative ideas in social thinking—and America is no exception to this creative decline that is sapping the vitality of the Western world. In this sense, white America has inherited a racial crisis that it cannot handle and is unable to create a solution for that does not do violence to the collective white American racial ego. The racial crisis in America is more than a question of what Americans are going to do about their subclass of exploited Negro wards. It is also a broader question: which way is America going as a nation, up or down? Beyond that, it is a question of which way is white civilization going? How do white people, Americans included, propose to accommodate themselves to an emerging world of non-white peoples over whom whites no longer have the right of unilateral dispensation? The racial crisis in America is an internal reflection of this contemporary world-wide problem of readjustment between ex-colonial masers and ex-colonial subjects. The so-called "democratic heritage" of the American tradition has served as historical camouflage to hide the fact that America participated in colonialism through its peculiar institution of slavery. Although a very special kind of colonialism, as we shall elaborate later, slavery was an organic offshoot of European subjugation of Africa and the New World. After the Civil War, the Negro was transformed into a semi-colonial people no different from any other semi-colonial people in South Africa or parts of Latin America.

The historical development of the relationship between the races in America has cultivated a strange and unique pattern of intergroup psychologies between Negro and white of various castes and classes. Many Negroes, especially those who aspire to leadership of one form or another, and the majority of whites have shown a very perverse tendency to overlook or deny exactly what America is as a nation. America never was the all-white nation that the national psychology pretends. America is and always was multi-racial, multi-national, and culturally pluralistic. People who try to deny this fact with talk about Americans all speaking the same language or sharing the same "customs" are merely propagating the myth about "assimilated Americanism." America shares the English language with Canada but they are two nations. The universality of Spanish in South America did not prevent the formation of several independent republics on that continent. If language has failed to break down the racial fences or assimilate the various American ethnic minorities, why cite the American language as proof of an Americanized ideal which America has never achieved? (And let us not mention the Indians.) Either we accept without further delusions that America is pluralistic and democratically adjust our economic, political, cultural, and administrative institutions to fit what is the human living fact and cease believing in the mythology of assimilated Americanism based on the dominant white Protestant Anglo-Saxon ideal, or the racial crisis will be more and more exacerbated. This would be the approach to an evolutionary path for social change in America.

It is possibly too late for this approach. It would require voluntary social planning and governmental intervention into the economy—the great bugbears of the free enterprise economic religion. America has grown up planlessly and chaotically, leaving her racial and ethnic minorities to shift for themselves while she cultivates the idea that America is an all-white Anglo-Saxon nation. This is a totally false image. A psychology, whether individual or national, that tries to deny the essential facts about its social origins is lying to itself and to the world. Such a psychology, individual or national, cannot deal effectively with social reality. America in its national psychology lies to itself that Anglo-Saxon and North European racial ingenuity plus the resources of a virgin continent built American capitalist democracy. America lies to itself that it was always, from the beginning, a democratic nation when its very constitution sanctioned and upheld chattel slavery. Moreover, America conveniently forgets that the first capitalist "free enterprise" banks and stock markets in the land were made possible by accumulated capital accrued from the unpaid labor of Negro slaves. But it would be too much to expect contemporary America to go back over its own history and reassess all these racial facts. Americans are not historically minded and the capitalistic free-enterprise mentality only looks to the future in terms of monetary profits. A program of socially administered evolutionary changes in our economic, political, and cultural life seems very remote. A racial "New Deal" would cause more of an outcry than Roosevelt's reforms, even though these reforms were evolutionary methods to ward off revolutionary threats.

If the realities of the American way of life lead us to rule out the possibilities of voluntary evolutionary social change along racially or ethnically democratic lines, we are then faced with the other alternative: revolutionary ideas and methods. But here we encounter a very unique and complex set of problems. For to transform the Negro rebellion into a movement with revolutionary approaches, ideas, and appeals is an immense intellectual and organizational problem. Moreover, it poses what amounts to a new question in America: What, precisely, is revolutionary in form and content? This is not a simple question to answer because the only concept of social revolution that has come out of Western thought since the nineteenth century is the revolutionary overthrow of capital by the combined forces of labor. This is ruled out of our considerations because of the reality of the American capital-labor alliance. To speak, then, of social revolution in the United States from the Negro point of view means a reinterpretation of the meaning of social revolution for our times. This may appear a startling statement but it is, in all evidence, quite true. In investigating this problem, we American Negroes must not lose sight of one fact about the

Western world and its intellectual traditions: New social frontiers do not cease to be simply because Western philosophers have no more answers for the problems of the world. Still, we Afro-Americans who have always been excluded to the fringe world of Western society can learn a lot from Western philosophers and pick up where they left off. In this regard, the theories of social revolution thought up by Western philosophers such as Marx and others are bankrupt, passé, and irrelevant in Western society today. Socialism has not come to the Western world through the revolt of the working classes of white nations. As a result, the whole Western world is in serious trouble because social revolution is today the prerogative of the colored peoples. Despite the fact that Western white Marxists may attempt to cast colonial and semi-colonial revolutions in their own Marxian image, it is a fact that these revolutions are all indigenous, original, autonomous and unique in themselves. Marx did not invent social revolution but, at the same time, this does not mean that we cannot learn many things from Marx. The failure of the Marxist revolution in Europe and America has led many intellectuals, especially in Europe, to attempt to reinvestigate and reinterpret social revolution. The Negro intellectual must do the same if the Negro rebellion is ever to become a revolutionary movement in its own right. The Negro rebellion can learn much from other Western critics of revolutionary theory and arrive at its own answers for its own situation. Albert Camus, discussing rebellion and revolution, had this to say:

> Rebellion is, by nature, limited in scope. It is no more than an incoherent pronouncement. Revolution, on the contrary, originates in the realm of ideas. Specifically, it is the injection of ideas into historical experience, while rebellion is only the movement that leads from individual experience into the realm of ideas. While even the collective history of a movement of rebellion is always that of a fruitless struggle with facts, of an obscure protest which involves neither methods nor reasons, a revolution is an attempt to shape actions to ideas, to fit the world into a theoretical frame.[1]

These words were written by a man who died relatively young, who had become increasingly disturbed and alarmed by the steady deterioration of the political, moral and spiritual reality of Western Europe. Originally a French Marxist, Camus recoiled in the face of the obvious collapse and degeneration of the Marxian revolution between the two World Wars and after. For our purposes, we need not go into this very complex question as to why the working classes of European white nations failed to make the hoped-for revolution. Our immediate problem is not Europe but America, where we live. However, it is enough to point out that the white capital-labor alliance that has taken place in America has its parallel in Europe where the white Marxist "revolutionaries" became less and less revolutionary the more the European colonies became truly revolutionary. At the root of the whole question of the degeneration of Western Marxism in Europe was the colonial problem. It was not the Marxist plan that colored colonies should become liberated before white socialism came into Europe. The fact that this is what happened threw the European capitalists, and the Marxists as well, into a state of confusion and panic. The Marxists in Europe talked like revolutionaries but their internal politics became more and more geared to the necessities of preventing their own capitalist societies from collapse as a result of colonial losses. In Algeria, for example, where Camus was born, it is a fact that many French Marxists, when the racial showdown came, turned against the Algerian rebel forces. These facts, and many more, were not lost on Camus, who was an honest revolutionary defeated and confounded by the utter betrayal perpetrated by his own revolutionary tradition and the degeneration of Western morality.

From Camus we are able to learn the most precise difference between mere rebellion and viable revolution. More than that, we understand why the Negro movement, which is a rebellion, has its "revolutionary" limitations: It is a movement without any unique ideas of its own. The key to the question of "unique ideas" is lost in the confusion of ideas, or better, the lack of positive ideas, of what America really is as a nation and the true nature of the Negroes' intrinsic relationship to the American reality. This is a problem that has not been adequately or honestly explored in all of its sociological ramifications. It could not be because, as we have pointed out, the national psychology of the dominant white ideal prefers to project the image of America as an all-white nation. (Look at American films, television, and the advertising media, etc.) More than that, since we are dealing with a society which, besides wanting to be called an all-white nation, is also the most extensively industrialized capitalist nation in the world, and also wants desperately to remain capitalistic in order to defend its "free" institutions by keeping Negroes excluded (white labor is not going to overthrow it), it behooves us to examine this American capitalism in order to determine just what kind of economic animal it is. What are its characteristics? What are its strong points? What are its weaknesses?

American capitalism is not the same as other capitalisms in the Western world because it developed according to its own peculiar geographical, social, racial, political, and cultural climate. Moreover, American capitalism helps to sustain and prop up other capitalisms. What is crucial for capitalism as an economic system is that beyond the United States capitalism has nowhere else to go in terms of development. America is the last hope of capitalism as a system. But in terms of revolutionary ideas, the Negroes' relationship to this American system is a unique one, since we are excluded, and also for other reasons not yet explored. One significant reason for this uniqueness is that social revolution today is a product of the underdeveloped sections of the world's colored populations where there exists no such highly industrialized social base. For the Negro, this presents a very novel situation; in fact, one of the most unique in world history.

We American Negroes exist in essentially the same relationship to American capitalism as other colonials and semi-colonials have to Western capitalism as a whole. Yet when other semi-colonials of the colored world rebel against the political and economic subjugation of Western capitalism, it is for the aim of having the freedom to build up their own native industrial bases for themselves. Our American Negro rebellion derives from the fact that we exist side by side with the greatest industrial complex the world has ever seen, which we are not allowed to use democratically for ourselves. Hence, while the Negro rebellion emerges out of the same semi-colonial social conditions of others, it must have different objectives in order to be considered revolutionary. In other words, we must locate the weakest sector of the American capitalist "free enterprise" front and strike there. Where is that weak front in the free-enterprise armor? It is in the cultural front. Or better, it is that part of the American economic system that has to do with the ownership and administration of cultural communication in America, i.e., film, theater, radio and television, music, performing and publishing, popular entertainment booking, management, etc. In short, it is that part of the system devoted to the economics and aesthetic ideology involved in the cultural arts of America. If the Negro rebellion is limited by a lack of original social, political and economic ideas to "fit the world into a rhetorical frame," then it is only in the cultural areas of American life that such new ideas can have any social meaning. What is meant here is that the only observable way in which the Negro rebellion can become revolutionary in terms of American conditions is for the Negro movement to project the concept of Cultural Revolution in America. Why this is so we shall proceed to show by a historical, racial, economic, and cultural analysis of the American Negroes' many-sided relationship to the American system.

∽

The Negro rebellion in America is destined to usher in a new era in human relations and to add a thoroughly new conception of the meaning and the form and content of social revolution. In order to make social progress the world as a whole must move toward unification within the democratic framework of a human, national, ethnic, or racial variety. A great stride toward this world ideal of unification through national variety has been achieved in the process of dissolution of colonial empires.

In America, however, we have an unsolved problem of a unique type of semi-colonialism. The Negro rebellion comes at this time to give voice to the long suppressed ethnic consciousness of the American Negro as he rises to the task to throw off his semi-colonial yoke. But this Negro rebellion, mistakenly called by some the Negro revolution, is not revolutionary because it projects no new ideas beyond what have already been ratified in the democratic philosophy of the American Constitution. These constitutional concepts about "freedom" are the heritage of a revolutionary movement ushered in by the industrial revolution of centuries past. Since our traditions of latter-day liberalism are unable to apply these concepts to the realities of race in America, social progress demands that new ideas of social revolution be introduced into the bloodstream of the American tradition. It goes without saying that these new concepts must be extracted from native American social ingredients.

Hence, we have projected the new concept of Cultural Revolution. We maintain that this concept affords the intellectual means, the conceptual framework, the theoretical link that ties together all the disparate, conflicting and contending trends within the Negro movement as a whole in order to transform the movement from a mere rebellion into a revolutionary movement that can "shape actions to ideas, to fit the world into a theoretic frame." What do we mean by Cultural Revolution? Stated simply, Cultural Revolution means an ideological and organizational approach to American social change by revolutionizing the administration, the organization, the functioning, and the social purpose of the entire American apparatus of cultural communication and placing it under public ownership.

What has this to do with the Negro's struggle for racial equality, and why should the American Negro assume the initiative for such a task? Because the American Negro is the only ethnic group in America who has the need, the motivation and the historical prerogative to demand such changes. Also because racial equality cannot be achieved unless the Negro rebellion adopts revolution-ary tactics which can enforce structural changes in the administration of certain sections of the national economy. Since the alliance of white capital and labor obviates any challenge to the economic status quo where the production of basic commodities takes place, the Negro movement must challenge free enterprise at its weakest link in the production chain, where no tangible commodities are produced. This becomes the "economic" aspect of the Negro movement. However, it is the cultural aspect of this problem that is most important in terms of form and content in new revolutionary ideas.

The Negro concept of Cultural Revolution demands that both the American national psychology and the organization of American cultural institutions be altered to fit the facts of what America really is. Culturally speaking, America is a European-African-Indian racial amalgam—an imperfect and incompletely realized amalgam. Therefore, the American racial problem is a problem of many aspects, but it is essentially a cultural problem of a type that is new in modern history. Until this is intellectually admitted and sociologically practiced, chaotic and retrograde racial practices and conflicts will continue in American society. That the Negro question in America is essentially a cultural question has escaped the attention of the so-called theoreticians and practitioners of sociology and political and social theory. This is why the concept of Cultural Revolution becomes an intellectual means of introducing a new set of ideas into American social theory. A basic reason why the cultural aspect of Negro reality has been overlooked, dismissed, and neglected is that most articulate and intellectually inclined Negroes are beguiled to think of culture solely in terms of the white Anglo-Saxon ideal, which is the cultural image that America attempts to project to the world. The American national psychology prefers to be regarded as an all-white nation, and the American cultural arts are, therefore, cultivated to preserve and reflect this all-white ideal. Any other artistic expression is regarded as an exotic curiosity.

If we examine this cultural side of the race question in America very closely, we will find that, historically and culturally speaking, the white American Anglo-Saxon cultural ideal of artistic and aesthetic practices is false, predicated as it is on the myth of Western superiority in cultural tradition, and conceals the true facts of native American cultural development. What the white American creative artist or cultural critic is upholding as "superior" is the Western tradition of cultural creativity stemming from European sources to which the white American Anglo-Saxon (and those others who try to be such and are not) never truly added very much this side of the Atlantic. The statement often heard that "America has no real culture" is not far from the truth.

But to say that white America has not been culturally creative or original does not mean that America as a racial or cultural amalgam has not been culturally or artistically original. The historical truth is that it was the Afro-American cultural ingredient in music, dance and theatrical forms (the three forms of art in which America has innovated) that has been the basis for whatever culturally new and unique that has come out of America. Take away the Afro-

American tradition of folk-songs, plantation minstrel, spirituals, blues, ragtime, jazz styles, dance forms, and the first Negro theatrical pioneers in musical comedy of the 1890's down to Sissle and Blake of the 1920's, and there would be no jazz industry involving publishing, entertainment, recording; there would have been no Gershwins, Rodgers and Hammersteins, Cole Porters or Carmichaels or popular song tradition—which is based on the Negro blues idiom; there would have been no American musical comedy form—which is America's only original contribution to theater; there would have been no foxtrot—which has formed the basis for American ballroom dancing (not to mention several other popular dance styles in the history of American dance). In other words, the Afro-American ingredients formed the basis of all "popular culture" as opposed to "classical culture" in America. We can see from this that "cultural" aspects of life in America are closely linked with the development of American racial mores. Moreover, since all of these popular art forms comprise those cultural commodities involved in multimillion dollar industries (which exclude or exploit Negroes as much as possible), there is an organic connection in American capitalism between race, culture, and economics.

Culturally speaking, the American intellectual community has arbitrarily dichotomized the national culture into exclusive divisions—"popular culture" and "classical culture." In American terms classical culture is the tradition of glorifying the artistic traditions of Western Europe in the seven arts and the desire to cultivate an American extension of this Western tradition. In this endeavor, Americans as a whole have not done very well. The white intellectual community of America is, and always has been, very painfully aware of this American deficiency. Hence, the recurrent complaint: "America has no real culture." What is meant is that America has no real tradition of a classical culture to match the ascendant European. This fact becomes glaringly noticeable today when America is called upon to demonstrate the cultural results of its "democratic heritage" to the world at large, which is amazed at how little this country has to offer. That the upper levels of the American cultural community is painfully aware of this was mentioned by the late C. Wright Mills a few years ago: "The United States is now engaged with other nations, in particular Russia, in a full-scale competition for cultural prestige based on nationality. . . . What America has abroad is power; what it does not have at home or abroad is cultural prestige."[2]

Despite the grievous lack of a classical culture in America, however, this country always has at its disposal a reserve cultural weapon and that is jazz music, the Afro-American cultural contribution to the national soul. In 1955, *The New York Times* carried a headline on its front page to the effect: "United States Has a Secret Sonic Weapon—Jazz." The article went on to say: "All Europe now seems to find American jazz as necessary as the seasons . . . American jazz has now become a universal language. It knows no national boundaries . . ." etc. The State Department is quite willing to use jazz as a cultural weapon because it hasn't got much else. The problem posed here is that jazz, in the view of America's white cultural elite, is a "popular" mode of cultural expression and does not make up for the serious lack of American "classical" cultural arts. The question then is why was jazz music never cultivated by musical America into an American school of classical music in the same fashion that European folk-music was incorporated into the European classical music tradition? The answer to this question is also the answer to the question: Why does America have no real culture? American jazz was never seriously developed into an American classical school of musical creation because American composers and critics never really desired it. For to elevate jazz into a serious classical school would have demanded that the whole body of Afro-American folk-music also be elevated and glorified. This would also mean that the Afro-American ethnic minority which originally created this music would have to be culturally glorified and elevated socially, economically and politically. It would mean that the black composer would have to be accepted on this social, cultural, economic, and political level. But this the white American cultural ego would never permit. The inescapable conclusion is this: At the bottom of the whole question of the backward cultural development of America, the cultural banality, the cultural decadence, the cultural debasement of the entire American social scene, lies the reality of racism—racial exclusion, racial exploitation, racial segregation and all the manifestations of the ideology of white superiority.

This whole question of race and culture in America is imbedded in the social roots of the historical development of native American cultural standards and institutions. For this fundamental reason the Negro civil rights movement, at this late stage of its development, cannot go any further; it cannot transform itself into a movement with a revolutionary set of ideas unless it incorporates a cultural program along with its economic, social, and political platforms.

Such a cultural program, however, must be two-sided. It must be concerned not only with the aesthetics of the form and content of artistic creation in America but also with transforming the economic, institutional, business and administrative organizational apparatus that buys and sells, limits or permits, hires and disposes of, distributes or retains, determines or negates, and profits from the creation and distribution of cultural production in America. This is the meaning, for our purposes, of Cultural Revolution. We maintain that without such a revolution the Negro movement has no point of departure from which to compel the necessary social impact to effect structural changes within the American social system.

Moreover, it seems to be historically determined, if one seriously analyzes and examines the peculiarities of American capitalism, that it is precisely the economic sphere of cultural communications in America that must be revolutionized for more humanistic social use before such changes take place in commodity production, political organization or racial democratization. The theoretical reasoning behind this assumption is that, if the world revolution now in process emerges from the conditions of social underdevelopment, then social revolution in highly developed societies cannot have those same motivations. This would be particularly true for the United States, whose industrial development is greater than that of any other society. When we clearly observe that Western capitalism has cultivated the new class alliance between white labor and white capital in the face of colonial and semi-colonial revolutions, it becomes evident that the old Marxian formula of the revolutionary class struggle between capital and labor is passé and obsolescent. Hence any theory of social revolution must be modernized with a new set of ideas, coming not from the whites, since that is improbable, but from the colored races. This is why the African nations are involved in the cultivation of new social, political, cultural, and economic ideas to fit their respective needs. It is incumbent upon the Afro-American to do the same within his own social context.

What is the precise connection between the Negro rebellion and the African revolution? It is partially answered by saying that the connection is precisely cultural. It could not be anything else but cultural—which already implies "racial" or "ethnic." It certainly is not economic or even political in any serious dimension. What is the meaning of "Negritude," the aesthetic concept projected by the Paris group of African intellectuals sixteen years ago when they organized the Society of African Culture? One of the resolutions of that organizing congress describes the idea of Negritude very succinctly: "The imperious necessity for proceeding toward a rediscovery of historical truth and a re-evaluation of Negro cultures" in order to "revive, rehabilitate, and develop those cultures so as to favour their integration into the general stream of human culture." When Leopold Sedar Senghor met with some Negro authors in New York a few years ago, he told these authors that the American Negro should seriously study the question of the Negro aesthetic in American culture. Leopold Senghor, who is also a leading African poet, is one of the major African intellectuals on the question of Negritude. The unfortunate difficulty here is that Leopold Senghor, who is not an American Negro, understands the implication of Negro culture in American historical development better than any of the Negro writers with whom he discussed the matter. These Negro writers did not understand what Senghor meant, and have not discussed the matter since.

The American branch of the Society of African Culture (AMSAC), which was supposed to take up the question of Negritude as it relates to the American Negro, is run by a group of culturally white-oriented Negroes who did not believe that the African concept of Negritude really applies to the American Negro and heaped ridicule on Negroes in AMSAC who fought for the cultivation of the concept in America. The real problem was that AMSAC's leadership did not know how to apply the idea. The failures of AMSAC on this aesthetic question of Negritude in America means that the theoretical link between the African revolution and the Negro movement in America has not been established in the politics of the Negro intellectual community in America. This link must be a cultural one for the basic reason that the exploitation practiced on Africans and those of African descent in the Western hemisphere has not only been economic, in terms of labor and natural resources, but it has also been cultural. In America the entire industry of popular music writing, publishing, and selling was established by white appropriation of the whole body of Afro-American folk music—the only original music in America with a broad human appeal. This music has been cheapened, debased and commercialized for popular appeal. The American music industry has been exploiting, cheating, stealing from, browbeating, excluding, plagiarizing Negro singers, jazz musicians, composers, etc., for decades and getting away with it. The cultural exploitation established by white America in the early years of the twentieth century by the white appropriation of Afro-American folk-music was the first great manifestation of the racist development in the economics of American culture. This racist cultural doctrine, once established in music, spread through the entire field of cultural expression in America. It has had its poisonous effect on American theater, both musical and dramatic, and a distorting influence on American dance. Today it is till rampant in the jazz fields.

The racial attitudes behind American cultural developments were the basic problem of cultural competition between white and Negro. The whites very quickly realized that from the lowly Negro in America came the only rich vein of untapped and completely original material for song, dance, music and theater. This was the motivation behind the creation of the blackface or burnt cork tradition by the whites. (Ironically, in the nineteenth century Negroes were forced to use blackface in order to compete with whites in the use of Negro theatrical material.) The economic benefits derived from the creative and artistic use of Negro cultural ingredients were reaped by the whites through the simple practice of cultural appropriation of aesthetic ideas not native to their own tradition. As a result there came into being a long line of white creative artists and performers who either enriched themselves or got their start by using Negro material—the Al Jolsons, the George Gershwins, the Amos 'n' Andys, Eugene O'Neill, Ridgely Torrence, Marc Connelly, and more, plus scores of plagiarizing white composers (including very big names). Booking agents and managers have for decades made millions by the shrewd exploitation and manipulation of Negro performers and creators over whom they held the life and death economic power to hire or fire.

We have only one Negro "cultural" spokesman today and that is James Baldwin. But he is not talking about culture. In fact, Baldwin does not believe in "race" and would rather not consider himself a Negro author, merely another American author who accidentally happens not to be white. This may sound very "modern" and "New Negroid" but it is negative in the extreme. Baldwin's literary power of expression exists precisely because he is black in America. For all of his gift of creative expression, Baldwin is another example of the process of negation visited upon the Negro intellectual who is overawed by the glitter and glamour of a steel-riveted and chrome-plated Western world in the last stages of cultural and spiritual decline. The tragedy of cultural negation inflicted on the Negro personality in America is that this process of negation induces the negated to negate himself.

Thus it is that the concept of Cultural Revolution brings together in America several seemingly separate and disparate historical trends and processes that started with the industrial revolution and lifted millions out of Europe and Africa and placed them in a fateful social juxtaposition in the New World. This revolutionary process has never really ceased. It has merely halted for a spell of decades only to appear again in new forms with new aims for different peoples and nations. In the beginning the revolutionary leadership came from European whites who ushered in the modern world. But today the revolutionary leadership is the "browns," "blacks," and "yellows." Black revolution in Africa means black revolution in the United States because Africa and the United States are historically welded in that fateful juxtaposition of races which went into their national make-ups in the beginning. America is not immune from those social forces that are changing the world. No nation can step outside of history, and each nation must pay its just dues to historical demands at the proper time or decline.

The Afro-American must understand that he is Africa's cultural contribution to "the general stream of human culture" as defined by the Paris Society of African Culture. He must understand that his social revolution is nothing if it is not cultural in content. He must understand that all social revolutions are at once social, economic, political, cultural and administrative. But, depending on circumstances, each specific revolution is couched in different central demands. In the United States the only kind of revolution the Negro can make is a cultural revolution, because he represents the only ethnic group who has a political right to raise such a demand. The Negro revolution can be economic, social, political, administrative, or racial in form, but it must be cultural in content. If it is not cultural in content it is not revolutionary, but a mere rebellion without ideas "to fit the world in a theoretic frame." It is only the cultural needs of the Negro that coincide with or are complementary to the main humanistic need that goes unfulfilled in America despite this country's economic and administrative achievements—the need for a thriving, creative, humanistically progressive national culture.

Cultural Revolution brings, for the first time in Negro history, a new class of Negro leadership into the arena of public affairs with a national program for social change. This class or social stratum is the Negro writer, dramatist, poet, actor, painter, dancer, architect, designer, composer, arranger, film technician, sculptor, critic, etc. Heretofore, this class among American Negroes has been divided and compartmentalized along craft lines. There has been little or no conception among Negroes of the crucial need for artists of all crafts to work together within one organization comprising all the arts. This lack of cultural unity on the intercraft level existed because of the lack of a comprehensive cultural philosophy among Negroes in the arts. The present "cultural" work among Negroes consists of "integration in the theater," "integration in the films," "integration in this and that," etc. This amounts to an inconsequential and dead-end cultural approach to American arts. Integration in the arts ignores the racist premises upon which the whole institution of the cultural arts in America is based. American culture is predicated on racial exclusion and the glorification of the white cultural ego. The entire economic and administrative apparatus of cultural communication in America is geared to, dependent upon, and motivated by racial exclusion and the cultural negation of the Negro, and, having no democratic or humanistic role to play in society, becomes of necessity more and more commercialized and more and more unable to deal with the living truths of American social realities. It is a foregone conclusion that a film industry that in unable to deal with the social truths of race relations in America is certainly not about to integrate Negroes in any phase of film production Therefore, it is the economic and administrative foundations of cultural communications in America that must be radically altered before the social role of cultural communications can be changed and democratized. Until this takes place in the cultural arts there will be no integration in the arts. It is the same thing as asking to join the dead and the dying at the gates of the graveyard of dead civilizations for any Negro to seek integration in American culture as it now stands. This is most certainly not our historical role in world culture. With all the indignities American culture has heaped on the Negro in the past with its blackface imitation, stereotypes, servant-role handouts, lazybone characterizations, the "Mammy" sagas, etc., we should now be embarrassedly particular about asking to be made more ludicrous by participation in the banalities of what passes for "cultural arts." For any Negro today to beg, with childlike and empty-minded mimicry, to have the Negro image further distorted by its inclusion in the whitefaced orgy of spiritual decadence that has corrupted and debased all the cultural arts in America, is to ask that the Negro participate with the whites in their senseless and insane debasement of every humanistic social value that ever came out of the Western cultural tradition. This tradition has come to a sorry end in America as practically the whole cultural outlook retreats from the social realities of America and the world at large into an idiotic ivory tower.

The time has arrived for the Negro creative artists to see that they have a special role to play in the Negro movement in terms of ideas relating to their respective arts, not as interim pinch-hitters for professional civil rights leaders. Rather, the Negro creative artist's role in America is the same as that already outlined by the Society of African Culture in its perspective for the African creative artist and intellectual:

> The mission of Negro men of culture within the framework of S. A. C. is to: (a) assert, uphold and enrich their national cultures; (b) decide the sense of events and cultural works in the world according to the bearing of these on their own life and destiny; (c) bring about an increasing awareness of their responsibilities as men of culture; face to face with their national cultures; face to face with general culture.

With regard to the present active social class of Negro creative artists, however, we are up against a difficult ideological problem. The majority of this group (excepting jazz musicians) are pretty much a-racial in their artistic or aesthetic preferences. Most Negro actors do not believe in a specifically Negro theater. Many Negro writers do not like to be designated "Negro" writers. The ethnic dance forms of the Negro have been abandoned by most Negro dancers of the modern school. With the exception of the jazz musician there exists no specifically Negro school of aesthetics. The fact that such an a-racial attitude exists among the creative artists representing an ethnic minority of eighteen to twenty million people is to be deplored. Here it is shown that the concept of integration is negative, one-sided—a negation of the idea of the social meaning of art itself. "Universality" cannot be used to mean the negation of one's own ethnic origins or the art ingredients or the cultural qualities of those origins. For a Negro artist to take this position means, in effect, that he is accepting as his aesthetic model the white standard in art and aesthetics. The American cultural wasteland has nothing to offer the Negro who is so bent on integrating into nothing. The political task of the Negro artist, then, is to fight for the over-all democratization of the American apparatus of cultural communication in order to make a place for the unrestricted expression of his own ethnic personality, his own innate creative originality. In other words, the Negro must become nationalistic in terms of the ethnic and cultural attributes of his art expression.

These ideas on Cultural Revolution are merely exploratory and are meant to open the question for general discussion. We are seeking definitive answers to the question: What is social revolution in the United States? In doing so, we must seek to inject new ideas into the Negro movement. We believe Cultural Revolution to be a vehicle for the expression of a set of new ideas. The basic social problems implied in the concept of Cultural Revolution are by no means new problems. They emerged in the latter part of the nineteenth century in America and became potent social, cultural, and economic factors that shaped American race relations into what they are today. Cultural Revolution is a new concept only insofar as we believe it to be the first definitive attempt to conceptualize these basic social realities into an ethnic or cultural (or even political) philosophy. More must be said about this concept. Simply to present it also raises a score of other questions that must be discussed.

NOTES

1. Camus, *The Rebel* (New York: Alfred A Knopf, 1954), p. 106.
2. Mills, *Power Elite* (New York: Oxford University Press, 1959), p. 334.

CHAPTER FIFTEEN

Rebellion or Revolution?
II.

Despite many new features of the present-day Negro rebellion, this movement has its roots in the accumulated experiences of the past fifty-odd years. But most of the younger, articulate "radical" elements of Negro leadership imagine themselves to be inspired by ideals whose existential relationships to the here-and-now need no other rationalizations. Thus the movement, while having many historical carryovers, is guided by individuals whose slogans reveal little awareness of historical ingredients that have gone into the making of such a complex social force as is the Negro movement today. As a result, the Negro movement's potential is compromised not only by the hard barriers thrown up by the establishment, but [also] by a leadership whose views about American realities are extremely a-historical, limited and oversimplified.

This leadership outlook has been able to mobilize a great variety of direct mass-actions, some scattered, others concerted. But it has not been sufficient in comprehension to carry these actions beyond the great impasse of the March on Washington. There the great Freedom clamor was absorbed in the emptiness of a great void and the protests became like echoes in a canyon that bounce about in mocking repetition. The march led not to a victory but to a crisis, and many are asking: How could it happen that the voices of Freedom could echo with such a hollow sound?

Part of the answer is that the Negro movement suffers from the serious disease of "historical discontinuity." For example, since World War I a series of world-shaking events, social upheavals and aborted movements have intruded and sharply set succeeding generations of Negroes apart in terms of social experiences. The youngest elements in the Negro movements today are activists, of one quality or another, who enter the arena unfortified with the knowledge or meaning of many of the vital experiences of Negro radicals born in 1900, 1910, 1920, or 1930. The problem is that too many of the earlier-twentieth-century-vintage Negro radicals have become too conservative for the 1940ers. Worse than that, the oldsters have nothing to hand down to the 1940ers in the way of refined principles of struggle, original social theory, historical analysis of previous Negro social trends or radical philosophy suitable for black people.

In the wake of the March on Washington one semblance of a radical idea did emerge out of the din of hollow protests—the Freedom Now Party as a vehicle for black political expression. But it is already evident from the discussions going on within this embryonic political movements that its leading voices are far from grasping the nature and scope of the problems inherent in the Freedom Now Party idea. The leadership of the Freedom Now Party inherits the peculiar disease of all Negro movements—historical discontinuity. This leadership would like to pick up the new banner across which is emblazoned "Political Action!" and go forward. But to what and where? How can the Freedom Now Party manage to fill the great void that greeted the March on Washington? The simple fact of raising the issue of a black political party does not mean that the views of those who raise it are any less compromised by historical discontinuity than those of others. For the problems facing the FNP are historically cumulative. It falls to the FNP to attempt to unravel the knot that binds Negro consciousness with the multiple strictures of ideological confusion and ethnic disorientation. A black political party that is going to mean anything in America has to be a party with an ideology that is persuasive enough to enable Negroes to cope with extremely difficult economic, political, and cultural problems peculiar to American society. But parties with such an ideology are not built overnight—as some of our superenthusiastic FNPers are prone to think. The Freedom Now Party comes into existence at the end of a fifty-year period whose experiences have, for all political intents and purposes, gone wasted.

Consider the fact that it has taken all these years, from 1910 when the NAACP was first organized to August, 1963 in Washington, to bring home the fact that NAACP methods (or variations thereof) are insufficient for achieving Negro aspirations in America. Did not Bayard Rustin, one of the leading generals of "marching" campaigns, admit (*N.Y. Times,* 12/2/63): "The civil rights movement not only reached an impasse with its current tactics but also had retrogressed in many cities to conditions that existed before this year's upsurge."

Mr. Rustin said more that that. We quote:

> Interviewed at Howard University . . . Mr. Rustin described the tactics of lying down in the streets to prevent the movement of trucks, and other forms of direct action, as "gimmicks." He said there was a danger that the civil rights organizations would become wedded to these gimmicks as ends in themselves.
>
> The civil rights movement had gone as far as it could with its original approach and the time had come to broaden the movement which, he added, faces the danger of degenerating into a sterile sectarianism.
>
> Heroism and ability to go to jail should not be substituted for an overall social reform program. We need a political and social reform program that will not only help the Negroes but one that will help all Americans. Only then can we win.

In *The New York Times* of November 12, 1963, other leaders were quoted:

> "Direct action efforts have failed," said the leaders of New York City's civil rights organizations. "Picketing and work stoppages . . . not the answer," said a Teamsters Union leader. "It's a political matter and it must be treated as a political matter."

Well, many of us black radicals knew this a long time before the March on Washington took place, but it was considered akin to racial treason to say so. The trouble is that leaders of Mr. Rustin's type have always been very late in waking up to the realities. When he advises Negroes to "shift tactics" he is tardy, because thousands of Negroes have already shifted to positions which it is very doubtful Mr. Rustin himself would take. And do you think that any of Bayard Rustin's co-strategists among the Big Six Rights General Staff (James Farmer, Whitney Young, Roy Wilkins, Martin Luther King, Jr., A. Philip Randolph, Bayard Rustin) will pay any heed to his late but sage advice? No! More marches are planned to state capitols and city halls and a proliferation of more "gimmicks." The great sit-in morality crusade will continue in a society predicated on immorality that breeds the pathological martyrdom of the jailhouse. The constant search will go on for new styles of "causes" with new martyrs and other Negro martyred personalities to romanticize in the left-wing press with new "defense" committees. This whole tragi-comedy of racial frustration is an indication that fifty years of protest has left the senior leadership bankrupt in terms of social and political imagination, trapped between the grave limitations of their philosophies and the crushing might of the establishment which they cannot dent.

There is no one leader or school of civil rights thought responsible for this state of affairs. It is the collective weakness peculiar to a class—a political disease endemic to the entire civil rights leadership. Except for an abundance of lawyers for the battle of attrition on the legal front, this class is not even technically equipped for reform. Who will replace E. Franklin Frazier and W. E. B. Du Bois in the social sciences? Where are the Negro economists, statisticians, etc.? Practically, the entire civil rights leadership reveals the propensity for loud protest and quiet status climbing; i.e. social opportunism. Thus Mr. Rustin's demand for "a political and social reform program" will fall on deaf ears and barren ground. What kind of social reform movement will come from a class which is characterized by a complete disdain for advanced social theory of any kind but has a strong affinity for the very social values of the establishment which it is alleged to be fighting against? Political and social reform Mr. Rustin demands. We wonder what Mr. Rustin will do to implement his own suggestion. The Freedom Now Party movement has to overcome fifty years of wasted experiences which have not left us a single school of social reform, radical or otherwise, to cure the crisis-ills of the civil rights movement. In order to advance towards Mr. Rustin's "political and social reform program" it is necessary to review history, because the seeds of the protest movement's failures lie hidden in the record of past decades. A movement that is not historically determined has little future.

All the evidence indicates that the roots of the current crisis of the Negro movement are to be found in the period between the end of World War I and the years of the Great Depression. This is what is meant by "historical discontinuity." For most of the social issues that absorb the attention of all the Negro radical elements today were prominently foreshadowed in these years. Yet the strands between the period called by some the "Fabulous Twenties" and the current Negro movement have been broken. The real implications of this historical discontinuity will not be appreciated unless one presents a panoramic view of that period. Consider what was happening.

In the early 1920's two of the great giants in the history of Negro leadership clashed in a bitter ideological conflict over the destiny of black people in the Western world—W. E. B. Du Bois and Marcus Garvey. The strange thing about this clash was that both of these personalities were strong advocates of two different brands of "Pan-Africanism" which neither one could cultivate in his own homeland. The West Indians did not back Garvey's nationalism in Jamaica, B. W. I., and Du Bois' first Pan-African Congress had to be sponsored by France—one of the leading imperialist powers—who turned over the Paris Grand Hotel. At home Du Bois was far from being a nationalist. At the time, he was editor of the NAACP's *Crisis* magazine, with a circulation of over 100,000 annually. The NAACP was then, as now, the leading integrationist organization among Negroes. But it is noteworthy that the word "integration" was not in vogue at the time as a synonym for "civil rights." Integration as a slogan appears to have gained wide usage during World War II and after because of the urgency of the campaign to integrate the armed forces.

The clash between Du Bois and Garvey was a bitter one. The former denounced Garvey as (to put it mildly) "bombastic and impractical" while Garvey scornfully relegated Du Bois to the Negro "cultural assimilationists" whom Garvey despised. That the Du Bois–NAACP philosophy and Garvey should so sharply conflict is understandable. But the fact that black nationalism should arise in the United States with such persuasive mass-potency raised many questions about the Negro movement in America which were not settled at that time or even understood. For the actions and reactions of both Du Bois and Garvey to black nationalism indicated that both were unable to deal with nationalist ideology purely within the American social framework where it is destined to play out its positive role. In this sense was the "Back to Africa" aspect of Garvey impractical and escapist in the same way as is the "Separate State" idea of the Muslims escapist. The tendency of Negro nationalism of all varieties to drift toward escapist solutions and ideals is the result of an inability to find the proper economic-political framework that has relevance to American realities. Truthfully, it would have been too much to expect the 1920 Negro radicals to be detached and objective enough to clarify the integrationist vs. nationalist tendencies and mold them theoretically into a political fusion. Dialectical processes have never really been understood in America. The two fundamentally basic trends behind Negro racial ideology in America, though sharply etched out in terms of organizational confrontation, got lost and went unresolved in the turbulence that seethed in American society during the "Fabulous Twenties."

～

World War I shook the very foundations of world capitalism in Europe and inspired liberating currents within the colonies. It sent Garvey to New York and

Du Bois to Paris in search of "Pan-Africanism." It uprooted southern Negroes by the thousands for the trek to the North to meet West Indians that many had never known existed. It sent Negro soldiers to France to fight for "democracy" and brought them back to march into a race war on the home front because the KKK had been revived again in 1915. The real semicolonial status of the Negro was grimly revealed and lynch-law raged across the country north, south, and west as black soldiers in uniform had to fight for their very lives, homes, and families. "We return. We return from fighting. We return fighting," said Du Bois' *Crisis* magazine as it echoed the temper of the times, and the NAACP opened up its great postwar protest campaign in 1919. Other organizations entered the crucial fray—the National Equal Rights League, the National Race Congress and the Commission on Interracial Cooperation, a Southern group. All during this time, more and more, Negroes were streaming north.

Though the thunder of racial wars boomed ominously, it cannot be overlooked that the post–World War I turmoil in America dug deep into the national consciousness, churned it up, and threw onto the open stage of life everything that was sick and ailing in the nation; i.e., in American capitalism. Both black and white were profoundly agitated and, unlike the 1950's and 1960's, were openly saying so in every conceivable way. Today the only real agitation is black. A. Philip Randolph's *Messenger,* "The only Negro radical magazine in America," preached "social revolution." A Harlem radical press evolved—*Challenge, The Crusader, The Emancipator,* etc. The Federal Government investigated "Radicalism and Sedition Among the Negroes..." The 1920's saw a genuinely serious questioning of the American national purpose, a great rash of individual quests for the relationship of man, the individual, to and in the collective badly shaken by world events. Sinclair Lewis' novel, *Main Street,* described the drab, dehumanizing effects of capitalism on American urban life which sent intellectuals by the scores escaping to emigré existence in Paris. Many a Negro soldier wished he had never returned. The twentieth-century revolution was continuing and it sent its currents into odd places.

Claude McKay, the West Indian poet and novelist, preceded Garvey in New York. He was uprooted and a poet-seeker on the move. So was Langston Hughes, out of Joplin, Missouri, who later worked his way to Africa in a romantic search for "lost identity." McKay found a literary home as associate editor of *Liberator* magazine, founded in 1919 by the leading white radicals of the time, one of whom was the famous John Reed, who had recently written *Ten Days That Shook the World.* Here McKay clashed with Michael Gold, who later became the main "cultural" commissar of the newly formed American Communist Party. McKay resigned. The white radicals on the *Liberator* staff made the first attempt to contact Garveyites in Harlem for an "alliance." They failed, and thus the incompatibility of Negro nationalism and white radicalism was first demonstrated. But McKay, too, rejected Garveyism and revealed that the black intellectual did not really understand what was happening and was forming the wrong alliances. The uprooted McKay, always the seeker, took off for Moscow to learn about the "new society" that was causing capitalist nightmares. He was well received, wined and dined, and much was made over the "American" Negro. He hobnobbed with the top leaders of revolution at the Fourth Congress of the Communist International which he described as "The Pride and Pomp of Proletarian Power."[1] The black radical always has reasons to doubt. After touring Europe, McKay returned *Home to Harlem* (his next book). Some left the United States and did not return for a long time. Josephine Baker, the famous singer-comedienne, came out of St. Louis, was briefly seen on New York stages in Negro shows, but left for Paris to become the famed attraction of the Folies Bergere and a household word in Europe. Some of us heard her perform in the North African desert in World War II, but didn't know her story then.

Creative things blossomed in the 1920's like flowers on a battlefield and the Negro, despite his economic and social disabilities, was going through another phase of his unique experience in the Western world. It was during the years of his harshest oppression on slave plantations that the most divine Negro spirituals were created. Similarly, during the post–World War I years when American racism reached its highest pitch in this century, Negroes again reached for another level of cultural attainment. For the 1920's ushered in the age of Paul Robeson, Countee Cullen, Charles Gilpin, Rose McClendon, and Jean Toomer, whose literary career was short but brilliant before he disappeared. The "New York Wits," a thriving literary movement composed of a blend of older and younger writers, won the critical spotlight for several years. Among them were James Weldon Johnson, mature and experienced, and the younger Wallace Thurman, Jessie Fauset, Rudolph Fisher, and others. Most of them were bitter, ironical and satirical.

Noble Sissle and Eubie Blake brought new stature to the musical theater with *Shuffle Along,* a sensation in 1921 which established a new vogue. Ethel Waters and the immortal Florence Mills sang and performed before thousands whose critical acclaim was boundless. The latter's career was cut short by her early death in 1927; the "peerless child artist" who became the "Little Blackbird" had sung a brief song. Florence Mills was the greatest, it is said, but she was representative of scores of Negroes of varying talents of that decade who appeared in search of fulfillment to light up the American cultural scene. Alain Lock, the scholar, chronicled that movement in his study of the Negro Renaissance, *The New Negro.*

American whites were also having a cultural revival and the process by which the whites intervened in the Negro revival, contained it, distorted it, and fastened the incubus of cultural paternalism on this Negro movement has not been told. The great symbol of this process was the folk-opera, *Porgy and Bess*—written by whites for whites who at first did not even think that Negroes were good enough to perform it. Its first recordings were by whites in "black-voice," and it represents the classic example of cultural exploitation practiced by whites on the Negro under capitalist culture. Its distorted social and aesthetic values have been projected ever since as the outstanding "American" musical accomplishment.

Briefly, this describes what the 1920's were like. The lynch mobs fought the Negro for his very life while the white aesthetes ran to Harlem and other places for the unique experience of warming their chilly souls and fingers by his cultural bloodstreams. White writers and aesthetes, such as Eugene O'Neill and Carl Van Vechten, the patron of Negro artists, discovered the creative power of the Negro "passion," hailed it, used it, exploited it, and sold it. The Communists and Michael Gold scolded the Negro artists for falling prey to Van Vechten's "bourgeois" corruption at the Harlem parties of the famous A'Lelia Walker, where white Bohemia from Greenwich Village and black Bohemia made "social" revolution. Of Van Vechten, Langston Hughes wrote: "He never talks grandiloquently about democracy. . . . But he lives it with sincerity and humor."[2] The Communists who did talk so much about "democracy" never understood the role of Negro art in capitalist society. Michael Gold, who was a great admirer of Leon Trotsky (that is, before Stalin expelled him from Russia), had hailed Trotsky's book *Literature and Revolution* when it appeared a few years before. In this book Trotsky had said:

> It would be monstrous to conclude that the technique of bourgeois art is not necessary to the worker. Yet there are many who fall into this error. "Give us," they say, "something even pock-marked, but our own." . . . Those who believe in a "pock-marked" art are imbued with contempt for the masses.

Michael Gold never believed this. The Communist white never understood real Negro proletarian art in the 1920's. It was the non-political whites who hailed "The Jazz Age" when the "real" Negro soul was revealed. One exuberant white music critic said that Negro music was an antidote to white "spiritual bankruptcy." But the roots of American spiritual bankruptcy were basically socio-economic, of which race was an ugly surface manifestation, and which was concealed by capitalism's booming prosperity. People could exist, if not really live in the full meaning of the word. Prosperity, especially in the North, made the newly formed Communist Party's appeal to white labor a one-sided dialogue between radical intellectuals and themselves. It was an oddly eclectic period when the elements of the melting pot boiled almost to the rims of the oceans. It was a decade of extreme poverty and riches, hopes, dreams, despair and disillusionment. Culture *did* boom. In fact, there were all the ingredients of "Cultural Revolution" in the making in America—the *real* American revolution of that time, which is yet unfinished. But the primitive Marxists of the 1920's did not comprehend that American capitalism's technological advances in mass cultural media—films, radio, and music records, etc.—was a new capitalistic feature to replace Marx's "religion" as the real modern opium of the people. Instead, in the intense debate on politics vs. art that was raging in the leftwing between John Dos Passos and Michael Gold of the *Liberator,* the Gold faction won out and subordinated the creative artist, who was already being crushed by capitalist culture, to the domination of a "politics" not even relevant to the America scene. Thus did the Marxist leftwing separate itself at the outset from the American mainstream; its influence was forever tangential. The Negro affinity with the leftwing during the 1920's was a mere flirtation and the nationalists went their own way. Radical artists and radical politicians split and went their own ways. As Genevieve Haggard, one of the leading radical ports of the time, put it in her book, *May Days:*

> It is the artist's fault because he is afraid of revolution. It is the propagandist's fault for giving the artist a job he cannot perform. . . . From now on, as long as this division holds our art will have not fertility.

This was written in 1925 as the poet reviewed what the *Liberator* radicals had accomplished before the magazine folded in 1924. And how true her prophecy had been for America! Claude McKay had already seen that Michael Gold's political position on the role of the radical artist was destructive and had resigned from the *Liberator.* The high water–mark of the 1920's had been reached. Negro nationalism went into decline after Garvey was jailed in 1927. A. Philip Randolph's *Messenger* folded in 1928. Two years later the "Fabulous Twenties" disappeared in the catastrophe of the 1929 economic crash. And all the great issues, trends and expectations that agitated and moved Negroes of the time were left suspended and unresolved in the memories of those who first flourished in that decade.

In the devastating pall of the 1930's depression the great issue among Negroes was sheer survival, which lessened the ardor for nationalism, and "protest" took on other survival meanings. Thus all Negro ideology from the 1920's, whether nationalistic, integrationist, separatist, or cultural, fell under the influence of "New Dealism," or the expedient lure of the white labor movement, or the mystique of the Marxist left given prominence by hard times.

Came World War II and a new generation of Negroes was caught up in another crisis of world capitalism; but the "historical continuity" between them and their elders of 1917 was already broken. The 1930's produced a generation who spoke another language. It was not understood that though the setting for the world conflict that was brewing was on another plane and in another key, the fundamental issues would always be the same in this century. Hence, nationalism the world over would become a universal theme of liberation that one would have to listen to. And the Negro in America, born in 1920, 1930, or even 1940, would hear the echoes of the Du Bois-Garvey conflict over the meaning of nationalism come back to him through other voices from other platforms. Only this time the Negro in America must resolve the conflict between integration and nationalism in a positive way once and for all.

Black Nationalism in America lapses into romantic and escapist moods so long as it depends on emotional slogans, the messianic complex for a leader, or empty militant aggressiveness. Nationalism the world over is being expressed and must be expressed through economic, political, and cultural institutions to make them conform to nationalist aspirations. That these questions are not understood among Negroes is more than obvious. But the ability of the Negro movement to proceed beyond its present impasse depends on the solutions to these problems.

NOTES

1. McKay, *A Long Way From Home* (New York: Lee Furman, 1937).
2. Hughes, *The Big Sea* (New York: Alfred A. Knopf, 1945).

CHAPTER SIXTEEN

Marxism and the Negro

The fact that the Socialist Workers Party (Trotskyite) announced in *The New York Times,* January 14, 1964, that it had nominated a Negro, Clifton DeBerry, to run for President allows us the opportunity to discuss in depth a question that has long been agitating many individuals, friends and foes, concerning the relationship of Marxism to the Negro movement in America today. We emphasize "today" because some years ago it was impossible to be objective about this, inasmuch as the Marxist movement as represented by the Communist Party was so indissolubly linked with practically everything Negroes attempted to do, it was impossible not to find a Communist or two under the bed if one looked earnestly enough. Some very relevant issues about Marxism were thereby distorted and confused by a barrage of heated denials and accusations about the "Red Menace."

The relationship between the Negro movement and the Marxist movement has gone through a succession of qualitative changes on both sides. Today the Negro movement has developed to its highest level of organizational scope and programmatic independence in this century. In the meantime, the dominant trend in American Marxism, the Communist Party, had declined to the low status of a weak, ineffectual sect creating a vacuum in "revolutionary" politics which the Trotskyites are desperately trying to fill. The eclipse of Communist Party Marxism went hand in hand with the decline of labor union radicalism in America. White labor (as differentiated from black labor) went conservative, pro-capitalist and strongly anti-Negro. This created a serious and practically insoluble dilemma for the Marxist movement because the theory and practice of revolutionary Marxism in America is based on the assumption that white labor, both organized and unorganized, must be a radical, anti-capitalist force in America and must form an alliance with Negroes for the liberation of both labor and the Negro from capitalist exploitation. No matter what the facts of life reveal to the contrary, no matter what the Marxists say or do in terms of momentary tactics, this is what the Marxists believe, and *must* believe or cease functioning as Marxists. For Karl Marx's dictum on this question was that "Labor cannot emancipate itself in the white skin where in the black it is branded." Today, the Trotskyites consider themselves to be the most "orthodox" of Marxists.

The fact that white labor in America today is clearly unsympathetic to the "emancipation" of either Negro workers or the "petit bourgeois" Negroes—or the "intellectuals," as the Marxists are fond of citing—poses, as was said, a serious dilemma for the revolutionary Marxists. On the other hand, the Negro movement's rise to the ascendancy as a radical force in America completely upsets Marxian theory and forces the Marxists to adopt momentary tactics which they do not essentially believe in. In short, they become opportunistic. Here we refer to the white Marxists. The black ones are another question which is currently personified in the case of DeBerry. The realities in America today force the Marxists to deal with the Negro movement as the *de facto* radical force, but this does not hide the fact that the Marxist movement is in serious crisis. Moreover, the greater the Negro movement becomes as an independent force, the more the Marxists must strive to ally themselves with the Negro movement, and the deeper becomes the crisis for the Marxist movement itself. For the "alliance" it attempts to forge with the Negro must be one in which the Marxists dominate in order not to be absorbed. This alliance is meant to build the Marxist party, *not* the Negro movement, in order to rescue the Marxists from their own crisis. In the Fall, 1963, issue of the *International Socialist Review,* the Trotskyites, in discussing the "Freedom Now" Party movement, said:

The present tasks of the SWP in connection with the Negro struggle for liberation are:

(4) To expand and strengthen the party's cadre and forces in the Negro organizations and the civil rights movements, by: (a) recruiting revolutionary Negroes and helping to train them for leadership in the party and mass movements.

Elsewhere in the same issue the Trotskyites said:

In the same way the influence of the colonial revolution . . . upon vanguard elements of the Negro movement has helped prepare the emergence of a new radical left wing. In all these cases, it is the task of revolutionary Marxists to seek to win the best elements of this newly emerging vanguard to Trotskyism.

The *real* issue at stake here is: Who is destined to be the dominant and decisive radical force in America—black radicals or white radicals? And this is a question that will and must be settled outside the scope of any existing theory, Marxian or otherwise, because there is no theory that covers this development. Such an American theory (if it is ever written down) will have to come from blacks. Hence we have the most unprecedented situation yet seen in the Western world—a Marxist movement with a time-honored social theory which does not work out in life with a mass following, and a viable Negro movement of masses in movement which is stymied because it has no social theory or program to take it further. World historical trends have brought both the old Marxist tradition and the new Negro movement face to face on either side of a profound impasse. The Trotskyites, being the most astute of all Marxists, attempt to bridge the chasm by nominating a Negro for President! This desperate gesture cannot cure the Marxian crisis by enlisting the Negro potential. Moreover, it is not the right remedy for what really ails the Negro movement at this juncture. It is the same thing as offering an impoverished man with a wife and ten children a Palm Beach vacation with some political V.I.P.'s and all the trimmings just "to get away from it all." What happens to the man's family? These are some of the reasons why the SWP's presidential announcement caused so much confusion, anger, and suspicion within the ranks of the Freedom Now Party movement concerning "white radical influence." For DeBerry also linked himself with the Freedom Now Party without the party's permission to do so—a well-known Marxian type of maneuver in Negro affairs.

As the Negro movement stops and gropes about for its methods of entering the next stage, this question of Marxism's influence will keep bobbing up in different situations. It is therefore necessary for black radical "thinkers" (as opposed to "strugglers" or "street-men" as some proudly call themselves) to get a clearer understanding of why the Marxists act the way they do and why they are in a crisis. The Negro movement is also in crisis despite its late achievements—a crisis which is linked to world developments broader than our own problems and with roots in events which predate us.

The crisis of Marxism in Europe and North America has its roots in the confused events of the Russian Revolution of 1917. In the case of the Socialist Workers Party, it was Leon Trotsky, its guiding revolutionary thinker, who first said that a socialist revolution was even possible in Russia. This was in 1905 when none of the Russian Marxists agreed to that possibility (not even Lenin). Trotsky was denounced as a ridiculous visionary for saying this, but later won other Russian Marxists over to his thinking. Thus Trotsky was actually the *theoretical* father of the Russian Revolution and Lenin was its chief architect and leader.

Marxism, as Marx himself developed it, did not foresee or predict a socialist revolution in a backward agrarian country such as Russia. According to Marx, the revolution he predicted had to come about in a highly industrialized nation which had necessarily created a large, industrial class of workers, well organized and well trained in the production skills of capitalist industry. The capitalist class of owners would get richer and more compact due to monopoly growths, and the working class would get poorer and poorer to the point where they would revolt and overturn the system and expropriate the owners. Recognizing full well that they were revising the original view of Marx, both Trotsky and Lenin then agreed that if a socialist revolution was possible in Russia—a large agrarian country with only a small degree of industrial development—then this revolution could not stand alone. It would have to be supported by simultaneous revolutions in the advanced nations of Western Europe.

Such did not happen. There *was* a revolution in Russia but it had to stand alone because supporting revolutions elsewhere did not succeed. The result was that the most important single event of the twentieth century was transformed into its gravest tragedy. Moreover, it put the Marxist parties in Western Europe, the United States and elsewhere in a serious dilemma—a dilemma which over the years has deepened into a series of crises. This is because every social revolution that has taken place since the Russian Revolution has also developed out of industrially backward, agrarian, semi-colonial or colonial conditions while the working classes of the advanced white nations became more and more conservative, pro-capitalist and *pro-imperialist*. Moreover, the very fact that the world revolutionary initiative had passed from white nations of the capitalist world to *non-white nations* of the colonial and semi-colonial world introduced another factor in revolutionary

THE ESSENTIAL HAROLD CRUSE

politics, the racial factor, which the Western Marxists never admitted should be a factor of any importance at all. Workers, in their opinion, regardless of race and national differences, should all think alike on the question of capitalism and imperialism. The Trotskyites still function under this grand illusion. This is why Clifton DeBerry, in the Social Workers Party's announcement in *The New York Times,* had to project his support of the Freedom Now Party on the basis that it is "a step toward independent political action by *labor* and Negroes." By this he means *white labor* and Negroes (emphasis ours). But the leaders of the Freedom Now Party never made any such pronouncement. The Freedom Now Party is a step towards *independent black political action.* Clearly, the Trotskyites do not really want this. Because Marxism is in a crisis in America, they must attempt to project the idea of the Freedom Now Party in their own Marxian image, with the old worn-out, discredited theme of Negro-labor unity.

The Trotskyist theoreticians realize very well that a truly independent black political party which functions irrespective of what white labor does or does not do will further deepen the already serious crisis of the Marxist creed in the West. It could show that Marxian ideas about capitalism in advanced countries are not to be taken seriously. A whole raft of Marxian formulations would be further called into question. In any event, none of this would be the fault of the Negro. Rather, it would be the fault of the Marxists for being dishonest with themselves and misleading generation after generation of innocents about the true nature of the Russian Revolution. What was this revolution? What did it achieve? The Communists and the Trotskyites, twin branches of the same withering tree trunk of Western Marxism, have been attacking and accusing each other over these questions for almost forty years. Why?

Let the Trotskyites tell it—it was because Stalin and the bureaucracy "distorted" and "betrayed" the "socialist revolution." But the Trotskyites have only inherited a problem in socialist theory and practice that Trotsky made for himself. Who was it but Trotsky himself who first claimed that such a revolution was possible? All the facts reveal that Trotsky got the very kind of revolution he actually made and deserved and then disowned it because it wasn't really "socialist." He accused the Stalin bureaucracy of "terrorism," of "smothering democracy," and "suppressing the opposition," of taking away the political power of the workers' soviets (councils). But it was Trotsky himself who set such precedents by ordering the brutal suppression of the Kronstadt sailors' revolt of 1921 long before the Stalin bureaucracy set in.

The Russian Revolution logically turned out just the way it had to, considering how and where it was achieved and what the social objectives were it set for itself. Trotsky helped formulate these objectives. Nothing was betrayed—it was the Russian revolutionaries who betrayed themselves, and the Russian masses suffered. After Trotsky's revolution it was imperative that the Communists industrialize a backward country in as short a time as possible, because there can be no socialism until there is enough of an industrial base to socialize (i.e., nationalize). Hence, all the political conflicts between Russian factions centered around the great, pressing problem thrust on them by their own revolutionary seizure of power: How to plan and administer nationalized property, most of which had to be built before it could be administered. This was no ordinary task and the nature of the revolution itself brought to the fore just the type of individuals needed to perform the operation—Stalin and his Stalinists, single-minded, dictatorial, brutal and practical. Not the Trotsky type at all. Trotsky opposed this natural trend of his own revolution and was expelled from Russia.

According to a strict interpretation of Marxian formulations, Trotsky tampered very loosely with Marxian "laws" and reaped the whirlwind. This premise of course absolves Marx of responsibility for the tragic, anti-socialist aspects of the Russian Revolution. The intent is to argue that if Marx was right about the workings of "historical laws" and Trotsky was a Marxist, then something was wrong with Marx's "historical law" formulations. Either this or Trotsky was a Marxist who gravely misinterpreted the functioning of Marxian laws. But it was Marx himself who insisted: "One thing is certain: I am not a Marxist." Meaning what? Are we to take it to mean that because his prophecies about advanced capitalist societies—the white nations—did not materialize, we are entitled to say that Marx was wrong because he failed to properly interpret the very laws he is credited with being the first to discover? If this is the case we then have a strong premise for taking Marx at his own word. If he himself admits he was not a Marxist, then who really was a Marxist after he passed away? Whose claim to be a Marxist must anyone take seriously?

We pose these questions because the Trotskyite nomination of DeBerry for President grows out of the Marxists' belief that the "historical laws" have preordained the Negro movement in America to be used as a kind of transitional social phase leading to the Marxian revolution. In this instance we are to suppose that the Trotskyites are applying the "methods and principles of historical materialism," i.e., the "laws" correctly "before the fact." But even to grant the Marxists, for the sake of argument, the validity of their own Marxian premises, we have to say that their application of the method is no more Marxian than others that failed to bring, in their opinion, Marxian results. This assertion might surprise or even shock the Trotskyites, coming as it does from non-Marxist radicals of the Negro movement. However, it is not that we are prejudiced against "Marxism" per se. We study Marxism in the same way we study objectively all social science schools of thought which claim to be scientific. What we strenuously object to are the methods that the Marxists use.

Fundamental to all Marxist formulations is the *dialectical method of theory and practice*. Marx made it amply clear that his method was dialectical; hence any approach to social life which is not dialectical cannot be Marxian. We would tend to agree with many, such as the late C. Wright Mills, who said of Marx in his book *The Marxists*, "His *method* is a signal and lasting contribution to the best sociological ways of reflection and inquiry available." [Emphasis Cruse's.] We make a distinction here between Marx's original *method* and the *applications* of his latter-day disciples, and we reject these applications precisely because they are not, in our opinion, arrived at by the dialectical method of reflection and inquiry.

How did Marx arrive at his conclusions about the role of the working class in capitalist society? Through the application of one of his prime laws of dialectics: *The law of the unity and conflict of opposites.* In Marxian dialectical processes, social phenomena, e.g., classes, ideas, institutions, etc., are not static, but proceed through constant development and change. Capitalistic production creates capitalists and workers (opposites) who come into conflict because their class interests are not identical. Capitalists exploit workers by not paying them their full labor value. Capitalists seek the highest rate of profit through intensified exploitation of the working class. The conflict of interests generates "class struggle," e.g., strikes. Marx observed that the basis of class struggle lies in a contradiction between the methods of production and the social relations of production (private property). These contradictions can be resolved only by a social revolution wherein the working class overthrows or otherwise expropriates the capitalists. This description of dialectics, while simplified, explains why Marxists have considered it to be the historic role of the working class in capitalist societies to usher in the socialist era.

Marx came to these conclusions about the working class in Europe over a hundred yeas ago, and these predictions still have not been borne out in the advanced capitalist societies of Western Europe and North America. Yet it must be stated that according to his own dialectical premise of analysis, Marx had every right to make such predictions. The abundant evidence in the social and political life of Europe in Marx's time pointed to revolution. Moreover, the failure of the social revolution to materialize in the advanced capitalist countries does not at all invalidate Marx's dialectical method. What does become invalid is the subsequent application of the dialectical method by the followers of Marx in the twentieth century. We say this because if we accept the premise of dialectics, then we accept the view that everything in social life is constantly changing, coming into existence, and passing away. But if this dialectical premise is "truth," why then is it assumed that everything in society is subject to the processes of change *except the historical role of the working class in advanced capitalist nations?* Why is this white European, North American labor movement itself exempt from dialectical change in terms of class position, ideology, consciousness, etc., and in terms of what other groups or classes this labor movement fights, supports, or compromises with in the "class struggle"? Has it not become abundantly clear that the white labor movement in the advanced capitalist nations has, indeed, abandoned the Marxian historical role assigned to it? And do we not, therefore, have the right to claim the European and American Marxists who still hew to this white working class line are practicing *mechanistic materialism* rather than *dialectical materialism?*

Classical Marxism rejects all forms of mechanistic materialism because it denies any genuine evolution in the sense of the emergence of new forms and new qualities of new things. Hence the very premise of dialectical thinking demands, in this instance, an admission that new forms of social consciousness can develop within capitalist societies which are of more political relevance than even the social consciousness of the conservative labor movement. Any other conclusion than this is manifestly anti-dialectical. Fundamental to the crisis in all the schools of Western Marxism in the advanced capitalist countries (the white nations) is the crisis that has long gripped the philosophical system of thought, the kernel around which the entire political, economic, cultural, theoretical and program-matic structure of Marxism must form. It is the crisis of dialectical materialism, which was conceived by Marx as a method which had to comprehend the reality of the world, but is no longer able to do so. The reality of world revolutionary events are running far ahead of Marxian theory.

In 1939, when the European white working classes were armed to the teeth along the borderlines of their nations ready to spread war and mayhem against themselves all over Europe and half the world, Trotsky, writing about "Marxism in the United States," could say with the most lofty detachment: "By the example and with the aid of the advanced nations, the backward nations will also be carried away into the mainstream of socialism." Here is expressed in the most graphic manner the supreme illusion of the Western (or in Trotsky's case) the "Westernized" white Marxist. They cannot let go of the *idée fixe* of the white working class "saving" the world's humanity. Rooted in their preconceived notions, their undialectical ideas, is the deeply ingrained "white nation ideal." Socialism becomes, like capitalism, a white-nation conception, the great white working-class prerogative. The "white man's burden" shifts from the capitalist's missionaries to the socialist's revolutionaries, whose duty to history is to lift the "backward" peoples from their ignominious state to socialist civilization—even if the whites have to postpone this elevation abroad until they have managed to achieve it at home. But in so doing, the white Marxist's dialectical conceptions of world developments become a distorted image of the reality that is taking place before their very eyes.

The dialectical analyses that Marxists project concerning world developments are, in truth, mechanistically gross distortions of the original dialectical methods of Marx, who was essentially true to his method for his own time and circumstances. It was not the fault of Marx that the world changes, for this was already explicit in dialectics. But the distortions of today's Western Marxism lie in the fact that Marxists treat dialectical materialism only from the standpoint of how the impersonal productive forces develop, how the material forces evolve in society to go through stages from feudalism to capitalism. Or further, how capitalism penetrates the underdeveloped world and brings the latter into the capitalistic network. But Marx pointed out that "In the social production which men carry on they enter into definite relations that are indispensable and *independent* of their will." [Emphasis Cruse's.] Which means that men are subject to the blind forces of the laws of social production unless they become socially conscious of what is happening to them. But how men become socially conscious is a problem of the theory of knowledge and reflection, which is an inseparable category in the dialectical method of social inquiry. If men did not comprehend the nature of material forces, they could not intervene in the process of these forces in order to shape events, i.e., to control blind forces. Thus men, or classes, or groups, or even nations cannot assume the task of "revolutionizing" societies unless they are strategically situated to do so and also have the necessary consciousness to shape events. In this regard, social developments can situate certain classes to shape events, give them the potential; yet such classes can remain without the consciousness or the will to make history. But there are always other classes, and it is the implied function of dialectics to correctly perceive which classes are being brought to the forefront of social consciousness by blind material forces. These classes will become the social force chosen by "historical laws" for historical roles, rather than preconceived classes that history has left behind.

Lenin dealt most thoroughly with how men or classes receive their sense perceptions of the real world; but Marxists today bypass this aspect of dialectics because they believe the social role of the "proletariat" alone settles this question for all time. White Marxists have tried to make world reality fit their dialectical preconceptions; but world developments require that dialectical conceptions embrace world reality. Such conceptions cannot come from the minds of Western Marxists whose philosophical views have become provincially rooted in the crisis-reality of the Western world and cannot transcend the conceptual limitations of that world. They talk revolution, but revolution is being made by others. World social developments are running ahead of their world social theory. William F. Warde says that the principles of historical materialism are applicable everywhere "provided they are applied with full consideration of the facts in each case." But the question Warde does not discuss is: Who is to determine this, those who are making the world revolution or those in the West whose dialectical views are anchored to the lethargy of the white working class?

The Marxian Theory of Knowledge (dialectics) implies that if the backward peoples of the world are carrying themselves into the mainstream of socialism instead of being led there with the aid of the advanced nations as Trotsky saw it, then the backward peoples must replace the white working class as the "chosen people" of the dialectical functionings of world society. Hence if "historical science" or dialectics is to be considered truly scientific, it must be developed and verified in life by the inclusion of the social experiences, the history, the ideas and political philosophies, and the points of view of the backward peoples. In short, it is the social realities of backward peoples that count today the world over. For it is their social consciousness that is determining which way history is moving. Dialectical materialism is no longer the philosophy of the proletariat (i.e., the European proletariat), as the Western Marxists would have it.

It is the fate of the Marxists to be imprisoned within their illusions and that is the source of their crisis. They cannot deal with the race question in America in terms of their dialectical method except superficially, which they must attempt to conceal by all too obvious practices of political expediency, such as the DeBerry nomination. This must, of necessity, bring them into serious conflict with the Negro movement itself, for the spiritual affinities of the Negro movement are not with the white working class of America whose status vis-à-vis American capitalism is qualitatively different from Negroes'. White labor's heyday is behind them in the history of the 1930's. The American Negro movement is currently a semi-colonial revolt that is more inspired by events outside America than within it. We can much better explain the Negro movement's relationship to world developments today by quoting Leopold Sedar Senghor, president of the African republic of Senegal, from his pamphlet on *African Socialism.*

We are not communists . . .

The paradox of socialistic construction in communist countries in the Soviet Union is that it increasingly resembles capitalistic construction in the United States of America. . . . And it has less art and freedom of thought.

But a third revolution is taking place, as a reaction against capitalistic and communistic materialism, and which will integrate moral, if not religious values, with the political and economic contributions of the two great revolutions. In this revolution the colored peoples including Negro Africans, must play their part, they must bring their contribution to the construction of the new planetary civilization.

Of the Negro American in this "third revolution" Senghor quotes Paul Morand as saying:

The Negroes have rendered an enormous service to America. But for them one might have thought that men could not live without a bank account and a bathtub.

The living facts of the world revolution today are more persuasive than any revolutionary theory that came out of western Europe after the death of Marx. We do not hold Marx accountable for any deviations or distortions that either history or men have imposed to detract from his doctrine. He was a towering product of his times and his conclusions about the society of men tore away the veil that hid the profound forces that moved societies. His forecasts have been negated by the very dialectical process he revealed; yet to say, nay insist, that history should act just the way Marx thought it would is to do an injustice to a great thinker and to imply that dialectics is a philosophical fraud, as many have tried to do (even some who called themselves Marxists). Neither history nor dialectics, which is history's inner clockworks, stands still. Neither is history prone to bestow special historical prerogatives on any special class of people forever. It is the peculiar juxtaposition of time, place, and social circumstances which decide who is going to play the role of prime movers of history. Considering this, we can well understand Marx's own assertion, "I am not a Marxist." It would have been a historical tribute to Marx's self-effacement if Leon Trotsky had admitted: "Though I played fast and loose with Marx's laws, I am no dialectician."

In America today, the Socialist Workers Party must strive to conceal the theoretical bankruptcy of Western Marxism by the highly questionable political strategy of entering into political competition with a Negro political party (which is not even established) by presenting a Negro candidate for high office. Some capitalists trying to crash in and exploit the Negro economic market could not have been more crass and opportunistic. But what is revealed here that is more striking than mere crassness is the unreality that hovers around much of what American Marxists do. Basic to all this unreality is the Marxist illusion about the "working class–socialist myth" as it concerns the Russian experience. For the Trotskyites to be forced to let go of this dead issue would be to force the admission that the Trotskyite Fourth International is and always has been rather utopian. For after the seizure of power in Russia by the Bolsheviks and the creation of soviets, the problem became more Kantian than Marxian. The Marxist revolutionary idealists assumed that Marxist elites, once in power, act in accordance with the Kantian "categorical imperative" and perform their functions according to an ethical code of "right conduct." This has been and always will be a problem of revolutions.

The hard American realities and the Negro movement force the Trotsky-ites to push into the background all these issues that once agitated the international revolutionaries years ago, and to depart from the book and play it pragmatically by jumping on the bandwagon of the black political party idea. But this cannot work. The Freedom Now Party will not permit itself to be used to save the Marxist tradition in America from its own illusions about the nature of social reality today. Clifton DeBerry's role as a Negro Marxist of the Western mold is a contradiction that cannot be solved within the context of the political, social, and cultural philosophy which the Freedom Now Party will attempt to shape. In view of what Leopold Senghor says on the matter of Communism, an American Negro Marxist becomes a rather misplaced figure in the real scheme of things. And his position is made all the more ridiculous if he is involved politically in beating the dead horse issue of Stalinism vs. Trotskyism. What can this really matter to the "third world" in view of the fact that Russia's place and impact on the twentieth-century revolution is established and well-known? Trotskyites in the West have been reduced to the role of ferreting out Stalinist vestiges in world revolutionary currents, analyzing the "distortions" of revolutions already made, and projecting an ideal of the "socialist revolution" that has never been seen or experienced, while rehashing Trotsky's theory of "permanent revolution"— an undialectical concept because everything, including revolutions, is a process of change and development. Trotskyites are the purists of the Marxist camp—astute, analytical, and possessed with the insight to refine, from their own point of view, every aspect of historical materialism. But they cannot escape the theoretical net of the crisis of Marxism in the West. Clifton

DeBerry is a mere pawn whom the Trotskyites can attempt to foist on the black political party wearing a king's crown that is much oversized.

The Negro movement possesses inner qualities of different degrees of nationalism and integrationism whose economic, political, cultural, and psychological implications are too much for Marxian theory today. To attempt to confuse these unknown qualities with the white labor mystique of the Marxian left would be to disrupt the natural development of the Freedom Now Party and confuse the real native issues of the Negro with the unreal and irrelevant view of the Marxists concerning American realities. Such intrusions will be fought with every weapon at the FNP's disposal.

The Freedom Now Party is predicated on the ideal of achieving independent black political power in the United States through economic, cultural, and administrative approaches. In this way, the Negro movement in America becomes aligned with the real nature of the world developments involving non-white peoples. In this realignment of world social forces the reality is that white capitalist nations, including all the different classes within these nations from upper bourgeoisie to lower proletariat, have become, in fact, bourgeois and relative middle-class strata vis-à-vis the non-white peoples who have become, in fact, the "world proletarians." This is the real outcome of dialectical processes in our age. If world unity of different peoples is ever to be achieved within a democratic framework, it must be sought along the paths of "social consciousness" that clearly reveal future possibilities rather than the dead ends of the past that we have encountered in radical politics.

PART FIVE

Post-Black Power Writings

CHAPTER SEVENTEEN

The Racial Origins of American Theater: A Response to Robert Brustein

(Unpublished)

Given Cruse's unique position as both playwright and historian, he was particularly qualified to respond to critic Robert Brustein's lament that the social fault lines of American life had produced a "balkanized" theater. Cruse, the long-standing cultural pluralist, made the argument that the failure to achieve that nebulous ideal of "national unity" in aesthetics was rooted in the primordial and unresolved racial conflicts of the nation's infancy. As late as 1996, Brustein's ongoing plea for a type of aesthetic patriotism elicited a similar response from playwright August Wilson.

Some months ago, Robert Brustein bemoaned the "balkanization" of the American theater audience and pondered the long-standing need for an American National Theater. He asked the question: How can a single theater hope to develop a body of plays and productions that transcend these national divisions and appeal to a general American public?

Given the true history of the American Theater, the sordid history of American race relations, and the shoddy fashion in which "Americans" have administered the ethnic group problem in the United States, one might just as well ask the question: How can we Americans develop a National Church, given the Constitutional edict that there shall be a separation of Church and State?

Although such a positive social goal of the "national purpose" was never implied or denied by our Constitution, Americans (Anglo-Saxons, that is) have successfully managed to separate "cultural" necessities and imperatives from whatever social goals the Constitution permitted as the consummation of National Destiny.

As one way of responding to Mr. Brustein's complaints, I will cite one writer's personal experience in the theater. Between 1950 and 1962, he wrote four full-length plays on Afro-American life. As for professional quality, none of these plays, as written, was very good "theater," as the expert practitioners of the theater craft would say. As everyone in the theater knows, good plays are not written but rewritten. In this writer's case, his four plays were never rewritten because in the Fifties, there existed no black theater institution of professional quality in New York in which black theater ideas could be refined. In such an atmosphere, the theater was unpromising except for the most dedicated diehard black dramatist. Loften Mitchell, the writer of the book for *Bubbling Brown Sugar,* was such a playwright.

This situation was brought about by a number of historical factors that Mr. Brustein, as trenchant as ever, hints at but only obscures. The prime factors were mainly racial. The main reasons behind the absence of an American National Theater are mostly racial factors. The ultimate "Balkanization of Our Theater Culture" stems from the racial, ethnic and religious consequences of the nineteenth century racialism that permeated the burgeoning American theater movement of the 1890's. Theatrical philosophies and practices in the United States reflect the pervasiveness of a generic kind of cultural psychology which is informed by an aesthetic response of racial superiority. People talk about "racism" as a "civil rights" category, overlooking the deep, almost inaccessible and often invisible aesthetic component of racism that informs all cultural standards and practices in the United States, including theater practices.

Before Mr. Brustein, or anyone, can presume to discuss the American Theater historically or aesthetically, or honestly, it must be first admitted that the Americans have made only one *original* contribution to world theater and that was "Negro Minstrelsy"—a seminal theatrical form of Afro-American-African derivation. Everything else in the American theatrical tradition was either brought over from England or imported from the European continent to be either imitated or refined by American playwrights, directors and actors. The irony of it all is that both blacks and whites have a long history of trying to deny the fact that the American musical is the true, native American theatrical form, and [it] is, form-wise, evolved mainly from the basic elements of the American (Black) minstrel form popular in the nineteenth century.

The modern American Theater movement, beginning in the 1890's, was built around plays, in the main, imported from [Europe] because Americans had very few playwrights of the high caliber of a Dion Boucicault. [. . .]

It is true that on the creative cultural front, the American creative intelligentsia could not be accused of not expending the effort in fending off the cultural hubris of the European. But it took the added intellectual spur of [. . .] George Jean Nathan and H. L. Mencken in the pages of *American Mercury* and *The Smartset* to delegitimize the flimsy dramatic dross that, since the Nineties, had passed for legitimate and fashionable theater. The acerbic Nathan fashioned a prominent career on the fine art of critical demolition of shallow American playwrighting, thus clearing the aisles for the entrance of Eugene O'Neill.

However, it is in his references to the career of O'Neill that Brustein obscures the operational prevalence of the main factor behind the thematic derelictions and failures of the American Theater, i.e., the race factor. It is more than significant that Brustein cites specifically the "later career" of O'Neill, when the fact was that O'Neill's later career was made possible by the achievements of his early career. His early career as a recognized major dramatist was established on the basis of two plays—*The Emperor Jones* and *All God's Chillun Got Wings*— *two plays based on the American race question.* In other words, O'Neill was launched as a playwright of national and international prominence by drawing on the American black dramatic idiom, thus bringing into theatrical focus two of the three major historical, racial and cultural components that comprised the primal [. . .] American nation.

The three primary racial and cultural stocks of this primordial, incipient national concept were White Anglo-Saxon Protestants, imported Africans and indigenous Indians. Thus began an epic, three-way racial and cultural encounter, the final outcome of which is not in sight. For his "stuff of drama," O'Neill drew on the theatrical potential of the black and white confrontation.

Now in terms of the cultural imperatives native to American theater practices and philosophies, O'Neill's use of the black idiom was legitimate whether or not one likes *The Emperor Jones* or *All God's Chillun Got Wings* (most blacks didn't like either). What *is* both awry and remiss about the American theater is that a black playwright would not have (could not have) written either play and gotten away with it. If a black playwright *had* written such plays with a similar point of view on the materials, he (she) would have been totally ignored by the same white audiences that hailed O'Neill, and would have been severely criticized by the same blacks who either upheld or rejected O'Neill, but for different reasons. The whites would have assumed (similar to the London critic in 1924) that a black could not possibly have the ability to write a good play, and ought not to be wasting his (her) time trying *even to dramatize black life.* The blacks would have objected on the grounds that such plays projected the unwholesome, uncomplimentary side of the black image.

Loften Mitchell is a Harlem-born and bred playwright of long-standing, going back to the late Forties. The most honest play Mitchell ever wrote was *The Bancroft Dynasty,* a play about early Harlem life. [It] was so truthful that even Mitchell's best friends in the Harlem theater circles advised him to "burn it!" It took him about thirty years of dogged determination to write successful "legitimate" plays based on black life and to wind up getting Broadway credits via a musical using "canned" music as the score.

The record of O'Neill's successes and the failures and frustrations of a Loften Mitchell (and others) accentuate the profound truth that the reasons behind the American failure to produce an American National Theater are basically racial. The real stuff of the thematic potential of the native American theater lies in the racial and cultural confrontation of the White Anglo-Saxon, the Afro-American and the Indian. It is within the social history of this tripartite racial confrontation that lie the genuine sources of thematic ideas for the missing "body of plays and productions" that Brustein imagines should "transcend (American) national divisions and appeal to a general American public." However, it is precisely such genuine American controversial themes that American playwrights (black and white) have been psychologically conditioned to evade or avoid.

From the point of view of the black-white racial and cultural confrontation, this psychological inclination to evade the disturbing implications of the "dramatic" conflict themes inherent in this historic confrontation partially explains [. . .] why so many white playwrights following World War I were drawn to [themes drawn from black life], producing the unnatural genre of "Negro Plays" by white authors. This trend essentially began in 1917 when Ridgely Torrence presented his three "One Act Plays on Negro Life" (*The Rider of Dreams, Granny Maumee, Simon the Cyrenian*). James Weldon Johnson called the event, "The most important single event in the entire history of the Negro in the American theatre" because it was:

> The first time anywhere in the United States for Negro Actors in the dramatic theatre to command the serious attention of the critics and of the general press and public.

However, this theatrical event was more prophetic and also fateful, and had more ramifications than Johnson was willing to concede for the kind of American theater that a Brustein would much later lament the absence of. Writing in the NAACP's *Crisis* magazine in October 1926, W. E. B. Du Bois cogently expressed the fact that American writers for the stage did not have the [public sanction] to write truthfully about American life. Citing the then current vogue of "Negro Plays" written by whites and the inevitable distortions of Negro characterizations, Du Bois asked—But why do white artists do this? He gave a most trenchant answer:

> White artists themselves suffer from (a) narrowing of their field. They cry for freedom in dealing with Negroes because they have so little freedom in dealing with whites. DuBose Heywood writes "Porgy" and writes beautifully of the black Charleston underworld. (Why?) . . . Because he cannot do a similar thing for the white people of Charleston or they would drum him out of town. The only chance he had to tell the truth of pitiful human degradation was to tell it of colored people.

But the irony was that the "colored people" who went to the theater in the 1920's, 1930's and 1940's did not like what white playwrights such as Heywood were saying about black character in the theater. Everybody knowledgeable about the American theater knows about the continuing controversy surrounding *Porgy and Bess,* the musical rendition of Heywood's "Porgy." Lorraine Hansberry's entrée into theatrical celebrity in 1959 was accompanied by an embittered condemnation of *Porgy and Bess,* the only American achievement in musical theater that has been accepted by the world as a "classic" piece of theater. The fact that this "classic" was written around a black theme was no mere historical accident, but is a generic result of the fact that America's only original contribution to world theater is the Negro minstrel, that America's only original contribution to world music and world dance is black music and black dance. These are the ramifications of American theatrical developments that Brustein and other critics fail to cope with in their assessments.

In seeking out the line of least creative resistance by circuitously incorporating the American race factor as a dramatic theme, white dramatists from O'Neill's 1920's through the Thirties and Forties confounded and retarded the striving black dramatist in their honest attempts to grapple with and master the intricacies of black character, black idiom, black tragedy and black comedy. In other words, in exploiting the black themes and popularizing them, the white writers created a funhouse of sentimental, tragic or comic stereotypes which the black writers dared not seek either to imitate or refute because neither black nor white audiences were conditioned to accept either approach. This black problem in the theater was not successfully met and overcome until the advent of the Sixties. Yet even in the 1970's, the black playwright has not been able to completely overcome the inhibiting influence of the "stage Negro" created by whites over the years. This is the main reason why black writers write so few good plays that are not "autobiographical." It has, so far, been the film media rather than the theater medium that has, to any degree, liberated the black writer from the restrictions of stereotype.

Hence, when Mr. Brustein cites the contemporary "balkanization" of the American theater, he is describing a situation that is, historically, ex post facto, [. . .] the original source of American theatrical malaise which is the *racial* factor rooted in the slavery experience. "Balkanization," as Brustein sees it, has to be seen as rooted in historical "ethnicity"—meaning European-derived ethnicity in America which, for the most part, is traced to the immigration of the post–Civil War decades. On the other hand, "balkanization" is, as Brustein says, reflected in the present-day audience response in which:

> A number of productions came and went . . . including a feminist musical, a one-man Artaud show, a one-woman evening of poetry and music, and two one-act black plays. Each of these productions attracted its own special audience, and each of these audiences seemed entirely independent, if not somewhat wary, of the others.

In addition, Brustein singles out "black audiences," "tourist audiences," "bridge and tunnel" audiences, meaning "blue-collar and white-collar people." For further clarification, he might have identified the ethnic background of these audiences which have "balkanized" the theater. For they are essentially unidentified ethnic constituencies in search of a theater with which they *might* identify in the way in which blacks identify with *The Wiz,* etc. They come to the theater with the silent hopes of encountering dramatic themes that somehow reflect their own psychology and life experiences. They usually do not find such rewarding experiences because, although the theater might be "balkanized" in terms of the splintered audience, as Brustein says, the theater does not offer the requisite variety of thematic material to accommodate the full range of the splintered tastes.

Moreover, Brustein's ideal of the American National Theater which does not exist, could not hope to accommodate the theatrical variety to meet the tastes of the "special audiences" for the simple reason that the American Dramatic ideals never fully accepted the legitimate nativity of such thematic ingredients as bona fide facets of an American National Theater idea. Nor, in fact, did it accept the Indian factor. Thus the racial negation in the American theater worked against blacks and Indians in one way, but against European ethnics in other ways.

The European-derived ethnic made many contributions to native Americana but not intrinsic theatrical contributions, as such. According to Carl Wittke, one of the leading chroniclers of European immigrant impact on American culture, these immigrants attempted merely to duplicate their old-world theatrical forms in the new American setting. In real terms of immigrant contribution to American cultural arts, Wittke remarked, "I do not mean to overstress their contributions." This was the same Wittke, the German American scholar who wrote *We Who Built America: The Saga of the Immigrant* in 1939, in celebration of the European ethnic's overall contributions to American civilization, who also pointed out that "Without the large Negro population of the Southern States, the one purely native form of entertainment and the only distinctively American contribution to the theater—the Negro Minstrel—would have been equally impossible."

It was significant that it took a German American intellectual immigrant to render this historically and culturally honest assertion about the origins of "native" American theatrical forms; an Anglo-American cultural historian would never have admitted that the lowly American blacks could have made any contribution to American culture [. . .] outside of the Negro Spirituals. However, Wittke had to admit that the European ethnic contributions to the American theater consisted of dramatic themes imported from Europe chiefly by the Irish, the Germans and the Jews. Hence ethnic drama consisted wholly of portrayals of ethnic life either in Europe or in America. Wittke said of the Irish, "Their plots are not without significance in the history of the American melting pot," an observation that applied to the late nineteenth and early twentieth centuries, [when] European drama had already been "classicized" by

Ibsen, Chekov, Shaw, Strindberg, Pirandello and a host of others. It was the importation of such plays from Europe that made the European tour of Mr. H. A. Jones such a newsworthy item for *The New York Times* in 1907.

[. . .]

Yet withal the theatrical inputs vouchsafed European ethnicity, [and] the basic tripartite racial encounter has not been fully reflected in the evolution of American drama. Decimated physically through a sustained genocidal assault, and later apotheosized for his stubborn bravery, the Indian was never immortalized in American drama. Hollywood, of course, compensated for this through its depictions of the Indian in the filmic folklorization of the mythical cowboy of the Western frontier. But seldom did the film do justice to the full dimensions of Indian character.

At one time, perceptive Americans attempted to confront the Indian saga in the theater. In an article in the March 1926 issue of *Theatre Arts Monthly*, Hartley Alexander observed that "Here in the New World is a source which, for variety of material and charm of motive, is quite comparable to the sources from which the Greek artists drew. This is true in mythic poetry, in decorative motive, and in melodic theme; and the materials exist not in one style but in several, each developed to a form splendidly expressive . . . We Americans, with our transplanted culture, have achieved as yet little more than a colonial echo of the ancestral arts, and so long as we lean heavily upon our European sources we are unlikely to more than faintly echo their forms."

Whatever the cultural historians are moved to say these days about our celebrated "Jazz Age" of the Twenties, at least the writers and critics (thanks again to Mencken and Nathan) were honest enough to boldly cite how the abrasive impact of Anglo-Saxon racism stifled the cultural arts by narcissistic exclusionism. Anglo-Saxon cultural supremacists refused to cultivate and water the gardens of America except where they chose to plant their own seeds. And even then they were parsimonious with the fertilizers because deep down they really did not have much regard for art or artists.

[. . .] Hartley Alexander [in the March 1926 issue of *Theatre Arts Monthly*], inadvertently revealed more serious flaws in American aesthetics than he intended when he asserted that the Indian motifs were "quite comparable to the sources from which the Greek artists drew"! The racially biased cultural history of the United States had not properly informed Mr. Alexander that the only theater institution in the United States that had the popularity that the Greek theater had in Athens was the minstrel theater tradition. [. . .] More than that, the *true* history of the Greek theater (not the Europeanized classical history taught in university drama schools) reveals that the Greek playwrights relied extensively on Ethiopian and African themes, actors and plot materials. In fact, the history of the American minstrel theater tradition (with its almost total reliance on the Negro idiom) shows that American minstrelsy was, historically, the closest simile of the Greek comic theater ever produced in the Western World since the fall of Rome. In American minstrelsy, the much-maligned and comically derogated fashion of "blacking up" or the "burnt cork" tradition should be seen as an American adaptation of the *classic Greek use of the mask in character impersonations.*

But since American minstrelsy was considered a rather crude, bawdy caricature of "niggers," the American theater tradition refused to glorify the minstrel by refusing to refine it. However, the Anglo-Saxon racial encounter with the transplanted African was an historical re-enactment of the ancient Greek encounter with Africans (Ethiopians). The great difference being that the ancient Greeks were not race or color conscious like the Anglo-Saxon 2000 years later. Thus, Greek dramatics incorporated the African theatrical idiom into their plays, thus enhancing both Greek and African originality. By contrast, the Anglo-Saxons in the United States appropriated the original elements of Afro-American theatrical ingredients [by "masking"] their faces [with burnt cork], and thereby denigrating blacks.

Thus it was that Hartley Alexander and other devotees of the Indian theme aesthetic were defeated by American cultural history of the nineteenth century. The "Greek" theater historical connection had already been consummated in blackface minstrelsy. Hence, Alexander's attempts to recreate the "Greek" idea of theater by way of the utilization of Indian motifs were met with the objection—"Indian stuff doesn't go"! "As a matter of experience," wrote Alexander, "producers look askance at any suggestion of Indian drama . . . having in mind paint and feathers; and when their common sense and knowledge are fortified by the nose-tiltings and superciliations of the critical highbrow (who is all for the Greeks, Gothic or Chinese art, as his case may be), he who advocates the Indian's place under the artistic sun is left to equilibrate himself upon his own heels." Hartley Alexander seems to have overlooked the historical fact that while the Greeks may have been prone to wage war and take slaves as booty, they did not appear to have contemplated anything so execrable and dishonorable as the kind of genocide the Americans inflicted on the Noble Red Man. To then wait until the twentieth century to glorify the Indian on a theatrical pedestal through the transportation of Greek modes was like visiting the scene of a bloody crime with bouquets and garlands. Americans weren't up to that, thus Alexander's aims to furbish up the Red Man for dramatic art perished during the hectic aesthetic soul-searching of [the] Twenties.

[In that same vein], the unique aesthetic fact of the Twenties was not so much the negative attitudes towards Hartley Alexander's idea for an Indian Theater, as was the more Greek-like American preoccupation with the "mythic" qualities of the black image in theater, music and dance. All the critics of the Twenties [. . .] were well aware that it was Negro theatrics, music, song and dance that captured the fancy of the New York sophisticates. [. . .]

And all of this aesthetic celebration of the Negro took place at a time when American society was saturated with attitudinal racism that was so pervasive, so deep, at times so vicious and vindictive that a black man who had managed to live through the Washington, D.C., race riots of 1919 declared that: "There was an antagonism between black and white men which convinced me of the eternal hatred of different kinds of men." In America, it seems that the black presence has been able to elevate aesthetic comprehension above the reach of the base qualities of the human soul where even the demons of race feelings hide their faces.

Outside of the Yiddish Theater, there has been no "ethnic" theater style in America comparable to the drama of black life. There has been no dramatic school of Irish life in America, nor German, nor Scandinavian, nor Italian, nor Greek (modern), nor Spanish, nor French, nor Polish. The traditional force of the drama of black life can be seen in the fact that the one well-known play about Polish life, *Anna Lucasta* by Phillip Yordan, was a failure until revised for black life by Abram Hill of the American Negro Theater during the Forties. Legend has it that the black version of *Anna Lucasta* made seven million dollars.

What is there culturally, aesthetically, dramatically so enticing about the black theme in the theater that, at once, repels the whites and then attracts them? In the theater world, it was a well-known adage that plays about black life are either box-office poison or else tremendous hits. W. E. B. Du Bois, cited earlier, explained this theatrical phenomenon in creative and aesthetic terms. Much later on, even Brustein, in his complaints about the seemingly dire effects of the "balkanization" of the theater audience, had to emphasize the importance of the impact of the black movement of the Sixties on the American theater and its divided audience:

> The (black) separatist impulse now seems to dominate dozens of special interest groups, each trying to elbow the other aside for power and influence, and we have become a nation of political lobbies instead of a people, dissipating vital creative energies in the formulation of petitions and propaganda.

What Brustein seems reluctant to stress is the fact that, artistically and theatrically (as well as socially), the separatist thrust of recent years came first from a black propagandist constituency both inside and outside the theater. In the theater, this "separatism" was essentially a manifestation of the struggle of the blacks to implant their legitimate theatrical image on the American national consciousness. This effort is of long standing in nineteenth and twentieth century American history. During this extended effort, the blacks have had to vie with the whites for the creative autonomy over the black's own theatrical ingredients. In the process, the Afro-American has, more often than not, been exploited by being caught in the toils of racial and economic integuments which control theatrical enterprise. Moreover, the blacks have been sorely hampered in this uneven contention by possessing a generically dual theatrical tradition with which even the blacks themselves have never come to terms. This dual tradition involves an original musical tradition (derived from minstrelsy) and a so-called "legitimate" tradition which is a syncretist adoption of the European forms created for blacks by American whites in the exploitation of black themes and dramatic ingredients. (Eugene O'Neill, Mary Hoyt Wiborg, Ira and George Gershwin, Dorothy and Dubose Heyward, Paul Green, Ridgely Torrence, etc.)

From the 1890's through the 1920's, black writers and composers attempted to refine the native black musical theater. The history of American musical theater conveniently neglects to record the many outstanding accomplishments of pioneering black writers and composers such as Bob Cole and Billy Johnson (later Cole and J. Rosamund Johnson), F. E. Miller and Aubrey Lyles, Bert Williams and George Walker, who were also top performers, Jesse Shipp (a director), Will Marion Cook (a student of Anton Dvorak), Leubrie Hill, Eubie Blake and Noble Sissle. From the pens and imaginations of these black theater pioneers came such memorable productions as: *Clorindy—The Origin of the Cakewalk* (with lyrics by Paul Lawrence Dunbar), *Jes Lak White Folks* (sic), *The Sons of Ham, In Dahomey, In Abyssinia, Bandanna Land, The Shoofly Regiment, The Red Moon, Darktown Follies, Shuffle Along, Runnin' Wild* (which produced the dance craze, the Charleston), *Liza, Dinah, Chocolate Dandies, Rang Tang,* and others.

[. . .]

This retarded black-white-over-black creative cycle in black drama was not broken until the advent of Lorraine Hansberry's *A Raisin in the Sun* in 1959, opening up the new-wave black drama of the Sixties and Seventies which introduced such new black playwrights as Joseph Walker, Douglass Turner Ward, LeRoi Jones, Lonnie Elder, Ed Bullins, Ron Milner, Phillip Dean and others. It was highly significant that soon after the debut of her play, Lorraine Hansberry delivered an attack on *Porgy and Bess* as "bad art" and on the stereotyped roles written by white dramatists for black actors. However, no sooner had the new-wave black dramatists of the Sixties and Seventies had their say, than back came the black musicals into a new vogue. Ossie Davis's *Purlie Victorious* and Hansberry's *A Raisin in the Sun* were revised into musicals, and highly successful ones at that. [Other attempts followed:] *Bubbling Brown Sugar* by Loften Mitchell, *Ain't Misbehavin'* (on Fats Waller's career), leading up to black versions of white musicals—*Guys and Dolls,* and the celebrated *The Wiz.* These two latter theatrical creations [signal the return of blacks] to their truly native theatrical form—the musical theater. Ironically, [. . .] the imitation of white musicals means that *blacks have run out of truly original musical themes.* Thus ends what Brustein viewed as the new phase of (black) separatist thrusts in the theater. [. . .]

However, Brustein, to be historically accurate, has to admit that what he perceives as "dozens of special interest groups" vying for power and influence in the theater came to the fore *in response* to black separatist assertion. [. . .] Women as a "minority" and other special interest groups such as the "gays" were soon to follow the blacks in a bid for "power and influence." However, Brustein should recognize that it was the WASPs who, theatrically, were the first "separatists" whose cultural exclusiveness succeeded in preventing and discouraging "special interest groups" from contributing to the realization of what Brustein *sees as missing these days, i.e., the American National Theater.*

[. . .]

It is historically clear that when and if the idea of an American National Theater ever sees fruition, such a theater will have to be national in scope and in administration, but, at the same time, multi-national, multi-racial, multi-ethnic, multi-cultural in theatrical and creative content. Nothing less will do.

CHAPTER EIGHTEEN

The New Negro History of John Hope Franklin —Promise and Progress

(Unpublished)

[. . .] **I**t has been some thirty-two years now since John Hope Franklin emerged as a major American historian. His legitimate place in the pantheon of American historiography brooks no quibbling demurrers. For a historian who is also Black to have accomplished what John Hope Franklin has achieved in mere quantitative output in the United States between the years of World War II and 1979 ranks with that of any historian, of any national group, of any historical tradition, of any period in history, from the age of Bancroft to the era of Commager, Boorstin, a Vann Woodward or a Hofstadter, that is to say, with any historian whose obligation was to illuminate a specific tradition. In this regard, everything is relative, and our judgments have to be guided with this relativity in mind.

When John Hope Franklin's *From Slavery to Freedom* appeared in 1948 in New York (and I specify New York), the book was a Godsend to that scattering of would-be scholars, critics, and activists of my own age group and racial background. World War II was but three years retired into History, and that war had served to close out an important era in American history—the age of Franklin D. Roosevelt's New Deal. World War II was a watershed in both American and world history. And so it was for American Blacks. [The Second World War was] a violent coda of international proportions to a domestic decade of black despair, of desperate challenges, of dubious rewards. Yet, for American Blacks, the 1930's had been a decade of rising awareness of the need to know the history of conflicts and issues pertaining to themselves. There had hardly been a period during which Blacks in America, both young and old, argued and debated history and international events more than they did during the 1930's. Due, in part, to the introduction of the radio, [that decade was one] in which knowledge of history and the ability to interpret the meaning of contemporary events became democratized. In the process, American Blacks, similar to everyone else, were goaded to think beyond the restricted limits of national and also group insularity.

However, in the special area of Black American history, there had been a paucity of available texts related to the issues that generation argued and debated. Black scholars had knowledge of such things, but my peers were lucky to be among those accepted into the educated inner circles where such knowledge was the medium of interpersonal exchange. Wise old Black men could afford to show off their world knowledge by quoting such books as Count Volney's *The Ruins of Empires,* a much-revered study of ancient history, but were not very enthusiastic about discussing such facts as American slavery. In Harlem of the late 1930's and early 1940's, older men talked about champion prizefighters, entertainers, obscure leaders in various fields, sometimes Booker T. Washington and W. E. B. Du Bois, but more often they asked the enlightening question "Did you know that . . . so and so . . . a black man, did . . . so and so . . . way back in 1895, long before you were born?" These older men in Harlem revealed that the American historian's craft had, for many years, served to obscure the very real record of Black American achievements in important areas of social, political, economic and cultural life. Hence, John Hope Franklin's *From Slavery to Freedom* appeared as the epitome of the grand statement about the Black past. Here, for the first time in our lives, was offered a textbook, massive in scope, authoritative, very nearly a compendium of Black History in the Western Hemisphere, with an extensive index, and a fulsome, informative bibliography. Here was presented the grand panorama of Black History spread out in all its dramatic evolution, in unadorned but highly readable prose that even a high school graduate could readily understand. *From Slavery to Freedom* was a reference book that not only filled in those annoyingly curious gaps in one's knowledge of things past, but opened up unrecognized avenues for further research and revelation. [It] was a landmark in Black historiography. A reviewer writing in the *Journal of Negro History* described it as "one of the most scholarly contributions of recent years to the field of literature dealing with the American Negro."[1] [. . .]

At the outset, any assessment of Franklin's work must first, I feel, consider the black and white climate of academic opinion in which Franklin emerged as a scholar. It was a peculiar racial and academic climate that made *From Slavery to Freedom* important despite what some critics would point out as textual weaknesses. For my generation, especially, the established icons in the study of Black History were W. E. B. Du Bois and Carter G. Woodson. There were a few other historians, but none as well known as these two. It was as if World War II had, in a manner of speaking, closed out the era of scholarly predominance of a Du Bois or a Woodson. In 1945, Du Bois was already 77 years of age, and Woodson, 70. The young black generation was a war generation, whose outlook had been rendered less insular, less provincial than its parents. Matters of importance tended to be more international in scope and more futuristic. Did the Black past in the postwar period seem as important as Black History had been to the arguers and debaters of the late 1930's? What John Hope Franklin was to later describe as the "New Negro History"[2] in 1957 was, then, already in the process of being written and expounded by a number of younger scholars, of which Franklin himself was one. An assessment of this article, "The New Negro History," and some of Franklin's subsequent writings is the main theme of this paper.

At this time, Franklin was already known to his colleagues for his study on *The Free Negro in North Carolina* (1943). Since this book was a publishable version of his dissertation, its retrospective optimism regarding the intimate nature of slavery in North Carolina can be overlooked, depending on one's point of view towards the Peculiar Institution. In any event, *The Free Negro in North Carolina* must have highly impressed Carter G. Woodson who took the pains to review the book himself in his *Journal*. Three months before Woodson's review, Franklin used some of his data on the Free Negro in North Carolina in an article titled "Slaves Virtually Free in Antebellum North Carolina." The justification that Franklin offered for this seemingly extravagant assessment of slavery in North Carolina was that: "The treatment of slaves in the ante-bellum South had almost as many variations as there were slaveholders." This truism about slavery, that it was not ever a uniform system of rigid oppression or benevolent paternalism, had been understood long before Franklin made the discovery in his investigations of "Slavery" and "Freedom" in North Carolina.

Slavery historians have each carved out staunch (and also academically lucrative) positions of "interpretation" around the various meanings of the truism. Slaves were virtually free in North Carolina, said Franklin. Later Ira Berlin would describe free Negroes as "Slaves Without Masters." [. . .] In any event, it appeared that, perhaps, Franklin's interpretation of his slavery data might offer some clues to what his point of view might be on *contemporary* events as *well* as on history. Woodson, for example, in his review of Franklin, praised him for offering "new interpretations" of "Slavery" and "Freedom." Thus, when one read Franklin's espousal of "The New Negro History" later on one hoped that Franklin might be presenting new ideas on the question of new "interpretations."

In the meantime, however, among the contemporary events of special interest to historians at the moment *From Slavery to Freedom* appeared were discussions relating to the annual celebration of "Negro History Week." Deeply involved in these activities were all of John Hope Franklin's professional colleagues in New York. Prominent among them were L. D. Reddick, then the curator of the Schomburg Library of Black History, and Harcourt A. Tynes of the New York Public School system. Tynes was president of the Harlem Branch of the Association for the Study of Negro Life and History (ASNLH), Carter G. Woodson's historical society. At that moment, the "Negro History Week" celebration, institutionalized since [1926], was being stepped up and widely publicized in New York. This was just about the time Franklin was beginning to receive wider public notice as a major historian, and his name was more prominently associated with Carter G. Woodson's ASNLH.

It so happened that at the time of the appearance of Franklin's history, the celebration of Negro History Week was beginning to attract the support of the political Left. Inspired by the rising prominence of Herbert Aptheker as a Marxist historian in the field of Black History, [the Left] had assumed the role of publicly espousing the importance of Negro History Week celebrations. In the February 11, 1947 issue of the Left *New Masses,* magazine, Herbert Aptheker published an article entitled, "Negro History Arsenal for Liberation"—"To Rescue the Negro People's past from oblivion and distortion is to arm for today's struggles." [Given] the considerable influence of the political Left in 1947-48, John Hope Franklin's book was destined to appear in the midst of an apparent three-way jurisdictional contest over who would have the most influential say, from an interpretive standpoint, about the content and thrust of the Black History being written in the postwar period. At that moment, the three opinion centers in the interpretation and the content analysis of written Black History were (1) the reigning Black Historians inside the Association for the Study of Negro Life and History, (2) Marxist Historians, e.g., Herbert Aptheker and the Foner family,

(3) those few Black and White academic historians and social scientists who supported Carter G. Woodson's ASNLH but not in a policy making role. In his article, Herbert Aptheker mentioned John Hope Franklin among the "excellently trained Black historians" of "our own day" such as: "Charles H. Wesley, L. D. Reddick, Luther P. Jackson, Lorenzo G. Greene, W. Sherman Savage, Alrutheous A. Taylor, Eric Williams, Horace M. Bond, James H. Johnson and, of course, the two grand old men of the crusade—W. E. B. Du Bois and Carter G. Woodson" who had, as Aptheker expressed it, "Been doing an invaluable job of spadework and pioneering." This article by Aptheker appeared just before Franklin's *From Slavery to Freedom* was released.

What struck me about Aptheker's article ["Negro History Arsenal for Liberation" (*New Masses*, February 1947)] was the unusual tone of militant commitment to "rescuing the Negro people's past from oblivion and distortion" coming from the political Left. It seemed to me that the Left was more militant about this issue than some Black historians mainly because they, the Left, couched the necessity of championing Black History for compelling "political" reasons. Thus it seemed to me that the Political Left was attempting to outdo the Carter G. Woodson group in the ASNLH in "politicizing" Negro History Week.

However, I then became aware of the fact that a controversy was brewing in certain Harlem circles over the significance of Negro History Week celebrations. It took two years for this brewing controversy to break out in print. *The New York Amsterdam News* of February 18, 1950, editorialized that:

> It is time to get rid of Negro History Week celebrations. We are confronted with a serious problem. We want American history presented as the total record of the past activities and experiences of all groups and races. We do not want it from any special angle. We do not want the reader of history to become prejudiced in favor of our special outlook.

At the same time, the *Baltimore Afro-American,* also on February 18, 1950, commented in this way:

> Many people think that Negro History Week celebrations should not be held. But as long as the historians of our school books, the editors of the daily newspapers continue to exclude the American Negro, and fail to show that he, too, is a normal part of this country, and has helped and is still helping to make it the great nation that it is—then of necessity we must celebrate Negro History Week.

This debate, coming when it did, was a revelation. It would not have occurred to me that any articulate sector of Black opinion would have questioned the validity of such an institution. For to question the validity of Negro History Week celebrations was tantamount, in my view, to questioning the validity of Carter G. Woodson's ASNLH and his entire career. In fact, to question the validity of Negro History Week was to question the academic and intellectual legitimacy of every historian who had committed himself or herself to the labors of producing histories, and other studies on American Blacks. Moreover, it raised the uncomfortable question as to what significance should be attributed to Franklin's *From Slavery to Freedom* beyond its value as good scholarship. Should not such excellent scholarship be of benefit to Blacks? Should not such scholarship be celebrated? But if so, how? And if not, then it would have to be concluded that scholarship might be of interest to the inner society of scholars, but beyond that, a study that charts the events of the long trek of Blacks from Africa to the Americas is only of marginal import even, one might say, to the educational and intellectual status of the Black elites, not to mention the status of Black people in general.

But it soon became clear that the problem was even deeper than the *Amsterdam News* editorial had suggested in its opposition to Negro History Week celebrations. What became clear was the very real, long-standing existence of a curious ambivalence towards Black History *qua* history, *even within the Black intellectual and academic tradition.* It was a naïve mistake to assume that every scholar and academic who happened to be Black thought the same as Du Bois or Woodson. The implications were disquieting, to say the least, for here was the spectacle of white historians such as Aptheker and the Foners demonstrating, what seemed to me, more militant support of Negro History Week than certain Blacks themselves. It was Aptheker in his *New Masses* article who attacked such white historians as Henry S. Commager, Allan Nevins, Dwight L. Dumond, W. J. Cash, Ulrich B. Phillips and William A. Dunning for what he perceived as their derelictions in depicting the role of Blacks in American history. By contrast, the reigning Black historians, unlike the militance of the Left, responded from what was clearly a defensive stance.

At the 35th annual meeting of the Association for the Study of Negro Life and History, held in Atlanta in October 1950, the Association came to grips with the problem. The *Journal of Negro History* for January 1950 reported on the proceedings as follows:

> During the discussion from the floor, the question was raised whether there was need for further special study of the Negro. Dr. John Hope Franklin and

Dr. (Rayford) Logan challenged this point of view, calling attention to the fact that if other journals and schools are not devoting as much attention as is needed to the subject, there is a continued need for the Association, the Journal and the (Negro History) bulletin; that the Journal (of Negro History) publishes a considerable number of articles by white scholars and many of the subscribers are white institutions and individuals.

At least John Hope Franklin had made his position clear on the matter. He strongly supported the continuing of the "special study of the Negro." Having read his *From Slavery to Freedom* pretty thoroughly by 1950, I could have expected no less from a historian whom I had never met, but whom I admired. Certain carping critics had chided Franklin for ignoring certain important areas, but at that moment it was not very clear to me exactly what those areas were. What mattered was that the historians with whom I was personally acquainted were in agreement with Franklin on the importance of the "special study of the Negro" and the celebration of Negro History Week. [. . .]

Later, a closer reading of the statements of both Franklin and his colleagues in the ASNLH regarding the continuation of Negro History Week celebrations revealed that their scholarly sentiments lacked a definitive ring of solid conviction. Their statements on the validity of a continuing "special study" of the Negro were couched in rather provisional terms. If the *Journal of Negro History* conveyed Franklin's and his colleague's sentiments correctly, then the need for a special study of the Negro existed *not* because they earnestly preferred it that way, but mainly because other journals and schools were not devoting as much attention as was needed to the subject. It was being suggested by Franklin and others in 1950 that if more major, prestigious (i.e., predominantly "white") institutions, universities, and journals would begin to accept the legitimacy of Black History (and by implication the whole range of Black-oriented social science) there *might* not exist any further compelling need for the ASNLH to serve the institutional role of the "official," monopolistic sponsor of study and research in Black History *qua* history. Of course, that sector of Black intellectual opinion that agreed with the *Amsterdam News* editorial believed that the time for deemphasis of Black History *qua* history had already arrived by 1950. The fact was problematic enough, but what was crucial here was the obvious trace of ambivalence toward the "Special study of the Negro" discovered in the very institution created by Carter G. Woodson for the express purpose of furthering the legitimacy of such study. Thus the defense of the "Special study of the Negro" by the self-proclaimed specialists was not inspired by the kind of unqualified convictions that looked forward to their continued hegemony over their special field of Black History *qua* history. It was not too long after the death of Carter G. Woodson in 1950, that the *Journal of Negro History* began to show a marked change in its content quality.

[. . .]John Hope Franklin did not, however, rest on his laurels. He went on his way to develop into what one may call the complete historian of his genre. [. . .] *The Militant South,* his third book, demonstrated in a convincing manner that an American historian who is also Black is fully capable of writing history [. . .] deemed "white," even if it is essentially "White Over Black," to paraphrase another historian [Winthrop Jordan]. If a derivative Southern historian could write a history of the South that discussed the crucial labor, class and caste, the cultural inpact and/or cultural influence of Blacks on the manners and mores of "Southrons" only in passing, because it was obligatory, and call it a history of events "as they really were," then so could John Hope Franklin. There were only three parsimonious references to "Negroes" as such in the index of this study. [. . .] Blacks were impersonally dealt with under the heading of "Slavery." However, "The connection between slavery and the martial spirit was almost universally recognized,"[3] wrote Franklin. Thus, the *real* ante-bellum South was far removed from the nostalgic romanticism of a Thomas Nelson Page with his retrospective visions of courtly gentry, contented slaves, chaste white women, magnolias and chivalry and transplanted cavaliers. [. . .] Franklin's *The Militant South* was a land of studiously practiced military propensity to political violence as an ingrained way of life.

[. . .]

Although as distinguished a Southern historian as C. Vann Woodward, curiously, did not cite *The Militant South* in his *The Burden of Southern History* (1961), Franklin's reputation was solidly established—so much so that influential white historians would later be able to say "Well, John Franklin is not really a Black historian, you know. He is an *American* historian!" Later on, William M. Brewer of the ASNLH would show signs of qualifying his earlier unqualified praise of Franklin's *From Slavery to Freedom.*

The occasion was Franklin's revised third edition, 1969: "The title is sort of a misnomer as Negroes are nowhere free in 1969," said Brewer. "A better title would be: A Cultural and Social History of Negro Americans, which would connote and denote what this work really is."[4] Brewer went on to further deflate Franklin's prestige balloon. He said there was a noticeable tendency toward "sweetness and light" here and there in Franklin's history. Franklin, he said, ought not to have allowed his publishers to claim that *From Slavery to Freedom* "Is the best book ever written about Negroes." Moreover, said Brewer, "The book is indispensable for any course in Negro history, but *utterly inadequate alone as a textbook.*" [. . .]

There were developing here, seemingly, some belated reservations about Franklin's work coming from that sector of Black opinion more solidly in favor of Black History *qua* history, i.e., in favor of the continued "special study of the Negro." William M. Brewer, who died several years ago, was a staunch member of that persuasion within the ASNLH. He would castigate members of the Black academic establishment for their coolness towards Black History *qua* history as a discipline. [. . .]

In light of all this criticism pro and con, the question posed from that point on was [the one raised by] William Brewer: *To what extent did John Hope Franklin actually help the special study of the Negro go forward?*

When Franklin published his article, "The New Negro History," in 1957, he appeared, at first sight, to be announcing the approach of a new era in the "interpretation" of Black History coming from himself as America's premier historian who is Black. However, on closer reading of this article, it appeared that Franklin was saying different things to two different audiences. The article was first printed in the *Crisis* magazine of the NAACP before it was reprinted in the *Journal of Negro History* (by permission). That in itself was significant. To the NAACP Franklin appeared to be saying:

> During the last two decades some significant changes have taken place in the writing, teaching, and study of the history of the Negro in the United States. On almost every side there has been a remarkable growth in the history of the Negro.[5]

The mention of "the last two decades" coincided, of course, with the appearance of *From Slavery to Freedom* in 1948 and 1957. However, the assessment Franklin made of those two decades might have been legitimate depending on one's historical frame of reference, except that his colleague, William Brewer, was not that enthusiastic about the Black History twenty-year harvest [. . .]

Brewer recognized no "seminal ideas" in John Hope Franklin's work. What did "seminal ideas" have to do with the problem of "interpretation" in Black History? Or more to the point, what did Brewer's reference to "seminal ideas" have to do with what Franklin outlined in his "The New Negro History" in 1957?

For one thing, [Franklin's article] did not mean to Brewer and certain other reigning members of the ASNLH what it might have meant for the reigning members of the NAACP. On the one hand, this article represented no historian's "interpretive" opposition to the guiding social tenets of the NAACP "racial integration" mainly because Franklin had already been integrated as an American historian who just happened to be Black. On the other hand, insofar as the ASNLH was concerned, his "The New Negro History" obviously attempted to promise new and "seminal ideas" in the field, but hedged all the way through with a succession of interesting commonplaces on the craft of history writing which, apparently, did not satisfy William Brewer and others within the Association. These, I gather, are some of the reasons for Brewer's not so muted criticism of Franklin's work up to 1969. Brewer argued that:

> The weakest portions of Dr. Franklin's work may be found in his *caution* and *leniency* with the "interracial cooperators and hustlers," white and Negro.
> [. . .] He has already received more adulation from white people than any American Negro excepting Booker T. Washington for similar reasons.[6]

Much of this sharp criticism [may] have been inspired by mere envy and jealousy growing out of Franklin's phenomenal successes. [. . .] However, it cannot be said that the totality of Franklin's work has been either provocative enough, original enough, probing enough to defend his immense reputation against the searching criticism of those among us who yearn for those "seminal ideas." [. . .]

[O]nly one year after *The Militant South*, Franklin could [write "so far as the *actual* history of the American Negro is concerned, there is nothing particularly new about it. It is an exciting story, a remarkable story. It is the story of slavery and freedom, humanity and inhumanity, democracy and its denial. It is tragedy and triumph, suffering and compassion, sadness and joy." Truthfully, the statement does a great deal in explaining] why his 28 books, 53 odd articles and monographs, plus some eight additional edited volumes, narratives and biographies hardly ever transcend the narrative and descriptive orthodoxy established in *From Slavery to Freedom*.[7] If prizes were awarded for sheer volume of work, John Hope Franklin would rest securely in every Hall of Historical Fame. [. . .] Yet his very choice of historical topic is governed in advance by his own philosophy regarding the function of history writing. His philosophy is explicit in his historiography, but is clearly spelled out in such an autobiographical sketch as "The Dilemma of the American Negro Scholar" (1963), in which he protests against those dominant tendencies in American intellectual and academic life that conspire to keep the Black scholar and intellectual out of the "mainstream" and restricted [to] "Negro Studies."[. . .]

> There emerged a large number of Negro scholars who devoted themselves almost exclusively to the study of the Negro . . . (They) alas, made an institution

of the Field of Negro Studies. (They became) the victim(s) of segregation in the field of scholarship in the same way that Negroes in other fields had become victims of segregation.[8]

Note that his assessment of the "dilemma" of the Negro scholar appeared seven years after the publication of *The Militant South* [which had gained Franklin a] "release" from Negro Studies, and thirteen years after his statement of 1950 in which he defended [. . .] the legitimacy of the "special study of the Negro." Moreover, between 1963 and 1977, [Franklin produced] approximately 50 books and articles, [. . .] approximately 31 [of which] deal with race, Negroes, and/or ethnicity. [Does] this quantitative output indicate that Franklin is experiencing an intellectual dilemma?

[. . .]

The contemporary problem in Black History is that not too many students of history are likely to glean much from Franklin's body of work and his philosophy beyond the fundamentals of the disciplines and the rigid requirements of certain historical research methodologies. These are important. However, the student looking for the "seminal ideas," the challenge of unique "interpretations," or anything resembling the unorthodox in the philosophy of history would be hard-put to find such intellectual qualities in Franklin's body of work.

[. . .]

In view of these observations regarding John Hope Franklin's "The New Negro History," it has to be concluded that when Franklin, in 1950, upheld the continuation of the "special study of the Negro" as a legitimate area for study and research for the historian who is black, he was already in the intellectual throes of questioning that position. If it is claimed that this shifting, ambivalent position is a generic result and unavoidable consequence of the peculiar nature of the field of historical studies in the United States, then it becomes an intellectual and "interpretive" problem that must be seriously discussed and analyzed.

[. . .]

NOTES

1. *Journal of Negro History [JNH]*, April 1948, p. 225.
2. Ibid., April 1957, p. 89-97.
3. *The Militant South*, 1956.

4. *JNH,* October, 1969, pp. 416-19.
5. Ibid., cited, April, 1957.
6. Ibid., cited, October, 1969.
7. Ibid., cited., April 1957.
8. Franklin, "The Dilemma of the American Negro Scholar" (*Soon, One Morning,* Herbert Hill, ed., 1963), pp. 62-76.

CHAPTER NINETEEN

Amilcar Cabral and the Afro-American Reality

(*Black World*, October 1975)

Amilcar Cabral, the architect of independence in the former Portuguese colony of Guinea-Bissau, like Cruse, subscribed to an analysis of liberation movements that placed culture in the foreground. Cabral's statement that "In certain circumstances, it is very easy for the foreigner to impose his domination on a people. But, whatever may be the material aspects of this domination, it can be maintained only by the permanent, organized repression of the cultural life of the people concerned" is only a degree removed from the introduction to The Crisis of the Negro Intellectual. *In those pages, Cruse writes "As long as the Negro's cultural identity is in question, or open to self-doubts, then there can be no positive identification with the real demands of his political and economic existence." Nevertheless, by 1979, the author was not sanguine about the state of Pan-African politics. The following essay details the shortcomings of the movement and the imperatives laid down by Cabral's liberationist theories.*

In order to deal with the applicability of Amilcar Cabral's cultural model to the Afro-American in a conclusive way, we must first review certain ramifications of Pan-Africanism in the 20th century. When the Black Power phase of the Sixties transformed itself into the Pan-Afrikanist romanticism of the Seventies, Amiri Baraka paid little attention to the fact that historic Pan-Africanism was never a political party movement. Nor was the Black situation in the United States the focus of its programmatic interests. Those interests were centered mainly, and primarily, on the African continental situation. But once the leadership of the Pan-Africanist Movement was transferred to indigenous Africans at the Fifth Manchester Congress of 1945, the Pan-Africanist program, as such, could not be transformed into a significant African land-base[d] program unless it immediately acquired a *political form* that was relevant to African realities. It was these imperatives that eventually pushed Kwame Nkrumah to found the Convention People's Party (C.P.P.) in June 1949.

George Padmore described these West African Gold Coast developments as "Pan-Africanism in Action" and related how Nkrumah, then the general secretary of the United Gold Coast Convention (U.G.C.C.), was forced to break with the "conservative" leadership of Dr. J. B. Danquah over the issue of "Self-Government Now" and form a more radical political organization:

> Loyally adhering to the decisions of the Pan African Congress, that organiza-
> tion was the key to power, the first thing he set about doing after breaking with
> the moderate U.G.C.C., was to form a country-wide party on a non-tribal,
> non-religious basis. This so alarmed the African conservative tribalists who saw
> their political careers threatened, that they appealed to the Chiefs and the
> British officials to suppress the C.P.P. as a "dangerous Communist conspiracy."
> But it was too late to invoke the "red bogey." *Party politics had caught on.*[1]
> [Italics Cruse's]

Seen in terms of the historical sequence of developments within the "African–Afro American–Caribbean" triangular relationships, this Gold Coast political development is highly significant with respect to the problem of political "form" and "content." The "Pan-Afrikanists" are so prone to be "carried away" with the excesses and flamboyancy of unassimilable "African" content that they pay no attention to "form." It is to be noted that prior to these Gold Coast events, most American organizations were called "con-gresses," "conventions," "movements" or other pressure forms, but *not* political parties in the parliamentary power sense. Another fact that should be noted is that concomitant with the W. E. B. Du Bois brand of Pan-Africanism, his call for a Black *political party* in 1916 was not answered until 1929, by Marcus Garvey in Jamaica, and until 1949, by Nkrumah in the then Gold Coast. The significance of all this is that the Black political party projected by Du Bois in 1916 was *not* in connection with his Pan-Africanist Congress line, but had to do with the special political circumstances of the Afro-American in the United States. What Pan-Africanist and "Pan-Afrikanist" scholars have failed to perceive is that, *historically,* the Afro-American *should have* established an independent Black political party at least by the time such a political form was established on the Gold Coast, *if not a decade or two before. That such did not happen was one of a number of unrecognized failures of leadership in the evolution of the 20th-century Black movements in the United States that was to effectively hamper the "Pan-Afrikanism" of the Seventies.* In the absence of established and ideologically grounded Black political parties in *both* the United States and Africa (not simply *ad hoc* movements like the ALSC)* programmed to national, regional, and international issues, the Afro-American is politically crippled in any attempts to pursue what are his historical responsibilities in the United States and in Africa. Without viable political institutions, the Afro-American cannot effectively influence American foreign policy on Africa. Why the ramifications of all this [are] so poorly understood is explained in the factual history of Pan-Africanism and Garveyism.

No doubt Baraka was inspired by this politically retarded situation to conjure up the notion of a "World African-Nationalist Pan-Afrikanist Party," which was like trying to build a tower by starting with the pinnacles in mid-air. Reading behind "Pan-Afrikanists" and their shallow views on modern Black history is similar to observing adolescents playing Kings and Queens in imaginary Black kingdoms of the mind, safely guarded "behind the veil" from the racist blight of world reality. This is why nearly everything they claim to have learned from the past leads to futility. The point is that Kwame Nkrumah, in 1949, in pursuance of the mandate of Manchester, was not so politically childish

---

*   *Ad hoc* "movements" fall apart. Most U.S.-based "Black nationalist" organizations are *ad hoc* and narrow in thought, with little staying power. The longevity and ability to consolidate and expand are limited by ideology that is a mixture of emotionalism, sentimentalism, messianism or goals that are usually millennial rather than politically realistic. U.S. "Black nationalists" usually avoid political organization. (ALSC: African Liberation Support Committee.)

as to attempt to form a "Pan-Africanist-World-Continental-Political Party"—
which would have been an egregious blunder of the first magnitude!

However, as Karl Marx observed long ago, men make their own history,
but not always in the way they would like at any given "point in time" (nor are
men always very rational about it). In retrospect, the Black political idea of Du
Bois in 1916 *should* have emerged in the 1920's. Ironically, the Garvey
movement itself obviously played a role as one of the factors that discouraged
the evolution of such a party idea, *but it was not the only factor.* All in all, it was
apparent that Black leadership had a difficult time catching up with *all* the
imperatives of their own movements. The (James W. H.) Eason–Marcus
Garvey split in 1922, and the concomitant uproar within and without the
U.N.I.A., indicated that Black leadership as a whole, including Garvey, was
unprepared to cope *politically* with the rapid emergence of many of the new
features of the Black experience as they unfolded.[*] The overriding persuasion
of the "American" question *vis-à-vis* the "African" question forced Eason to
oppose "Garveyism." This "American" priority was reflected in the manner in
which the international repercussions of World War I had not only urbanized
thousands of Blacks by uprooting them from agrarian and semi-agrarian
moorings, but had also "proletarianized" many thousands of them. Moreover,
these mass migrations had also transplanted the Black "cultural" heritage from
its Southern origins into an urbanized and more secularized sociological setting.
It was this development that prepared the ground for the so-called "Harlem
Renaissance," a Black cultural phenomenon that, even today, has not been
definitely interpreted. Historically, the "Harlem Renaissance" first poses the
complex and important question of the relationship between various aspects of
Black culture, Black politics and economics. Thus the Black cultural Twenties
prefigures in actual *social practice* what the Amilcar Cabral politico-cultural
model describes theoretically in the Seventies for another Black/white (African)
context. Historically, the Harlem Renaissance presented the politico-cultural
ingredients in the Afro-American context and posed the issues in a fashion, and
in the kind of social context, that Cabral, of course, would not. In the *historical*

---

[*] The much magnified achievements of Garvey cannot be understood unless exam-
    ined from all angles and within the context of the totality of all sides of the Black
    movements of the 1920's. An excellent contribution to this end is found in Wil-
    son J. Moses—"Marcus Garvey—A Reappraisal" (*Black Scholar,* November-
    December 1972) pp. 38-49. Moses wrote: "My attack on Garveyism is not an
    attack on Black nationalism . . . it is an attack on the closed-mindedness that
    dominated Garveyist thought and that dominates the thinking of many modern-
    day Black nationalists." p. 47.

sense, the United States was the setting in which the *political* implications of
Black culture *should* have been worked out. In this "developmental" sense, Black
culture—as an *African derivative*, colliding and intermingling with the cultural
carriers of Euro-American (with the dominant Anglo-American) ingredients of
European derivatives, in a highly developed capitalistic and technological
society like the United States—is far removed from the politico-cultural reality
of Guinea-Bissau. But unlike Cabral, the cultural leadership of the Harlem
Renaissance did *not* produce a politico-cultural theoretical model.* Yet, the
belated arrival of a model such as Cabral's can, in a *theoretical* fashion, aid us
in reassessing the Harlem Renaissance, Garveyism, and a number of related
political and economic problems pertaining to the Twenties and after. In
pursuit of this analysis, we shall have to put aside momentarily the fact that
Baraka adopts the Cabral politico-cultural model because Cabral was a
"Marxist-Leninist." For in our consideration of "Marxism-Leninism" (as a
European intellectual product) we must keep in mind that European Marxism-
Leninism did *not* produce a politico-cultural model, but a *politico-economic-
class model.* That this was so is crucial to our understanding as to why European
"Marxist-Leninist" models have been so inapplicable to many features of the
Black experience, *especially the cultural.* However, as pointed out earlier, the
crucial factor for us is that the Amilcar Cabral model *is an African model,* and
as such it must be dealt with *historically.* Before we proceed, then, it is necessary
to briefly examine what Amilcar Cabral meant by "culture." He said:

> The culture of African peoples is an undeniable reality; in *works of art* as well
> as in *oral and written traditions,* in *cosmological conceptions* as well as in *music
> and dance,* in *religions and beliefs* as well as in the dynamic balance of economic,
> political and social structures created by African man . . .

However:

> The fact of recognizing the existence of common and particular features in the
> cultures of African peoples, independent of the color of their skin, does not
> necessarily imply that one and *only one culture exists on the continent.* In the

---

* In this historical sense it is better understood why the aesthetic or spiritual idea of
"Negritude," first conceptualized by African and Caribbean poets, actually had its origins of creative practice in the Harlem Renaissance writers' expressions. The Cabral
politico-cultural model arrives as a further refinement of "Negritude" which should
aid in clearing up disagreements about the concept.

same way that from an economic and political viewpoint we can recognize the existence of several Africas, *so also there are many African cultures* . . .

Hence, Cabral concluded that "In the perspective of developing the economic and social progress of the people" the following objectives must be sought:

Development of a popular culture and of all positive indigenous cultural values; development of a national culture based upon the history of the struggle itself; constant promotion of *political and moral awareness* of the people (of all social groups) as well as *patriotism* of the spirit of sacrifice and devotion to the cause of independence [. . .]

[. . .]

Throughout, Cabral talks about "The need for such an analysis of cultural values . . . to mobilize and organize the people, under the direction of a strong and disciplined political organization. . . ." He points out that, "The analysis of cultural reality already gives a measure of the strengths and weaknesses of the people when confronted with the demands of the struggle."[2] In passing, the writer must point out the similarity of the writer's own views on "culture" to Cabral's thesis on "cultural analysis": "*Thus it is only through a cultural analysis of the (Black) approach to group 'politics' that the errors, weaknesses and goal failures can cogently be analyzed and positively worked out.*"[3]

The above quotes by no means exhaust the thoughts of Cabral on the question of "Liberation and Culture," but are cited as a theoretical point of departure in a determination of the relevancy of the Cabral model to Afro-Americans. Moreover, the Cabral thesis on culture might be of some intellectual service in clearing up a lot of incompetent thinking and puerile confusion emanating from the minds of certain "Black nationalist" militants who simply cannot comprehend what is meant by "culture" in Black terms in the United States.[*]

During the Harlem Renaissance, no one recognized the politico-cultural implications of the period better than Du Bois, both from an intellectual and intuitive response. He attempted to spell out his perceptions in a number of instances, but few of his contemporaries even grasped what he was saying.[4] The real reason for this intellectual and critical lag was that the Black leadership contingent, in addition to being Du Bois' perceptive inferiors, were just 10 years or so removed from the Amenia Conference[**] with barely enough time to heal the wounds of the Washington-Du Bois rift before they were confronted with another leadership emergency—in the person of the perversely flamboyant, bull-headed and egotistical Marcus Garvey. This leadership, coming out of Amenia, was just as unprepared to cope with Garveyism as they were hard put to work out new leadership principles. They would have been just as hard put if Garvey had never arrived. On the other hand, Garvey was just as incompetent to deal with the Afro-American leaders as the latter were ill-prepared to deal with Garveyism, as James W. H. Eason, William Pickens, Emmett J. Scott, and many others, were soon to discover.[†] Garvey's uninhibited bravura simply caught the Amenia Conference graduates off balance as he pursued his utopian misadventure. His successes appeared all the more convincing because they were gleaned from a racial situation which for him [was] circumstantially accidental. Certain

---

*   In *The Crisis of the Negro Intellectual,* this writer's views on the aesthetic, creative and artistic elements of Black culture in the United States are shown to be the same as Cabral's. My views were, however, attacked by Robert Chrisman as follows: "Cruse never defines his vision of culture, or culture itself, for that matter." Later, he says—"Most often, Cruse appears to use culture in the aesthetic sense of the word to indicate the literary, dramatic, musical and philosophical values of black people . . ." Elsewhere, Chrisman asserts—"It is unfortunate that he limits his consideration of culture to the aesthetic realm, for the total culture of a people is composed not only of its arts and philosophy, but also of its tools, work habits and survival patterns." (See *Black Scholar,* November 1969, p.78). Ernest Mkalimoto argues in a similar vein when he complains of the "no small amount of confusion enfulfing the manifold uses of the term 'culture.'" He then insists that "It is mandatory that the term be stripped of all ambiguities as a necessary prelude to its transformation into a genuinely scientific concept." "Afro-American Cultural Nationalism" (*Journal of Ethnic Studies,* Vol. II, No. 2, pp. 1-10.) The Cabral politico-cultural model shows that, despite the prevalent ambiguities and confusions surrounding the term "culture" (which are understandable), the perceptions of Afro-Americans such as Chrisman and Mkalimoto are the conceptual results of *a priori* judgements derived from social-change thought-systems (European Marxism-Leninism, *etc.*) which never included cultural factors in their politico-economic class analytic models.

** Editor's Note: In 1916, a year after Booker T. Washington's death, the NAACP's Joel Spingarn invited leading Blacks to his summer home in Amenia, N.Y. The participants, who achieved a surprising degree of consensus without Washington's divisive influence, passed a strongly worded resolution (drafted primarily by Du Bois) pledging to fight for civil rights far beyond those advocated by the Washington camp.

†   Mary Church Terrell, an Amenia participant, wrote that, "No one who was present could forget the 'Amenia Conference' . . . an effort to induce colored people of all shades and varieties of opinion to thrash out their differences and unite on some definite program of work. There were sixty leaders, men and women from as many different camps." (*A Colored Woman in a White World,* Washington, D.C., 1968) p. 195. In this autobiography, Mrs. Terrell does *not* mention Garvey.

conditions which Garvey inadvertently discovered set the stage for Garveyism, but Garvey did not create those conditions. Garvey's charisma and success actually concealed the fact that he had aroused a movement that had more potential than Garvey himself ever understood.* Using the Cabral politico-cultural theoretical model,** one can even today understand much better the ramifications of the Garvey movement *vis-à-vis* the Harlem Renaissance, plus the leadership outcome of the Amenia Conference.

NOTES

1. Padmore, *Pan-Africanism or Communism?*, p. 158.
2. Amilcar Cabral, "National Liberation and Culture" (1970 Eduardo Mondlane Memorial Lecture) University of Syracuse, February 20, 1970. (Italics added.)
3. Harold Cruse, *The Crisis of the Negro Intellectual,* 1967, p. 14.
4. See W. E. B. Du Bois, "Criteria of Negro Art" (*Crisis,* October 26, 1926) pp. 290-97.

---

* Ida B. Wells (Barnett), who, because of frictions with the NAACP and Du Bois did not attend the Amenia Conference, wrote of her talks with Garvey in Chicago in 1916-17. She relates her suggestions, advice and assistance given to him. She concluded: "Had Garvey had the support which his wonderful movement deserved, had he not become drunk with power too soon, there is no telling what the result would have been . . . Perhaps if Mr. Garvey had listened to my advice he need not have undergone the humiliations which afterwards became his. Perhaps all that was necessary in order to broaden and deepen his own outlook on life." (*The Autobiography of Ida B. Wells,* University of Chicago Press, 1970), pp. 380-2.

** Amilcar Cabral, the founder of the African Party for the Independence of Guinea and the Cape Verde Islands (PAIGC), led the decade-long armed struggle which culminated [in 1974] in the formal recognition of Guinea-Bissau's freedom from Portuguese rule. A Marxist whose theories were firmly grounded in the practical considerations of struggle and ultimate control of a land-base by oppressed people, he set forth his views in a series of articles and lectures published in the United States by the Monthly Review Press under the title *Return To The Source: Selected Speeches by Amilcar Cabral.* [. . .]

CHAPTER TWENTY

The Pan-African Constituency and The Black Electorate

(Methodology & Pan-Africanism, *Black World*, January 1975)

Cruse chronicled the meeting of the National Black Political Convention in the pages of the journal Black World. *In the series excerpted here, he analyzes the ongoing travails of the organization and its attempts to create a viable, "pan-political" umbrella that would encompass the diverse persuasions within Black America. In the essay that follows, Cruse analyzes both the shortsightedness of the "Black Power" ideology as espoused by Stokely Carmichael (Kwame Ture) and Charles V. Hamilton and chronicles the demise of the short-lived consensus between Black liberals and Black nationalists that was, perhaps, the NBPC's signature achievement.*

During January 1974, [Congressman] John Conyers attended a political meeting held in Newark where Conyers voiced grave concern over the state of mind of the Black electorate. At this meeting, Conyers highly commended Imamu Baraka for organizing the affair, and, at the same time, called for a move toward a "third party." He was quoted as saying that, "It is very important that blacks in the top echelon of political leadership nationalize their constituency."[1] By "top echelon," Conyers referred, of course to the 16 Black elected officials in the Congress known as the Congressional Black Caucus, the most prestigious assemblage of Black legislative power in the country since the tense and troubled heyday of Reconstruction. As a member of the Caucus, Conyers advised that, on the matter of nationalizing constituencies, he was speaking only as one member.

This Newark meeting, called by Baraka, was for the purpose of choosing a slate of candidates for office of mayor and Newark's nine councilmanic seats in preparation for the election scheduled, then, for May 1974. This meeting involving Conyers and Baraka was, among other political issues, indicative of Baraka's break with Kenneth Gibson, the Black mayoral incumbent, who, subsequently, won reelection without any support from Baraka. Conyers, however, praised the Baraka-inspired meeting as an example of the "extremely pure democratic process" and as an example of "democracy in its purest sense." He went on to say that the Caucus was a starting point for building a leadership for the nation's 25 to 30 million Blacks, "especially since we are almost 200 years late coming into the political process." The two-party system fails to provide Blacks with sufficient representation, said Conyers. He urged, therefore, that those involved in the Newark meeting take an active part in the upcoming National Black Convention at Little Rock, to help promote the third-party proposal.

Even in the face of the very obvious difficulties that block the road to a Black third party, Conyers' remarks had a ray of hopeful and encouraging light that would imply—"Let's get on with it, we have nothing to lose but our chains of loyalty to the Democrats and Republicans and our decades of unrequited votes." But Conyers immediately cast a sobering shadow of doubt over the issue when he declared that even though a Black agenda was developed at the nation's first Black convention in Gary in 1972, "One of the sad truths that came out of Gary is that most Black people aren't ready to endorse the Black agenda within the two parties."[2] He then added:

> "This is because at this point there's no black elected Democratic leader in the nation who can run off the Democratic Party ticket and win."[3]

One must seriously consider that what Conyers says here is probably the truth about the Black electorate's political outlook today. But what is even more disquieting is that both Conyers and Baraka (and other convenors) actually went through all the motions of the Little Rock convention knowing full-well that the issue of a Black independent party was already a rhetorical matter settled in the negative. A great many others who had attended the Gary convention also were aware that the Black independent party idea was a lost cause in 1974. This probably accounted for the drastically lowered attendance at Little Rock. Thus, the question remains: What did the convenors hope to achieve by staging the Little Rock convention? Was it a mere obligation because it had been planned as a follow-up to Gary? Such a routine justification could be acceptable, except for the fact that so many Black elected officials, including the prestigious Representative Charles Diggs, stayed away. Although everybody knows why they stayed away, their reasons nevertheless need to be reviewed. One Black journalist who maintains that the Little Rock convention was not only a great success but an "unappreciated milestone," claims that it was but an extension of the mandate of Gary, 1972:

The Gary convention established a national mechanism through which city regional, and state caucuses could be established to provide black people—all black people—an instrument of political expression, education, and mobilization on a nonpartisan basis.[4]

For this reporter, Little Rock demonstrated that the "national mechanism" was, indeed, functioning, however much it was in low gear. And he, then, concluded that the reason why so many Black elected officials stayed away was because, "Some public office holders and national leaders are simply not ready to endorse a national political public address system for blacks."[5] In an earlier column, this same reporter had said that "The decisions to turn this (Little Rock) convention into a giant workshop on 'voter mobilization' techniques could be the most 'revolutionary' course chosen by blacks in the last thirty years."[6] Perhaps this *was* the only realistic purpose that brought all the convenors to Little Rock; perhaps this *was* the only "hidden agenda" that made any sense, given the present objective Black political situation. Certainly, most of the resolutions that made the floor were not much different from those ratified at Gary, and one, like the Arab-Israeli resolution, was perversely rhetorical, divisive and strategically unwise in addition to being politically unnecessary. In view of this it appears that Mayor [Richard] Hatcher's oft-stated goal of maximizing the work of voter-registration in the expanding terrain of Black elected officials was the only goal that was underscored at Little Rock, if indeed even it was. In any event, Hatcher called the convention a success, and he must have had his reasons inasmuch as there has been a 152 percent gain in Blacks elected to political office over the last five years. Moreover, by the time John Conyers traveled from his Newark meeting with Baraka in January to Little Rock in March, Conyers had changed his mind about the Black independent party. "There is definitely less discussion at this time of a third party," said Conyers, who conducted a workshop in campaign financing. "That is an enormous undertaking. Our primary purpose is to bring together the broad spectrum of black political views to organize grass roots politics. Talk of a third party is still premature."[7] So, ultimately, Conyers and Hatcher fundamentally agree on what *has* to be, at least for the present pre-1976 election boom, the main strategy of the National Black Political Convention: the more intensive organization of grass-roots voting potential laying fallow in the district strongholds of growing Black elected officaldom. For practical political purposes of augmenting office-holding power, it is the most logical and pragmatic policy to follow. The question is, however, will such a policy serve to help solve some of the dilemmas of a representative like John Conyers?

Even if we accept the expediency of Conyers' vacillating position on the independent Black party issue, his dilemmas remain operational. If it is true, as was asserted by the reporter mentioned above, that "some public officials and national leaders are simply not ready to endorse a national political public address system for blacks," then how does Conyers hope to tackle the issue of getting "the top echelon of political leadership to nationalize their constituency"? Part of this "nationalization" process is the hard grind of intensified voter registration drives in *all* the districts. How much do the BEO's, taken as a whole, really desire such a thorough plowing up of the electoral acreage? In this regard, it is interesting to note that Conyers' own First Congressional district of Michigan, which is a Detroit district, had the second lowest number of congressional votes cast from a Michigan district in 1970. The First Congressional was also the hardest hit by the Detroit urban uprising of 1967. However, Conyers' voting record on Capitol Hill is rated Grade A by the Liberal consensus which places him in the category of a "progressive" in political philosophy (Being Black and from Detroit, how could he be otherwise?). Conyers is able to support both "Black capitalism" and cross-district school busing with equal fervor as Black progressivism. Yet, with all this going for him, the gap between Conyers and the bulk of his own grass-roots district constituency drew from him the very candid assertion that "most black people" aren't ready to endorse either the National Black Agenda or the idea of forming an independent party. But the gap operates both ways, because Conyers also pointed out that the top echelon BEO's are equally as unenthusiastic about an independent Black party as the Black electorate because they know that "no Black elected Democratic leader in the nation . . . can run off the Democratic ticket and win."

In terms of the future of Black Politics (say from now to 1984), the dilemmas of a John Conyers, and his own assessments of these dilemmas, a number of problematic questions are posed. One is this: To what degree would a dramatically stepped up voter-registration drive in heavily Black districts entice the top echelon BEO's to attempt to "nationalize" their constituencies? Further, would this hoped-for expansion and consolidation of these district constituencies constitute a potential step forward in the direction of a Black independent party? Would such an incremental expansion of the aggregate electoral base inspire a brave member of the top echelon BEO's to run independent of the conventional two-party ticket with the daring hope to "win"? Given the current state of mind of the top echelon BEO's, the answer is probably an emphatic no! And one of the reasons for this candid appraisal of the BEO's is that the reason they are in politics is *only to "win."* Today, "winning" is the strategy trap that will forever forestall the consolidation of a Black independent party constituency. "Winning" is the perennial goal of conventional American politics—the be-all and end-all of aspiring to and holding political office. But a Black independent party must set out to build up and sustain an ongoing constituency around a select number of programmatic issues, from one election year to the next, whether the party "wins" any elective office(s) or not. In this regard, the Pan-Africanist, Owusu Sadaukai, is about 90 percent correct when he forcefully argues that there is much more to Black politics than electoral campaigns. It is this all-consuming issue of "winning" which basically separates the top echelon of BEO's from the challenge of Conyers' call to "nationalize" the Black constituencies. Conyers is as much aware of this as anyone, which further compounds his dilemmas. Another apparent feature of Conyers' dilemmas is his strange and seemingly strong political attachment to Imamu Baraka.

[The journalist] Chuck Stone surmised that the future of the independent third-party thrust depended upon whose viewpoints prevail—Baraka's Hatcher's, or Dellum's. What has apparently happened since Little Rock is that Hatcher's post-convention strategies have prevailed, at the same time that Baraka's ideological clutch-hold on the National Black Political Convention has also prevailed. . . . If we are permitted to cite the defection of Charles Diggs from the National Black Political Convention as one indication, then it is also clear that even those few top echelon BEO's who once supported the National Black Political Agenda have abandoned open ties to Baraka. But where does this leave Conyers? In defending himself against the criticisms of Hatcher for failing to attend the Little Rock convention, Diggs replied that perhaps a National Black Political Convention is too huge an umbrella to cover the large variety of political groupings within the Black community. "Maybe we are fooling ourselves," he added. [. . .] "National and local elected officials were critical of the convention's program because it was not relevant to their needs." As for himself, Diggs objected "being automatically folded in under the so-called Baraka formula," meaning the Baraka-enforced change in the rules regarding selection for delegate status.[8] [. . .]

Here is more evidence of Baraka's "clutch-hold" on the convention process, the ideological bottle-neck of the National Black Political Convention as a "new form." Diggs complained bitterly that the Baraka-enforced rules change were "one of the major reasons for the lack of black elected officials at the convention." "Here are people with a proven constituency," said Diggs. "They are leaders by their election to public office. The rules were okay two years ago (at Gary). Why aren't they now?"[9] The catch here is that Imamu Baraka is *also* a leader! To be sure, it is not by virtue of elected office, but by dint of his complete sway over a disciplined Pan-Africanist constituency in his own hometown. When Imamu Baraka, as LeRoi Jones, abandoned the degenerating and dangerous scene of Harlem Black nationalist politics of the late Sixties and retreated to Newark, it was more of the "Prodigal's Return" than his poetic sensibilities that suggested the title *Home* for his next book! Thus the Pan-Africanist constituency that Baraka proceeded to build in Newark has now emerged as the most crucial constituency in the politics of the National Black Political Convention. The proven political leaders mentioned by Diggs cannot cope with this constituency in the arena of the National Black Convention. Yet, because of the defections of Diggs and the top echelon BEO's, the National Black Political Convention as a "new form" is left dangling in awkward internal disarray, clinging to a semblance of organizational viability only because the viewpoints of Hatcher have prevailed to give it a claim to continuity. Where does all this leave Conyers? Diggs? Baraka?—*vis-à-vis* the NBPC? Programmatically, it is Diggs who should be closer to Baraka than Conyers in view of Diggs' intimate and official role in the affairs of the House Sub-Committee on African Affairs, his watchdog function into the affairs of South Africa and the role of American corporate business investments in that land of racial *apartheid,* his leadership activities in the African-American Conference of Africa and the African Liberation Day activities of May 1972. For a brief spell, it seemed that neo-Pan-Africanism in the United States had found a genuine representative in the halls of Congress. However, Coleman Young, Detroit's Black mayor, has implied that this interest in Africa surfaced only after Diggs became chairman of the sub-committee on

Africa in 1969. "Where was he when the United States was all over the Congo? When Nkrumah was deposed (with possible CIA involvement)?" asked Young. "He hasn't identified himself with militant anti-imperialist groups until the last few years."[10] [. . .] Diggs can very well move away from Imamu Baraka's Pan-Africanist constituency in Newark with impunity, but in Detroit, says one source, "Black nationalist movements are strong . . . , among them the Pan-African movement and the Republic of New Africa. While their programs are more third party and separatist oriented, Diggs must find ways to relate to them. Of the three or four senior members of the Black Caucus, Diggs is more likely to be pressured."[11] [. . .] At any rate, Diggs' move away from the National Black Political Convention is his declaration that the top echelon BEO's is his true home, the only real constituency to whom he must pay his dues of loyalty.*

NOTES

1. *Newark Star-Ledger,* January 20, 1974.
2. Ibid.
3. Ibid.
4. Vernon Jarrett, "Black Convention of 1974: Unappreciated Milestone" (*Chicago Tribune,* March 24, 1974).
5. Ibid.
6. *Chicago Tribune,* March 14, 1974.
7. *Chicago Tribune,* March 17, 1974.
8. Washington, D. C., *Afro-American,* March 30, 1974.
9. *Afro-American,* Cited, March 30.
10. Citizens Look at Congress, Ralph Nader Congress Project, "Charles C. Diggs, Jr." p. 15.
11. Ibid., p. 9

---

* [This is not published in its entirety. The concluding sentence "At any rate . . ." appeared in an earlier paragraph in the original version. This editorial change was made in order to conclude the essay in light of other sections which were omitted due to space considerations.—W. J. C.]

CHAPTER TWENTY-ONE

Review of the Paul Robeson Controversy

(*First World*, 1979)

Occupying the disparate niches of artist, intellectual, activist, and denizen of the Left, Paul Robeson's outsized life elicited commentary from virtually every corner of American society. Like Malcolm X and W. E. B. Du Bois, Robeson had, in the years following his death, become community property—a multifaceted figure whose life and intellectual output could be claimed by any number of diverse, and often antagonistic, political elements. A flood-tide of ink was spilled attempting to define Robeson as Black nationalist, Left internationalists, or liberal integrationist. Harold Cruse dealt with Robeson in The Crisis of the Negro Intellectual *as a metaphor for the broader tragedy in Negro life "which is essentially cultural." Moreover, according to Cruse, Robeson—and his relationship with the Left—typified the dilemma of the black artist. Laboring under the influence of white liberal benefactors—since there were no autonomous black institutions to support their work—black artists were, in Cruse's view, consistently compromised. In this regard, the Communist Party was only degrees removed from the upper-income Negrophiles who*

underwrote the Harlem Renaissance. Correspondingly, the "social realism" move-
ment of the 1930s did as much to distort the realities of Negro life as the primitivism
and black exotica that characterized the preceding decade. Twelve years later, Cruse
returned to the subject of Robeson, writing in response to historian Sterling Stuckey's
well-known arguments regarding Paul Robeson as Afro-American cultural nation-
alist. Cruse, it is safe to say, disagreed.

The article in Volume 2, Number 2 of *First World* by Sterling Stuckey and
Joshua Leslie, "Reflections on Reflections About the Black Intellectual" was both
a calamity, in terms of scholarly execution, and a belated revaluation of the fact
that *The Crisis of the Negro Intellectual* (1967) was not written in vain. If nothing
else, *The Crisis . . .* , 12 years later can inspire even shallow "reflections" on the
part of Stuckey (with help). Since he is not known for excessive output of
wordage beyond the limits of his Ph.D. dissertation, [. . .] these delayed
"reflections" border on the phenomenal. But the total results represent an
embarrassing excuse for serious thought. Such an incoherent pastiche of
intellectual subterfuge, dishonest evasion and negative obscurantism merits the
dignity of a response only for the fact that the piece *does* raise a number of
controversial issues that should have been clarified, if not resolved, ages ago. The
fault is mine.

One overriding fact behind Stuckey's misguided missile is that he never liked
The Crisis . . . as a book. But then, *The Crisis . . .* was not written with the
expectations that it would be smothered with affectionate academic embraces of
the Stuckey persuasion. It was anticipated that two salient issues would continue
to rattle the Stuckey type of mind—the Paul Robeson question and the problem
of "Black Culture." All of the other "reflections" can be dismissed as petty
conceptual knit-picking. Stuckey's "culture" notions are antiquarian.

First it is important to note that *The Crisis . . .* devoted only 17 pages (out
of 565) to Robeson. Those 17 pages have caused more agonized recriminations
from Robeson zealots than my uncomplimentary remarks about Robeson's
Communist Party friends—and for good reasons. Debating unresolved issues
surrounding the impact of "Black Culture" was one of the main reasons for my
writing *The Crisis . . . .* More than that, the career of Paul Robeson personifies,
more than that of any other Black-culture hero of the 20th Century, the complex
ramifications of the Black cultural experience. However, the key, underlying
problem in dealing with the Robeson issue is that Black intellectuals, as a class-
segment, do *not* possess a *functional* concept of culture within which to frame
their vague, conflicting, contradictory sentiments, notions, tastes and aesthetic

responses to the creative and interpretive problems related to the *artistic* elements of Black culture. In other words, Black intellectuals do not possess a cultural methodology that is both critically functional or historically grounded in the *evolutionary* aspects of culture.

Because of this serious flaw in the Black intellectual tradition, I committed what is essentially the gravest error in *The Crisis*. . . . The error was to assume that my critical references to "culture" would be interpreted as an attempt to open up discussion around the fact that we possessed no *cultural methodology* that is (politically) functional. It is significant that, 10 years ago, Robert Chrisman attacked this weakness, and Sterling Stuckey repeats it with the jibe: ". . . Cruse . . . hardly ever discusses Black culture as such and never defines it." It is not worth the bother to call attention to Stuckey's sophistry on this point. One need only read my chapters on "cultural democracy." More edifying on this problem is to point out that a bellwether of Black historical opinion such as the *Journal of Negro History,* from 1916 to 1970, hardly ever deals with Black cultural issues which highlights the lack of a cultural methodology in the Black intellectual tradition. This journal emphasizes political and "social" history but *not* cultural history. This also explains, in part, why the *Journal of Negro History* has never seriously dealt with a major figure such as Robeson. What it all means is that Stuckey (and Chrisman before him) and I are arguing about the same thing, but approaching the same cultural phenomena from different critical perspectives and personal experiences. [The absence of cultural methodology makes this unavoidable.]

But in coping with the Robeson controversy, it is necessary to be clear as to *which* Robeson one is talking about. In my view, there are essentially five phases to Robeson's life, roughly 1898-1920, 1921-1931; 1932-1940, 1941-1957; 1958-1976. The Robeson I am most concerned with was the Robeson of 1939 (his return to the U.S.) to 1976. This is the disputed Robeson, the controversial Robeson. This is not the pre-1940 Paul Robeson about which there can be little dispute as to the man's stature. By 1940, Robeson was considered to be "The Most Important Negro in the World." Regarding this assessment, I have no argument. Robeson supporters, very naturally, construe my criticisms as "attacks" on Robeson. I maintain that, after 1940, Robeson opened himself to the vulnerability of the type of criticism against which no single leader, no matter how great, is exempt. There has never been a single "leader" of any race or nation that was perfect, infallible or all-wise in the virtues of directing the destiny of peoples, nations or races. Paul Robeson was no exception, especially after 1940.

Sterling Stuckey's approach to Robeson is to apotheosize the multifaceted persona of Robeson into a unified, synthesized image that was all of a piece, *sui generis*, and was not the ultimate product of a unique evolution—an evolution which, in itself, merits a probing criticism. For it would be impossible to cope with the problems of the lack of a cultural methodology on the part of Black intellectuals today, unless historical culture-heroes such as Robeson are critically assessed within the context of *their* cultural evolution. Anything less is merely the methodology of Hero-Worship represented by the Sterling Stuckey enthusiasm, which adds up to poor history.

It is for this reason that Stuckey's (and Leslie's) article is so flagrant with ahistorical assertions, such as, for example, the petulant argument over the relative importance of Harlem, New York, to Black America of the 20th Century. One need only to be reminded that without Harlem there might have been no Paul Robeson, the famous actor-singer. It was the great migrations of World War I that in 15 years had established in Harlem the largest single Black community in the entire United States, if not the world. Without this "Cultural Capitol of the Black World,"[1] there would have been no Black semi-pro theater in the YWCA in which a Paul Robeson could have been discovered by Greenwich Village whites who took him downtown to star in a famous drama; who, later, organized his first concert of "Negro Spirituals" and launched him on the road to international stardom. Aside from the fact that it wasn't *Blacks* who did this, but *whites,* this evolution of Robeson is also significant for the fact that Robeson never consciously sought out and pursued this path to stardom on his own. Robeson's own wife, Eslanda, described Robeson adequately when she wrote:

> (Paul) read law occasionally with his class-mates and friends, but did not bestir himself to find a job. Paul was very lazy. He was not a person to think out what he would do or wanted to do and then go out and try to do it. There was no trace of aggressiveness in his makeup.[2]

A few years later, Robeson admitted, in an interview following his theatrical successes in England, that he couldn't explain his success:

> (Eugene) O'Neill and others repeatedly asked me to do the "Emperor (Jones)."
> I didn't want to. I was too interested in the law. At last, however, I fell for it.
> I played the "Emperor" and the London critics said I was one of the great actors!
> Soon after I was persuaded to sing in public. I did after much discussion.
> Immediately I was proclaimed a great singer! I had never sung in public before;
> I had never had a lesson in singing in my life!
>
> I simply couldn't understand it. I didn't sing these spirituals in any tradition,
> because I didn't know any tradition. I knew the songs from the time I was a

child and they were mostly songs sung in unison by a lot of people. I just sang them as I felt their meaning.[3]

This interview took place in London in 1928 during the phase in Robeson's evolution when he had been decidedly an *apolitical* individual, with no more special pride in race (or African descent) than numerous other Harlem Blacks of his generation. In his 1976 monograph on Robeson, "*I Want to be African,*" Stuckey tries to portray Robeson as a (Black) Nationalist that sprang full blown from his family womb of race nationalism, ideologically prepared to pursue the "Ends of Nationalist Theory and Practice, (from) 1919 to 1945." Thus it is not strange that Stuckey finds nothing to quote from Robeson on this "nationalist" reference until 1935! It is also significant that Stuckey quotes nothing from Eslanda Robeson's book about her husband written in 1930. If Robeson had been as "nationalist" as Stuckey makes out, between 1919 and 1930, Mrs. Robeson would certainly have revealed this in her book. This is neither a "criticism" nor an "attack" on Robeson to make this important point. It is merely to put the real facts of Robeson evolution in their proper focus. In 1928, out of Robeson's own mouth came the words, "I did not sing these spirituals in any tradition *because I didn't know any tradition.*" I translate this statement to mean he also did not know *any musical tradition before he was encouraged to exhibit his natural singing voice.* [. . .]

The first time I ever saw Robeson in a film was in *Sanders of the River* at the Harlem Alhambra. I suppose it would also be "impertinent" to say that I thought Robeson was an ass and damned fool for appearing in such a film. Of course, Stuckey, having been a mere *two years old* when *Sanders of the River* was made in 1934, would have to consult The New York Times Index in order to appreciate the temper of the times. Even then, as his history writing reveals, he probably would not have appreciated the fact that my first reaction to the great Culture-Hero was not very complimentary. [. . .] It is, however, not an "attack" on Robeson to say he disgusted me for appearing in that film. After all, we had Black actors during the Thirties who consented to play in more execrable films than *Sanders . . . ,* because they had no choice (if they wanted to be in films). With Robeson, however, he *had* choices and was *not* starving. Yet, with all the "Black Nationalist" consciousness that Stuckey ascribes to the hero, he consented to appear in a film depicting the colonialist point of view on Africa!

[. . .]

As for Robeson's musicality, I was, admittedly, very careless in my assertions on this point. I was not about writing a definitive critique of Paul

Robeson, thus I made these music references, merely in passing, as part of my general observations of the man's musical point of view, tendencies and philosophy. In making these comments in *The Crisis* . . . , caution should have suggested that I elaborate more on these statements, or else not make them at all. However, had the scholarship on Robeson *now* available been available to me in 1965-1967, my random statements on Robeson's musicality would have been even stronger and more explicit. Excerpts from Philip Foner's recent *Paul Robeson Speaks* strengthen my original contentions.

Black music is an integral, in fact, dominant artistic and creative element in Black culture, and Paul Robeson was one of the great communicators of Black musical culture. It was said by connoisseurs of concert music that Paul Robeson and Lawrence Tibbet (white) had the two greatest bass-baritones in the United States. Robeson was *also* an actor, but never received any extended training either as an actor or singer.

As a singer, Robeson's stated preferences were "Negro Spirituals and Folksongs." However, Robeson's *acting* accomplishments were on the *classical* level, since Shakespeare's *Othello* is a *classical* drama. [. . .]

[I]n Paul Robeson, one encounters what I consider a contradictory and intellectually inconsistent attitude towards the creative implications of the evolution of Black music up to the 1920's. [. . .] When interviewed by a reporter in London, 1933, on his musicality, Robeson said he would sing to his audiences in Russian, Hebrew, or Chinese, but that he would never sing again in either French, German, or Italian:

> I will not do anything that I do not understand. I do not understand the psychology or philosophy of the Frenchman, German, or Italian. Their history has nothing in common with the history of my slave ancestors. So I will not sing their music or the songs of their ancestors.[4]

My comment: Paul Robeson had a right to determine *his* personal *taste* in music, as a concert singer. However, in 1933, his personal *taste* in music was no proof that he understood the psychology of Russians, Hebrews, or Chinese, any better than he understood the psychology of Frenchmen, Germans or Italians, inasmuch as he had not acquired, in 1933, any extensive living experience in the context of any of those European, Asian or Middle Eastern cultural contexts. Note that Robeson did not abandon the "English" scene of London for the Russian scene of Moscow until 1935.

In this same interview, Robeson continued:

I fail to see how a Negro can really feel the sentiments of an Italian or a German, or a Frenchman, for instance. So I really can't see where the achievement is in singing in an opera in any of these languages. Of course, if there were a great opera written by a Negro on an African theme, I should say it would be just as insignificant an achievement for a white opera singer to give a credible performance of it.

I believe that one should confine oneself to the art for which one is qualified. One can only be qualified by understanding, and this is born in one, not bred.[5]

First, note that Robeson did not, in this interview, cite the possibility of a "great opera" written by a "Negro" on an "*Afro-American*" theme! *This studied omission is central to this debate*, inasmuch as Robeson never, once, visited Black Africa, for an "understanding" of a cultural context he wasn't "born" in. The main point is *not* to argue with Robeson's (or anyone else's) *personal taste* in music. [. . .] But given Robeson's exceptional musical abilities, and given the Black Cultural context in which he emerged, given his educational background, it is *not* "impertinent" to point out that there were both jarring and intellectually unjustified inconsistencies in Robeson's cultural views, especially in music. On the face of it, no matter how great or exceptional were Robeson's *individual* accomplishments up to 1933, his critical judgments on black music (and European music) were out of line with the wide cultural range of both creative and interpretive challenges *and* imperatives facing *all* Blacks in America in the creative fields of music, literature, theater and dance.

In 1931, Robeson had elaborated on his musical views in a *New York Times* interview, in which he said:

Wherever large Negro audiences welcomed him, there was a demand for the inclusion of the German, French and Continental classics on his programs. "It always makes me unhappy to do this," he went on. "I prefer a program made up of spirituals, because I know therein lies our sound and enduring contribution . . . By accepting the white man's music we are passing out of the scene as creators and interpreters . . . Either we must encourage (and) preserve our folk music, or we must leave this country, . . . and go to Africa, where we can develop independently and bring forth a new music based on old roots.[6]

[. . .] Note, *again*, that Robeson, by clear inference, dismisses the possibility of the Afro-American composers of his time (1930's) to "*Develop independently and bring forth a new music based on old roots*" in the United States! Why Paul Robeson would conclude, in 1931, that Afro-Americans would have to go to Africa to preserve and develop Black folk-music is difficult to understand or even justify when Afro-American composers *were* involved in the process of preserving and developing folk music right under Robeson's nose since the 1890's. *Why did not Robeson make reference to these composers?* Why did Robeson repeatedly reveal a negative attitude toward Afro-American creativity? [. . .]

What Robeson was implying (from 1931 to 1933) was that other Black concert singers of his generation were *achieving nothing at all* by singing "in any opera in foreign languages" (i.e., French, German or Italian) which suggested that Marian Anderson, Jules Bledsoe, Roland Hayes, Caterina Jarboro, Todd Duncan, Lillian Evanti (plus all those forgotten hopefuls studying music and voice) were proving nothing at all beyond the fact that they had good voices. However, it was perfectly permissible, and "culturally apropos," for *him,* Robeson, to learn Russian so as to be able to sing selections from the Russian opera, *Boris Godunov,* which is one of the great *European operas* out of the Russian *classical* tradition. [. . .] If one would apply Robeson's logic on the classical opera to the reasons for his mastery of *Othello,* as classical theater, one would, according to him, have to conclude that his performances of *Othello* had no substantial, "cultural" meaning at all, beyond the fact that Robeson could act as well as sing.

Deep confusion of values here!

However, the audiences who applauded Robeson's mastery of *Othello* as classical drama, did not do so as a response to the blase notion—"Well, all it proves is that Robeson is just another Black actor who can really act." Not at all! The audiences applauded Robeson because he, as a Black actor, was demonstrating conclusively that here was a Black man who could master English *classical* drama.

[. . .]

It would be historically blind for one to justify Robeson's views on "Negro Folk Music" in the face of the challenges that Blacks had to confront on both the cultural front and in the *educational* arena. Robeson's views on "Negro Folk Music" were at odds with his own generation of Black concert singers, *and also his own generation of Black composers.* The other famous Black singers, *all* of them, were accomplished in *both* "Negro Folk Music" and European classics, including opera and other forms of concert music. It could not be otherwise. [. . .] Simply because Robeson, as one exception to this educational process, received no extensive training in music (because of his natural voice), was able to gain fame *only* on the basis of "Negro Folk Music," in no way justifies his implied derogation of Black singers whose repertory included European music. But Robeson had to know that, in order for him to be able to match the repertory of a Marian Anderson or a Roland Hayes, he would have had to submit to considerable study, training or coaching. With the kind of voice Robeson naturally possessed, it required no extensive coaching to manage a repertory of "Negro Folk Songs." All he really needed was what he had, his able accompanist, Lawrence Brown.

In defense of his intellectually awkward position on "Negro Folk Music," Robeson insisted that his aim was "preserving the unique contribution of his race to the music of America." (This was, of course, *after* his discovery in 1928 that he really did represent a tradition!) He thought of himself as opposing those Blacks who were "ashamed" of the Spirituals, which was an indication of more vanity, inasmuch as not *all* Blacks were ashamed of Negro folk music. Maud Cuney Hare, in her definitive study of Black music (1936) cited the activities of numerous Black music societies engaged in preserving the Spirituals. The original group was the Fisk Jubilee Singers, who, from 1871 to 1932, gave concerts in the United States and Europe. In 1932, the old group was replaced by younger sisters, and the Jubilee choir continued. Moreover, practically every Black concert singer sang Black folksongs and Spirituals during the Twenties and Thirties.

Whatever one might think of Robeson's rationale for singing only folksongs, writers, dramatists, dancers, poets, etc., could not have conformed to Robeson's artistic criteria for the Afro-American creative tradition. For it would have meant that a talented writer would eschew the "modern" novel or short story in favor of slave or plantation folktales or narratives for plot materials. Playwrights would have reverted to minstrel show plots for new plays, Dancers, in the 1920's would have rehashed the Juba dance, the Buzzard Lope, the Eagle Rock, the Camel Walk and not produced the Charleston or the Lindy Hop, or the choreographic schools of Katherine Dunham or Pearl Primus. Poets would have gone on imitating Paul Lawrence Dunbar or Sterling Brown in their predilections for "Negro Dialect Poetry" or refined Negro folk poetry idiom. On this point, one should reread Darwin T. Turner's study on "Paul Lawrence Dunbar: The Rejected Symbol."

The argument here is that the 1920's presented the Black intellectual, the Black artist, writer, composer, singer, dancer, actor, painter, poet, educator, student, and critic, difficult challenges which the Afro-American had not faced prior to World War I. In order to win approval, status, respect, recognition in the arts, in the social sciences, in literature, in music, in philosophy, education, in whatever, a Black candidate had to measure up and master the knowledge, the experiences, the techniques, the research, the theories and practices of these disciplines as they related to *both* the American and the European experiences. It is safe to say that if W. E. B. Du Bois had not spent time at the University of Berlin learning the very latest in German scientific social science methodology that Du Bois would not have produced *The Philadelphia Negro* when he did (not to speak of his Atlanta research studies). For Du Bois to have rejected German methodology for the "cultural" reasons that Robeson scorned German opera would have been ridiculous.

However, let me reiterate: to say all of this is *not* an "attack" on Robeson, *per se*, but a *criticism* of the intellectual and cultural context that produced Robeson. Robeson, himself, was merely one reflection of the cultural contradictions, flaws, discrepancies, confusions and obscurantism that permeated the cultural responses of *both* Blacks and whites during the 1920's and thereafter. *The cultural* effects of the 1920's experience are still with us; the problems posed by the 1920's have not been resolved in terms of cultural criticism, cultural methodology, cultural analysis. In his apotheosization of a Culture-Hero such as Paul Robeson, a historian such as Sterling Stuckey only confounds in 1979 what was already compounded in 1929, further compounded in 1939 when Paul Robeson *had* to return to the United States because he had been forced out of England and Europe by the Hitler menace and World War II (Not because he really wanted to come home!) [. . .]

Robeson's studied preferences for "Negro Folk Music," coupled with his singular rejection of (German, French, Italian) opera (while at the same time, by implication, extolling Russian opera) is interpreted by me as indicating that Robeson did not think very highly of Black composers who, unlike his accompanist, Lawrence Brown, attempted to build "extended" compositional themes on the "Negro Folk Music" base.

[. . .] Sterling Stuckey's description of Robeson as personifying the substance of "Black Nationalist" theory from 1919 onwards proves that Stuckey is a poor cultural historian for not recognizing the fact that there existed a "Black Nationalist" school of music composition which Robeson did not acknowledge. [. . .] What would one say of an accomplished Black actor who did not acknowledge the existence of Black playwrights and their written works! [. . .] In all his published statements, from 1921 to 1939, Robeson never acknowledged the work of a single successful Black playwright. [. . .]

Long before the 1930's, when Robeson arrived in Russia to be enthralled by the Russian intellectual, creative and cultural mystique, Russian composers [. . .] had succeeded in "classicizing" Russian folk-music. [. . .] If Paul Robeson felt such a keen sense of "cultural" affinity between the Russian experience and the Black experience in the U.S. [. . .] it is quite evident that he wasn't perceptive enough to cite and compare *all the historical and cultural parallels* peculiar to both the Russian and the Afro-American evolutions in creative culture and to respond to them as would befit an individual of his educational background and international status. After all, Robeson had the responsibilities, the opportunities, the options and the obligations to accomplish much more than he actually did towards educating his *own* people (especially Black creative artists) in the realities, the problems, the challenges inherent in developing Black *creative* culture. [. . .]

It was true that the Russian serfs under the Czars were "slaves" in much the same fashion as were Black slaves in the ante-bellum South. It was also an interesting coincidence that Emperor Alexander II issued his revolutionary "Edict of Emancipation" that liberated the serfs in 1861, at the beginning of the American Civil War! Thereafter, the musical content and styles of Russian peasant and Afro-American folk-music revealed striking similarities in mood, structure and tone. It was also culturally striking that both the Russian and Afro-American folk-music traditions produced "nationalist" schools of advanced music composition. It was this music from the Russian "nationalist" school that the Russian singers of Robeson's caliber were singing long before Robeson went to Russia. *In Afro-American terms, Robeson's interpretive accomplishments lagged behind Afro-American creative accomplishments in music compositions.*

For example, Maude Cuney Hare, and Eileen Southern, both leading music historians and Black professional musicians, deal at length with what Southern described as "The Nationalist Movement in the United States," in Black music terms. Eileen Southern writes:

> Almost the entire first group of post-slavery black composers, i.e., those born before 1900—may be regarded as nationalists in the sense that they consciously turned to the folk music of their people as a source of inspiration for their composed music, whether in the fields of concert music, show music, or dance and entertainment music.[7]

[. . .] In describing the work of these composers, Southern writes: "Most of those who achieved distinction . . . were excellently trained; they had studied at Oberlin, the New England Conservatory, and the National Conservatory of New York . . . Consequently, they knew how to write music in traditional European style and, indeed, often did so, particularly when they wanted the music to sell. But they reserved much of their creative energy for Negro-inspired composition."

[. . .] The life-span of these "nationalistic" composers coincided with Robeson's singing career from the 1920's through 1939—[Harry] Burleigh, (1886-1949) [Clarence Cameron] White (1880-1960), [R. Nathaniel] Dett (1882-1943), [John Wesley] Work (1873-1925), [Charles] Cook (1869-1944). Between 1875 and the year of his death, 1943, Harry Lawrence Freeman composed 14 operas bearing such titles as *Voodoo* (1928), *The Zulu King* (1934), and *The Slave*. In fact, the entire group of (Black) "nationalist" composers devoted their craft to the rendition of "Negro Folk Music" into symphonies, cantatas, operas, tone poems, oratorios, *etc.,* yet a thorough examination of all of Robeson's pronouncements on Black music reveals that Robeson was unaware of the work of *most* of these composers, or else did not consider them worthy of mention, even in terms of his own concert role.

∼

The historian Sterling Stuckey responded to Cruse's criticism by saying: "In examining the hundreds of news items on Robeson during his years abroad, Cruse would have been hard pressed to find a single one in which Robeson's concern for Africa and Black American culture was not the theme—even in those articles featuring Robeson on the society pages of Black newspapers. Such themes, moreover, continued to dominate coverage of Robeson throughout the decade of the 1940s."

NOTES

1. James Weldon Johnson, *Black Manhattan* (1930), p. 9.
2. Eslanda Goode Robeson, *Paul Robeson—Negro* (1930), p. 73.
3. Philip Foner, *Paul Robeson Speaks—Writings, Speeches, Interviews* (1978), p.77.
4. Foner, p. 85.
5. Ibid. On this musical point note that Giacomo Meyerbeer, a German, had written an opera in French, *L'Africaine* (The African), which was premiered in the United States December 1, 1865. The African queen in this opera was named Selika. In 1880, Mrs. Sampson Williams, a Black female coloratura soprano, adopted the professional name of Madame Marie Selika, and, along with her baritone husband, toured Europe giving "classical" concerts. As late as the 1930's, Mme. Selika was a voice teacher in Harlem, New York. From the French point of view, Meyerbeer's *L'Africaine* was as legitimate as was Shakespeare's *Othello* from the English point of view, and also from Robeson's point of view in interpreting the "Moor" of Venice. (See: Maud Cuney Hare: *Negro Musicians and Their Music,* pp. 222-240.
6. Foner, pp. 81-82.
7. Eileen Southern, *The Music of Black Americans* (1971), p. 283.

CHAPTER TWENTY-TWO

"Letter to Ralph Story"

(Unpublished, September 10, 1986)

This letter was written in response to a paper that Ralph Story, a colleague of Harold Cruse at the University of Michigan, wrote about connections between Afro-American writers, their aesthetic output, and the sociocultural climate in which their work is produced.

Dear Ralph Story:

I've read and re-read your paper "Extra Literary Conditions for Afro-American Writers" with great interest, but with some critical reactions. It is a very good paper in and of itself. My suggestion is that you do not probe the "extra literary" extensively enough. More than that, I feel you do not give enough critical insights to the problem of black writers' thematic content and the insufficiencies most evident in their overall thematic content. Not only are black writers frustrated by the extra-literary factors you cite which are problematic enough; they are also disadvantaged by the self-imposed limitations of their thematic and topical content. I speak as one of those black writers you cite.

A writer (novelist, fiction, etc.) black or white is either a social critic, inadvertently or by design, or he (she) is nothing to be remembered. Black life is problematic life to a greater degree than other group lives (and so are black-white relations). Thus, black writers, if not "social critics" (after the fashion of a Balzac, for example) do not live up either to their calling (or their potential) as novelists or fiction writers. This is, of course, only one critic's opinion. Serious novelists (black or white) are either controversial or they matter very little. Serious fiction writers cannot write simply to "please" their intended audience. A serious black fiction writer cannot aim to please either blacks or whites (or both) at the same time. Today the proposition goes even further—black writers of fiction cannot write to please either *gender* and claim to be a "serious" writer. . . . This I think explains Chester Himes who was, in my view, a serious novelist and "social critic," thus nobody liked him very much—neither blacks or whites.

During the 1930's and 1940's some publishers would object to manuscripts by blacks on the grounds "They have an axe to grind against whites for their treatment of blacks." This was the "protest novel" that Baldwin once criticized in one of his essays. Richard Wright's *Native Son* was not cordially accepted by most blacks because the novel was not really a "protest novel" of the axe-grinding variety. It was the unabashed "Dostievskian" work of a genuine "social critic" who did not care what either blacks or whites actually thought about his portrayals. A novelist in creating "character" (black or white), must be prepared to depict the "good" and the "bad," the "moral" and "immoral," the "positives" and the "negatives" of character(s) and how these character traits impact [on] "society." The writer as "social critic" must depict life in this manner or else be a writer of little consequence. I recall that Theodore Ward, a black dramatist of the 1930's and 1940's, once gave me a problem to think about. He said I want you to think about this proposition—"Why do you think that black people will never be able to produce a black Henrik Ibsen (or a Shaw, or a Dickens)? Think about this and when you understand why some day, come and tell me your conclusions." The reasons have nothing to do with the fact that Ibsen, Shaw and Dickens are 19th-century writers, but with a writer's *social point of view* on social and human reality.

Black women writers, generally, do not measure up as serious "social critics" in the manner of, let us say, a Mary McCarthy, because their main literary objective is to glorify or enhance the blighted image of black womanhood which, in their view, needs revamping according to the impulses of the new black Feminism. Thus there are no "bad" or "immoral" or "dishonest" or "crafty" or "scheming" or "opportunistic" black women characters. Black women are all victims of "male oppression" (i.e. both black and white males). However, Ann

Petry in her 1940's novel *The Street* accomplished a pro-black female novel with the same quality of literary finesse as Toni Morrison, which is to say without feminist axe-grinding against black men. But this feminist literary quality among black women is a rare quality.

My view is that black writers (male and female) are inflicted with a thematic flaw. Their lack of the "social critic's" capacity is revealed in their lack of "objectivity" in their failure to deal perceptively with the black middle class, taking a leaf out of the literary work of a Balzac or a Sinclair Lewis. A Sinclair Lewis novel like *Kingsblood Royal* (about race) unfortunately could not be written by a black writer. E. Franklin Frazier's sociological analysis of the black middle class has provided a compendium of endless thematic material for black novelists which they shy away from as if it were forbidden territory. Which leads me to conclude that the roots of the black writer's "Extra Literary Condition" lie more in themselves than in the conditions imposed by the white-dominated publishing world. Black writers share the values of the black middle class (even as they write about the black working classes) to such a degree that it blunts their literary perceptions of social reality.

A good example (in my view) is Ralph Ellison who, inexplicably, you do not include implicitly in your essay. Why? What precise "Extra Literary Conditions" have prevented Ellison from producing another significant novel since *Invisible Man?* It is my conviction that Ellison opted for the life of an "Extra Literary Condition," an energy-consuming professorship that afforded him (and Fanny) ample financial supports for a comfortable, unchallenging, middle-class existence. (Fanny wouldn't allow for anything else, in my view!) Note the fact that Richard Wright, Chester Himes e.g., were supported in their literary careers by white women, not black women. This is an "Extra Literary Condition" of no mean importance, if one wants to explore the entire range of [factors] impacting on black male writers.

You mention the attempted collaboration between Langston Hughes and Zora Neale Hurston with the assertion that Hughes reflected a sexist and chauvinistic attitude toward Hurston which undermined their collaboration. However, I would disagree without knowing all the factors surrounding their relationship. First of all, Langston Hughes was a homosexual and had no (black) woman problem to contend with. Hence, Hughes lived a lifetime of literary pursuits absolutely free of the constraints and demands of a black woman mate or "significant other," as they say today. Hughes was a free and unfettered freelancer which is what a successful black writer *has* to be (whether male or female). This applies also to James Baldwin, the free-roving homosexual. I am not being either prejudiced or derogatory in saying this. I knew Langston Hughes very well—we moved in the same circles and were present at the same parties many times. I also know Baldwin, but not as well as I knew Hughes.

I am quite sure that Alice Walker and Toni Morrison, e.g., if pressed enough will claim that being tied to a black male would restrain and restrict their freedom of expression, their liberty, in the development of their talents (in which they would probably be right). This *is* an extra-literary factor not to be ignored when discussing black writers of any kind. (If a Harold Cruse had remained tied to his first mate, Cruse would never have been free to be the literary free-lancer who indulged in his years of writing and research leading to his writing of *The Crisis of the Negro Intellectual.* Cruse's mate split because Cruse walked out of a lifetime sinecure, a civil service job with the Veterans Administration. Once free of the civil service job as the ticket to an upward mobile salary over the years, Cruse became a free-lance journalist and writer. Cruse wrote four unsuccessful plays, three unfinished and bad novels, numerous unpublished articles and reviews. This was Cruse's schooling.)

Further afield, Frantz Fanon would never have become the celebrated literary revolutionary married to a black woman from his hometown in Martinique, who would have led him straight to a respectable middle-class psychiatric practice in Paris's "Right Bank" (not the Left). In my day, I hung out with fledgling black writers during our extra-literary struggles with empty pockets and hustling exploits for nearly twenty years. I can tell you that the majority of them had to avoid the hang-ups with black women wives or girlfriends whose general attitude was—"That writing ain't going to bring home the bacon. You'd better get out and get a job in the post office, or if worse came to worst, drive a taxi." (I can tell you that most of these black male writer experiences would make good satirical novels!) Further afield, Lena Horne married white in Hollywood as she recently revealed to Shirley Eder of the *Detroit Free Press* because her first husband, who was black, "Couldn't get me no jobs." Further afield, the only black creative men who could stay married to black wives, without hang-ups and restraints, were jazz musicians. Jazz musicians worked at their craft and free-lanced for the most part all their lives. But I could tell you some fantastic stories about their marital relationships (which would make great novels, which black writers won't touch!).

Back to Hughes and Zora Neale—Hughes did not need women. But you should know that Zora Neale had sexual "deviations" which she had difficulties in suppressing. I suspect that black males couldn't deal with her sexually, and she couldn't deal with black men very well. I know some of the facts about Hurston, but not all. Thus, I don't think it was a problem of Hughes's "sexism." The problems she had in collaborating with Hughes were part of a general black writer's problem.

Over the last fifty years, black writers have shown a congenital inability to collaborate in writing anything. This I experienced as a bitter fact of life. You cannot name one example of a successful black writing team since Sissle and Blake of 1922. White writers (especially Jewish writers) have produced a number of successful collaborating partnerships—Nordhoff and Hall, Kauffmann and Hart, Rogers and Hammerstein and many others. I seriously doubt that Alice Walker would have worked with a black screenwriter for *The Color Purple* even if the white producers would have allowed it, which they didn't and wouldn't have. These are part of the extra-literary conditions that explain why a Langston Hughes who wrote novels, poetry and plays, never collaborated with a black musician, lyricist or book-writer to produce anything of note.

I bring up this question of literary collaboration because the literary traditions of black Americans include much more than the "novel" or "short story." Blacks did not seriously take up the novel as a creative form until the 1920's. [Prior] to that, black writers, as such, also wrote for the theater. Your review of the writing career of Dunbar leaves out the fact that Dunbar was involved in extensive collaboration with other black writers in writing for the black theater. From a critical standpoint, latter-day black literary critics, such as yourself, have been influenced by the intrusion of a false dichotomy which is supposed to exist between the "novelist" and the "dramatist." Traditionally, the generic black literary form was not the novel but the play, especially the musical play. It was for this reason that Langston Hughes, a 1920's product, wrote plays, as well as novels and poetry. Hughes and Hurston fell out not over the collaboration in writing a novel, but over writing a play. It was the false separation between the drama and the novel pursued by the Harlem Renaissance writers that helped to exacerbate the black writers' ongoing problems and dilemmas. You are correct in suggesting that white liberal "patronage" was both an unavoidable but debilitating influence over fledgling black writers. But the consequences ran deeper than most of us want to either admit or investigate.

Consider the fact that the great Paul Robeson, a singer and an actor of great fame, never acted in a play, or sang a great role in either a play or a musical, or opera written by black writers. However, Paul Lawrence Dunbar, a poet and novelist, collaborated with the Johnson brothers, James Weldon and Hall, and Bob Coles in the musical theater long before the Harlem Renaissance novelists appeared in the 1920's. It is true that, for them, "extra-literary conditions" did exist due to the limitations of the black audience, which was practically non-existent. But the emergence of the black novelist, per se, was like a stillborn birth. A Jesse Fauset, e.g., was just as limited by her own Philadelphia elite, middle-class conventions, as she was by a limited audience composed of blacks who couldn't or wouldn't read books even if they had the money to buy them. She wrote about the middle class, but she could neither criticize nor satirize the black middle class (or the white) to any degree in which she would be taken seriously. For example, she didn't have the necessary perceptions to even satirize the white liberal class of Harlem Renaissance "patrons" to the extent in which Van Vechten satirized the blacks in "Nigger Heaven" who were the recipients of white liberal patronage. If she had "socially" criticized her own Philadelphia black middle class, she would have been rejected by her own class in the same fashion that a Thomas Wolfe was rejected by his own community in North Carolina who put him down for writing honestly about them in *You Can't Go Home Again*.

In the 1920's, American society wasn't ready for black writers any more than it was ready for white writers. It wasn't until Sinclair Lewis wrote *Babbitt* [that] Europeans actually believed Americans could write anything worth reading. It wasn't until Eugene O'Neill appeared [that] Europeans believed Americans could write dramas. Americans had an inferiority complex about literary creativity. Note that Americans cannot cite a single play written before Eugene O'Neill that is remembered enough for a revival. Few American novelists of the 19th century are recognized in Europe with the exception of Mark Twain, and perhaps Stephen Crane or maybe Jack London. Henry James was really an expatriate in London. The traditional attitude of Americans toward their own literary creativity is transferred toward blacks. Americans are still amazed (and sometimes resentful) at the idea of blacks writing novels, etc. It has been an attitude that blacks subconsciously adopt toward themselves. This serves to further inhibit black writers from venturing into thematic territory which they sense is prohibited. [. . . text unreadable]

Ellison had the whole literary world at his fingertips to conquer with his considerable craft, but he hasn't done it. Why? I think that a real critical analysis of Ellison's failure to repeat after *Invisible Man* is one of the keys to the collective failures of black writers as a group in 1986.

The issue is worth debating. This is all that I can say for now. There are other facets of your paper that I could discuss at length, but I will postpone a more extended discussion [until] some other time. Again, I think your analysis can be greatly extended and your insights enlarged upon.

Sincerely,

Harold W. Cruse

CHAPTER TWENTY-THREE

Interludes
with Duke Ellington

(Unpublished, 1982)

Although written in 1982, this essay echoes ideas expressed in the "early writings" section of this book because of its relevance to Cruse's early, formative experiences regarding black culture—particularly the theme of cultural autonomy, which remained at the fore of his thinking for the duration of his career.

During the post–World War II era, many of us younger Harlemites had the opportunity to meet the famous Duke Ellington. For some, like myself, the Duke [personified] the kind of sophistication we would have liked to attain—to imitate in other aspects of our limited way of life. Duke's music was "intellectual," symbolizing a mental quality we would have liked to display in our manners, our dress, our love affairs, our creative work—"Sophisticated Lady," "Mood Indigo," "Take the 'A' Train" and so on.

The most convenient place to meet the Duke was at the Apollo Theater or the Harlem Opera House on 125th Street, our Harlem "Main Stem." When Duke played at these theaters, they were always to full houses. During the interludes between "sets," when the usual featured movie was about to be screened, the Duke had the engaging habit of remaining in the orchestra pit to "Hold Court" with his admirers. His players would [. . .] "split" the scene for a breather. Looking back at it now, these were Harlem's dying days as the "Cultural Capital of the Black World." I can hazily recall the first time I paid to see a Duke Ellington show at the Apollo Theater. [. . .] It's impossible to recall either the year or the season [. . .]—it might have been either before WWII or after that I saw a certain show. This is because one's memories of all those fantastic shows at the Harlem Opera House or the Apollo Theater now blend into one unbroken continuous stream of vaudeville virtuosity lasting over a period of about 15 years. This stream of memory recall of the Harlem musical scene is peopled with such illustrious personalities as Cab Calloway, Don Redmond, Earl Hines, Tiny Bradshaw, Louis Russell, Blanche Calloway, Louis Armstrong, Count Basie, Ella Fitzgerald, the Nicholas Brothers, and many, many others. At any rate, the first time I saw a Duke Ellington show at the Apollo, the famed singer Ivy Anderson broke down in the middle of her rendition of "In My Solitude" and cried so bitterly [that] she had to be led off the stage. Whatever emotional trauma Ivy Anderson underwent that afternoon on the Apollo stage few in the audience could ever intimately know, but, in a youthful flash, it opened my eyes to the immense tragedy that lurked behind the flashy fronts of Negro entertainers. Ivy Anderson's public-stage loss of emotional control spoke volumes. It was probably a case of unrequited love compounded by the cruel, undemocratic vicissitudes of the Black entertainer's role of pleasing variegated audiences while, at the same time, burying their unhappiness and, perhaps, sense of unfulfillment behind the glare of the footlights. In any event, Duke Ellington rose to the occasion as Ivy Anderson was led, whimpering in tears, off the stage, and played a stream of Ellington orchestrations. I was deeply impressed.

Later on, my first personal communication with Duke occurred when he was holding court with some Harlem admirers in the Apollo orchestra pit after a show. The Duke liked to meet his "public" firsthand. During these interludes, he was often assailed: "Man, you still playing them same old riffs I heard you play five years ago," a young critic would say. "Man, I'm doing the best I can," Duke would reply in defense.

Very early on I perceived that, in numerous ways, Duke was very self-effacing. He was never arrogant nor overbearing in the display of his creative importance in the field of jazz music avant-gardism. Ellington, as I early perceived, was a genius with a congenital innocence about the impact of his original creativity. At first, Ellington's studied self-effacement regarding his creative originality was beyond my comprehension. In the late 1940's, I did not understand the intimate details of the Black entertainer's life behind the footlights. The main fact I did not comprehend, the prime economic imperative behind the Black entertainer's public face, was that he/she had to first please the white audience, the white critics, the white entrepreneurial investment dollar. Blacks, in the aggregate, had no power-leverage of any importance in the decision-making process of a Black entertainer's ascent to the level of fame of a Duke Ellington.

I was to learn this distasteful fact in 1952-53 when I first privately met the famous Duke behind the glamorous scenes of show business and its interpersonal realities. From 1951 to 1952, I was engaged in the laborious writing of my first full-length play—a "music drama" about the 1890's. When this play was finished, I presented it to the Greenwich Mews Theater in Greenwich Village, not with any hopes of getting it produced there since the stage dimensions were not large enough for such a production, but to get the script criticized by expert theatre people on how to rewrite the thing.

On the executive board of the Greenwich Mews was Rochelle Wall, a woman professionally active in advertising as a press agent, among other things. Rochelle Wall went wild over this script—much to my surprise—and took over the script, intending to push it. The script needed a score of incidental music and Wall said that there was only one person who could do justice to the script and that was Duke Ellington.

I reacted with disbelief. I was more interested in the play than the music which I felt an unknown composer could just as well handle. I told Wall that being a "nobody," a great musician like Ellington wouldn't give me the time of day. Wall said, "Look, Harold, if you want to do anything big, you must *think* big. I'm going to get this script to Ellington. I know his manager." [. . .] Later she gave me this fellow's phone number and told me to get in touch with him.

In the meantime, I was wavering between blasé doubts and hopeful star-gazing that maybe, just maybe, this contact might prove to be something "Big"— one never knows. This was a part of learning the real facts about show business.

About two weeks or more later, Rochelle Wall made contact with Ellington's "manager" and a date was set up for me to meet with him in his hotel room in what I think used to be called the "Manhattan Towers" on Eighth Avenue and the upper Forties. The hotel was not too fancy, but commodious. Mr. X. had a comfortable suite and was very cordial. He offered me a drink and looked me over. Finally, he produced my script and said—"Did you write this?"

I said yes, observing that he found it hard to believe. "It's remarkable," he said, "and I think this is something Duke Ellington ought to see." He and I talked for about an hour and a half that night (1953) and what came out was that this fellow was something of a power behind the scenes in the jazz world. [...] What his exact connection was to Duke, I never found out—I was too innocent to grasp the importance of that. But he talked admiringly about the script. He called it a "masterpiece" and all that. He couldn't get over the fact that *I* had written such a "fantastic" drama. Actually, the script was a "grand" idea, but that was all. In its present form it was not really "playable;" it needed drastic revisions, which it never got. As written, it did not require a complete musical score, but only incidental music. At any rate, Mr. X agreed heartily that Duke should read the script, and agreed to set up a date for me to talk to Duke about it.

As I recall, a couple of months passed. Mr. X called me and said that Duke was to go on television one evening and that I was supposed to meet with him in the TV studio before the show for a talk about the script. This was during the early days of TV broadcasting, before the time when live TV shows were broadcast with the smooth finesse we see today. The studio was on Lexington Avenue. [...] I went to this studio full of enthusiasm about meeting Duke and his band. [...] I had never seen a TV studio. When I got there, I received my first shock. The Duke was *not* playing with *his* band but with a miscellaneous combination of white musicians. The TV show was presented around the personality of Duke at the piano backed up by unknown musicians. I was sorely disappointed in seeing this done. It struck me as crass exploitation and misrepresentation, which I did not like at all.

But when I was introduced to Duke by Mr. X, I got another letdown. The Duke was his usual self at the piano practicing up on his "riffs" and snatches of melodies. When Mr. X presented me, Duke reacted as if I was the Great Mr. So and So he had never met. The Great Duke was completely under the thumb of Mr. X. If Mr. X said I was important, then I was *really* important. Here I was overwhelmed at the honor of being introduced to the Great Duke, and here he was almost speechless in the face of a nobody who his manager was presenting as a somebody. Frankly, I was embarrassed. Mr. X gave Duke the script with an expansive fatherly admonition—"Duke, I want you to read this play. It needs music. Harold, here, is a great writer—a wonderful talent." Duke took the script very meekly, looking at me as if he didn't know what to say. "I'll look it over," Duke said after a while. I stayed through the show. Later Mr. X advised me that I would have to wait a while, but he'd let me know when I'd be able to see Duke again about the script. I saw Rochelle Wall afterwards and told her what happened. "See, I told you, Harold. You have to think big when you want to do something Big."

In the meantime, I was carried away with the possibilities of this contact with the Great Duke. Maybe I would make it; maybe this was the first real break I would stumble upon. Maybe—maybe—maybe—who knows. Both Rochelle Wall and Mr. X were impressed with my play, but inwardly I knew better. *The Delta Rose* (the name of the play) needed expert revisions, which I was not able to do without expert help. I *knew* this, but Mr. X did not. Like most people in the music field, Mr. X did not really understand the theater. He was probably impressed with me as a writer. Jazz musicians do not deal with writers. Writers are another breed from jazz musicians and apart from their world. They know no more about playwriting than a playwright knows about how to direct a jam session. That was *the* problem, and I readily sensed it after talking with Mr. X the first time. *But I had made an important artistic managerial contact.*

About a month later, I got word from [Mr. X] that Duke would be playing a week's date at Birdland on Seventh Avenue in midtown and that I would be able to meet with him one night at Birdland to talk about the script. When the date was set, I was instructed by Mr. X to come to Birdland early in the first set, give my name and a table would be reserved for me free of charge. I was elated. I told all my friends about it. *I thought I was almost in—with the Great Duke.*

It was a cold, damp, nasty evening in the winter of 1953 that I showed up at Birdland full of anticipation. At the box-office I was told that I had a reserved place. Once inside, I found that the reserved place was a very long table with about a dozen places for a collection of other special guests. I felt more important. We were seated close to the orchestra stand just off to the right [of the stage]. All food and drinks were free—on the house. They were an interesting bunch of special friends of the Duke, hangers-on, show-biz people, etc. The house filled up—every table occupied when the Duke came on for the first set. Duke played everything out of Ellingtonia. He was supreme that evening. I ate and drank as if at a feast at the Gates of Show-Biz Heaven! The first set was over, the orchestra went backstage. The Birdland crowd thinned and filled again during the break. When the Duke returned for the next and last sets, the place was jammed again. Duke played more Ellingtonia—it sounded as if his repertoire was not only endless, but full of scores nobody had ever heard before but the Duke himself.

What a jazz evening that was for me! Finally, it all ended. Duke and the band went backstage. Birdland emptied. My reserve table guests left one by one. I sat there, alone, wondering. Then came the clean-up crew. They swept, wiped, and mopped. They piled the chairs on the empty tables all around me as I sat alone. They all gave me curious looks as they stepped around me closing down Birdland for the night.

It was already well after midnight. I didn't know what to do. Duke was backstage holding court. I saw a lot of famous singers and jazz artists coming and going in and out of Duke's quarters. [. . .] It was my first inside glimpse into the internal culture of the jazz world. In that world I saw that the Duke was really the King. When the Duke played an engagement, all the jazz world came to him after hours to discuss [their] problems, personal and professional and God-knows-what, with the Duke—the King. Jazz musicians' wives moved in after hours to chaperone their husbands and get them home out of the clutches of female predators. It was fascinating to watch as I sat there alone in an empty Birdland, but wondering—What do I do now?

Finally, after the cleaning crew had left, Mr. X showed up. He said, "Harold, didn't you see Duke yet?" I said, "No, I'm just sitting here waiting my turn." He said, "Come on in and let's talk." Mr. X escorted me into the Duke's dressing room. Inside, the Duke was alone with [. . .] a tall, statuesque, light-skinned beauty [that I assumed was his wife]. I knew nothing at all about the Duke's intimate personal life with women. This woman with him [. . .] was in a very bad mood this evening. Duke was sitting as if undecided whether his next jazz arrangement would be upbeat or smooth and mellow. [The woman] wanted him to get up and go home. [. . .] Anyhow, Mr. X got to the point. "Duke, you remember Harold, here. Well, he wants to talk some more about the script." I then noticed that Mr. X still had the script, which meant that Duke hadn't read it. Mr. X handed Duke the script. He opened it up and started to scan through it. That was when [the woman] intervened and said, with a tone of voice that was full of impatience, contempt and artistic illiteracy, "Duke, what the hell are *you* going to do with *that* thing?" Duke looked up at her with the same meekness that he had shown me when Mr. X first introduced us at the TV studio. Duke said, as he looked sidelong at me and Mr. X, *"All I want to do is read this thing and see what's happening, Baby."* She said peremptorily, "Duke, come on out of here and let's go home."

The Duke looked at me and Mr. X as if to say, "Well, *this* is what's happening right now." He put the script in a folder with music scores. Mr. X looked at me, and I looked at [Duke] and said "Okay, Duke, hope to see you again" and said goodnight and left. [. . .] Show business is all hopes, dreams, and chance. [. . .] It was really an impossible script as I look at it today—29 years later. The story idea was, and still is, a great one. If I *had* had as great a dramatic execution as Duke had in his sphere of symphonic jazz, *The Delta Rose* would be a masterpiece. But the script died that evening at Birdland with the Duke. I never heard from Duke or his "manager" again. The play script became a dead issue—I never revised it.

CHAPTER TWENTY-FOUR

Letter to Adolph Reed

(Unpublished, June 11, 1986)

Dear Adolph:

You'll pardon the tardy response to your correspondence. However, I've been extremely busy in putting the finishing touches on my own book, among other projects.

I've spent some time off and on in reading and rereading the pieces you sent. The Du Bois piece is the most interesting. The review piece on Cornel West leaves me kind of up-in-the-air simply because I'm not familiar with West's book *Prophecy Deliverance*. Eventually, I'll have to read the book, but not now.

Really, I can't argue at all with your perspective on the political thought of W. E. B. Du Bois. As you point out very correctly—Du Bois appears "as a champion who can be appropriated on an equal basis by any and all political tendencies." However, it is my conclusion that the totality and variety of Du Bois's thought is reducible to one common denominator in terms of philosophy. My conclusion is that Du Bois was fundamentally a cultural pluralist in terms of the black experience on the various political, social, economic and cultural levels in which he viewed Blacks in America and the world. It was for this basic fact that he was either hailed or opposed by such divergent tendencies as the NAACP and Garvey or the Pan-Africanists. None of these really understood the consistent ideological thread that ran through Du Bois's thinking. None of them understood that either Blacks in the U.S. or in Africa could or would ever be completely segregated for all time, nor completely "integrated" in the foreseeable future. The Black advocates of Garveyite (or Islamic) separatism and integrationism (assimilationism?) were and are just as "poles apart" in terms of social philosophy as they were in missing the central implied theme of Du Bois's thoughts. As far as nations go in the international arena, the contemporary international problem today is the problem of the coexistence of a multiplicity of nation-states. And so [unclear] weaker nation-states that there is the problem of plural coexistence of various racial and cultural group divergences. In fact, both in the international and intra-national contexts, there exists no other political, economic or cultural options open as a functional means of survival.

It is my belief that because Du Bois had to function as a spokesman under such severe and persistent duress from 1900 until 1963 that his antagonists (both black and white) never allowed him to expand on or completely refine his vision in a free, open exchange of ideas that took into account *all* of the racial, economic and political realities of the U.S. (or Africa!).

I think that one of your key observations (p. 441) regarding Du Bois's thinking is very relevant here:

> Precolonial Africa appeared in Du Bois's Reconstruction as a series of societies
> moving in lockstep toward collective teleological goals. He paid little attention
> to likely internal conflicts within his contemporary African unity, and took for
> granted the coordinating apparatus both in its existence and its progressive
> formation.

The key word here is "teleological" (as opposed to dialectical). When one remembers that most of us black activists and/or intellectuals of the Sixties tried to invoke Afro-American "unity" with the same "teleological" expectations, it serves to bring Du Bois's thinking back to being historically grounded in its native and natural milieu—the United States and its black minority.

Another key assertion you make regarding Du Bois is that "Du Bois sought to work out a program that accepted segregation as given." One might interpret this position as also "teleological," but I think it would be as unjustified and erroneous as the previous assertions that because of his peculiar brand of racial politics, B. T. Washington accepted Southern racial segregation as a given. In both cases, it is my contention that Washington and Du Bois considered segregation as very real *but not* preordained (teleologically) to continue as [the] permanent state of race relations. In terms of race relations, it is my belief that both Washington and Du Bois were inherently more *dialectical* than their critics were either prone to or intellectually capable of seeing or admitting. Coming from any direction, the responses to both Washington and Du Bois were simplistically and unabashedly *pragmatic* in the most vulgar and narrow-minded American sense of what Charles S. Peirce, the philosophical founder of American pragmatism (as interpreted by John Dewey) really meant. For Peirce, pragmatism really meant "the meaning of an idea was to be found in an examination of the consequences to which that idea would lead."

For anyone to have claimed that Du Bois's idea of the "consumer cooperative organization" strategy was merely and only a strategy for accommodation to racial segregation that would last for all time, and was, therefore, inappropriate, was to sorely miss the point of its future implications.

Du Bois's concept of the "consumer cooperative organization" would have been applicable to either a capitalistic or socialistic national economic system, contrary to all the arguments of both the apologists for capitalism or the advocates of "socialism" as the only, ultimate, solution for the black economic, political and cultural condition. For no matter what the dominant philosophy of economic organization, whether socialist or capitalistic, American blacks would be relegated to the very bottom of the ladder in terms of who, what race, what ethnic group, class or elites would be most favored when the economic rewards were distributed. (E.g., how many recognizably black Cubans does one see representing Cuban blacks up there at the Fidel Castro level of elite control of the socialistic economy?) In fact, statistically there are *more* American blacks in the high, political and administrative echelons of the American capitalistic system of government than there are in the Cuban socialistic system of government. This happens to be a very real contradiction that is also rather inexplicable. This is also the more contradictory when one considers the arguments of the radical socialists who say that racial injustices endemic to capitalism can only be eliminated under "egalitarian" socialism. (This also applies to sexism—percentage-wise, there are more women in politics, holding political office, more women writers, artists, entertainers, professors, businesspersons, etc., than there are in Cuba, Russia, China or in Third World countries.)

More to the point, I think it is inaccurate to suggest that Du Bois "accepted segregation as a given" because it further implies that Du Bois accepted segregation as a permanent arrangement and therefore sought a permanent accommodation with it. This amounts to an undialectical observation. I think that any assessment of a minority group issue over time has to be grounded in the idea of (social) strategy and group tactics. Any analysis of this sort has to be inductive or else the social reasoning cannot be dialectical. To suggest that Du Bois "accepted segregation as given" (which is what his shallow NAACP critics charged) is to lapse into deductive reasoning. More than 25 years after most of the discriminatory laws have been abrogated and discriminatory practice outlawed, blacks still maintain racially separate black churches. But I would be erroneous to suggest that because blacks still maintain separate churches, they are accommodating themselves to racial segregation. There are other (dialectical) reasons behind the maintenance of these separate black churches. In fact, the existence of these separate churches was one of the reasons Du Bois regaled [*sic*] the NAACP for not clearly and cogently explaining what the hell they thought they meant by segregation.

You quote me as identifying Du Bois with the "integrationist tendency" in the history of Afro-American thought (pg. 433). Maybe I did, but that was because Du Bois willingly allied himself with a white liberal dominated "civil libertarian" protest movement because he had no other choice in 1909-1910. But keep in mind here that in 1910, the concept of "integration" was completely unknown and unvoiced. From 1910 until 1940, nobody inside or outside the NAACP mentioned the word "integration" in terms of social policy. The word "integration" did not enter the lexicon of the NAACP until after World War II. In fact, the word "integration" was first widely used in connection with blacks in the military. The demand of the NAACP was to eliminate separate black army units and "integrate" blacks into the general army units. This was how "integration" entered the civil rights repertory.

Du Bois was calling for "economic cooperatives" and "self-help organiza-tion" among blacks as far back as 1918-1920. You are quite right in highlighting Du Bois's preoccupation with "pride in race" and the references to the fact that the Negro "is primarily an artist," etc., etc. However, his article "The Criteria for Negro Art" in the *Crisis* for October, 1926, shows that Du Bois's interest in Negro art was not limited to the "primitive."

For now, allow me to suggest that I think that the more pertinent and revealing clues to an assessment of Du Bois are be found in his monthly *Crisis* magazine articles and statements. Here is the *real* Du Bois. The *real* Du Bois is not to be discovered through the second-hand treatments [. . .] in the writings of Brotz, Broderick, et al. I feel that there is need for a comprehensive review of *all* of Du Bois's *Crisis* magazine writings, excluding what other writers (including Cruse) say *about* Du Bois.

Another thing, I think that more attention needs to be given to the ideological dynamics behind Du Bois's break with Booker T.—W. E. B. and Booker T. were of one mind up to around 1898 when the fight broke out between BTW and [William Monroe] Trotter over the Afro-American League (Council). What is to be made of the fact that Du Bois's inability to get money for his Atlanta [Conferences] inspired him to break with the position of BTW because the latter was getting all the money from the Carnegies, Schiffs, the Baldwins and the Rosenwalds, etc.?

As an exploratory reassessment of the Du Bois political, racial, and cultural saga, your piece is very good. I think that it merely opens up the historical vistas for a more in-depth analysis of Du Bois. The complexity of Du Bois serves to conceal a very consistent, dialectically logical stream of evolutionary philosophy.

More on this later.

Sincerely,

Harold

To be continued
P.S. I am also reading your book on Jesse Jackson. I have studied C. Vann Woodward's review in *New Republic.* More on this later. [. . .]

PART SIX

From
Plural but Equal
(1987)

CHAPTER TWENTY-FIVE

Conclusions

A summation of the twenty-six years since the 1954 *Brown* decision would have to call 1980 a watershed year for blacks. Only twenty years remained in the twentieth century, and only ten years were left to fulfill the Afro-American League's T. Thomas Fortune's prophecy that the civil rights struggle would occupy a century. Indeed, the ninety years that elapsed between Fortune's declaration and the end of the Carter administration in 1980 had not been an exercise in black leadership child's play. On the contrary, it had been an evolutionary saga of black leadership factionalism, contention, and rivalry; opposition and alliances; classism and its social prerogatives; nationalism and separatism versus integrationism and assimilationism; left versus right; black conservatism versus the white liberal left wing and conservative paternalism; Pan-Africanist (and later) Third World internationalism and Afro-American minority-group particularism. But since the harsh banes of racism and racial segregation were the common foes of all these factions, class alignments, and ideological divisions, internal disunity slowed down black progress on all fronts—political, economic, cultural, social, and educational. If the black struggle was not an exercise in child's play, it did trivialize crucial issues caused by a factional disunity that rendered black leadership an exercise in the futility of *political* subordination. This process culminated in the anomaly of more blacks being better off economically, and more being worse off, than their predecessors had been from 1900 to 1960.

Although on the average blacks are better off in the Eighties than their forebears, the tasks they face from now through the year 2000 will be more difficult—calling for more organizational skill, political ingenuity and imagination, intellectual endurance, hard work, and application of thought than before. Historically, the main spokesmen to represent anything approaching a *national* consensus appeal in the twentieth century have been Booker T. Washington, W. E. B. Du Bois, Marcus Garvey, A. Philip Randolph, Martin Luther King, and, recently, Jesse Jackson. T. Thomas Fortune was eclipsed early on by the political and racial consequences of being a "stillborn" leader during the dubious racial decade of *Plessy v. Ferguson.* Du Bois, Randolph, Garvey, and their contemporaries faced the "Crisis of Negro Leadership" first evident in the post-World War I period. Thus, King and his protégé Jesse Jackson would personify, both as participants and as advocates, black progress in all social advancements, underwritten in the main by the civil rights engendered by the black-white liberal-Democratic party alliance.

Jesse Jackson's emergence following King suggested the possibility of things to come in the Seventies *and* the Eighties. An assessment of Jesse Jackson as a leadership symbol can dispense with the hero worship that rightly belongs to King. King himself was unprecedented and unexpected among the black leaders produced by the Fifties and Sixties. Jackson has brought back into focus the economic factor that was downplayed and reduced to a nonfactor in black civil rights affairs. This was the philosophy of *noneconomic liberalism.* Tactically, noneconomic liberalism had been one means of expunging from the programmatic movement of the procapitalist, free-market ideals of the Booker T. Washington school in favor of constitutional legalism. Unsettled racial conditions in both North and South up to the New Deal obviated any serious debate how blacks would fit into the capitalist, free-market economy except as a cheap labor pool. The New Deal further discouraged economic debates by instituting the federal budgetary innovations of the welfare state. Under the economics of the welfare state, all talk of "black capitalism" became visionary, or at least irrelevant to black economic survival.

It took Jesse Jackson to reintroduce the notion of a black capitalist *clientage* class sponsored by white corporations as an extension of civil rights clientage into economics. More precisely, Jesse Jackson's People United to Save Humanity (PUSH) aimed to revitalize the latent energies of economically deprived black communities. As a description of PUSH operations noted: "Jackson began to direct the flow of white corporate profits earned in the ghetto into black banks as a means of strengthening the black communities' meager economic foundations."[1] PUSH was an extension of Martin Luther King's Operation Breadbasket. In King's conception, Operation Breadbasket was aimed at securing more jobs for blacks at the non-entrepreneurial level.[2] Jackson transcended the scope of King's plan by introducing large corporations to invest directly in black communities at the entrepreneurial level. Jesse Jackson realized the black economic dream of Booker T. Washington after some seventy years.[3] But in the process, Jackson developed the style and momentum for a qualitatively new brand of black leadership. Although PUSH's economic accomplishments would not even begin to dent the surface of growing ghetto poverty at the class level, Jackson's leadership could *politicize* the issue of black economics. During the transition from civil rights politics to the politics of black ethnicity, Jackson's leadership would emphasize the necessity of combining black political organization *with* black economic organization. However, his burgeoning leadership potential would be contained within the range of the fortunes and misfortunes of the Democratic party. Or, more precisely, within the black-white liberal-Democratic party coalition.

Neither the NAACP nor the National Urban League was bold enough, or sufficiently unrestricted by sanctions of *noneconomic liberalism,* to confront the seat of economic power in the manner of Jesse Jackson. The traditional civil rights leadership was in a programmatic bind. Once the ambiguity of the Fourteenth Amendment's equal protection clause became even more indistinct in the process of universalizing both civil and economic rights, the traditional civil rights leadership had nothing substantial to fall back on but the legislative stratagem of a Humphrey-Hawkins full-employment bill. Only a vast federal outlay could have given this full-employment bill any pretense of wiping out unemployment (whether of blacks, whites, or other minorities). Moreover, the corporate leaders from whom Jesse Jackson wangled financial backing for his black business clients were politically unsympathetic to federal funding of full employment programs. Corporate leaders are predominantly advocates of conservative fiscal policies. Thus, the only hope for passing the Humphrey-Hawkins bill lay with the Democratic party, and the entire civil rights leadership and black elected officials were, and had to remain, party loyalists. Hence, the Carter presidency became the last chance for any favorable congressional act on Humphrey-Hawkins. With record-high unemployment levels in the black communities, civil rights leaders, as champions of black progress, had to press for black rights that had become much more economic than civil. Then Carter, who owed his election to the "balance of power" of the black vote, began to hedge his support for the Humphrey-Hawkins bill:

> It started off as legislation that would have made the Government the employer of last resort for the unemployed. The question now is whether the Humphrey-Hawkins full-employment bill, after all the compromises, ended up as a political symbol of last resort for President Carter, Congressional liberals and the Congressional Black Caucus.[4]

But along the line, the sponsors of the bill had to give ground on the definition of full employment. Both Carter and the sponsors agreed that the primary emphasis should be on creating jobs in the private sector. But in its last stages, what the bill left "unresolved [was] how much money the Government is to spend on programs directed to people and places with chronically high unemployment—teen-agers, blacks, decaying inner cities, regions, states."[5] Ultimately, directly due to the swing of public sentiment to the right, the Humphrey-Hawkins bill became one of the domestic issues that helped defeat Carter; it also brought to a close the long reign of the Democratic party as the sponsor of liberal legislation in the stopgap or long-range economic interests of the underprivileged.

Although the category of the economically underprivileged included a larger proportion of the population than blacks, legislative controversies involving government spending centered around the plight of the blacks, not other minorities. The blacks would become the vanguards of social protest, first for themselves and then for other minorities. Blacks would also become the most prominent scapegoats for most of the conservative backlash from critics of liberal public policy. Ultimately, the combined factors that went into this burgeoning backlash from the right pushed Jesse Jackson to take the unprecedented step of running for the presidency in 1984.

With the decline of the Democrats in 1980, black leadership as a whole had nowhere to turn politically. Having been lofted by a considerable black consensus as the leader of the Seventies, Jackson had nowhere to go but up as a means of sustaining at least the symbolic justification for his leadership appeal. As King's immediate successor, more by self-propelled design rather than by consensus, Jackson mobilized his own supporters. When the politics of welfare state economics dwindled under the assault of Reaganomics, leaving Jackson's civil rights colleagues stranded, Jackson pursued his only option, the *leadership summitry* in the open field of electoral politics. However, in bidding for the highest political office in the land, Jackson had to be launched like a helicopter from a rooftop rather than as a turbojet from an airfield. The analogy here refers to the jet-propelled presidential electioneering that was the prerogative of a Walter Mondale, a John Glenn, and a Gary Hart. Which is to say that Jackson's presidential bid was launched without the backup of a well-cultivated and prepared political base. Jesse Jackson's *nonexistent political base was the figment of the black independent political party structure that was not formed during the black political conventions at Gary, 1972; Little Rock, 1974; or Cincinnati, 1976.* Because no black independent political party was formed from 1972 to 1980, Jackson's maverick impact on the political culture would be limited. He had no option other than to restrict his potential within the constraining folds of the Democratic party, which had been holding the black vote in ransom since 1936.

The subsequent Reagan Republican sweep demonstrated the dismal fact that the Democratic party's attachments to (and strategical need for) the black vote had evolved into an electoral liability. The Democratic party's identification with blacks was by no means a moral indictment, but a *political* indictment from the point of view of those of the electorate who labeled blacks as the most palpable scapegoats for a hot issue, too much government spending on social programs. Hence, running for the presidency as a black (unheard of racially and politically apocalyptic), Jackson had to criticize the front-runner, Mondale, for failing to address issues important to blacks, while at the same time promising to support the Democratic party ticket on demand.

In doing so, Jackson posed problems for blacks that would not have been solved even if the 1984 election had been won by Mondale or ended in a tie. In playing the politics of "loyal opposition" with the Democrats, Jackson sought to cajole them into a platform emphasis on black interests, while bidding for personal inclusion in the high echelons of Democratic party leadership. Which meant that neither Jesse Jackson nor the civil rights leaders had seriously faced the implications of Carter's defeat in 1980. What more could the Democrats do for blacks that had not already been done or tried? Thus, for Jackson and the civil rights leadership to justify both their demands on the Democratic party and their loyalties to party principles, they had to bring a set of *new ideas* to the party.

The political victories of Reaganism were due to the Democratic party's having run out of ideas. Both the national economy and the social foundations of the entire American society were beset by severe functional strains and stresses. During the Sixties, the civil rights movement itself had disrupted the foundations of society and removed the placid camouflage, revealing festering elements below the surface—an un-American degree of poverty, the organized roots of crime and corruption, widespread family disorganization (especially that of blacks), the terminal stages of urban decay, the advanced stages of interethnic enmities and competition, the degradation of national agriculture (a crucial black issue), and a bloated military budget that resulted directly from a foreign policy that not only gave a low priority to domestic problems but was also a long-run detriment to national interests. The list of domestic exigencies was endless. The decade of the Seventies, while crucial for black interests, was also a decade of a growing national emergency that called for a drastic reordering of domestic priorities. However, with the 1984 presidential campaign, it became increasingly clear that, despite all the good liberal-Democratic party intentions, the Democrats had neither a program with a potential for such a drastic reordering of domestic priorities, nor an electoral mandate for the program even if the party were politically solvent. The growing insolvency of black civil rights leadership only fortified its dependent belief that the Democratic party was still politically solvent enough to project a black issues-oriented program. Jesse Jackson, the unprecedented political maverick, thought the same thing.

Jesse Jackson, in his bid for the presidential nomination, could not break cleanly with the tradition that kept the black vote tied to the fortunes of the Democratic party. Although he had a clear option of turning his voter-registration campaign into a double-barreled political venture by organizing voters into an independent party, he skirted that challenge by projecting the idea of the Rainbow Coalition.

This Rainbow Coalition was, in part, Jackson's admission that the coalition that comprised the bedrock of the Democratic party was either inadequate and unrepresentative or else politically insufficient to propel the party toward victory in 1984. At the same time that he called for a Rainbow Coalition, Jackson did not, or could not, espouse a political program in opposition to or different from that of Democratic party. The Rainbow Coalition was an interesting political idea because it promised a brand-new party alignment. An important, even crucial, segment of this coalition would, of course, be the black voting bloc. In Jackson's view the only possible avenue for expressing the black voting bloc's independence from the two main parties would be within the Rainbow Coalition. On the one hand, the name itself, Rainbow Coalition, would spell out the group's pluralism. On the other hand, Jackson's idea implied that the existing Democratic party coalition in support of Walter Mondale had lost its powers of political persuasion. Ultimately, the results of the 1984 election indicated that the Democratic party—the party of FDR, Truman, Kennedy, Johnson, and Carter—had reached the end of the line as the liberal-left-wing axis of the traditional two-party system. And since the conservative-right-wing fulcrum of electoral politics, the Republican party, offered no future for realizing the aspirations of the black majority consensus, what loomed as the political hope for the black minority?

The only option left was to organize an independent black party. The ultimate aim of this black party would not be solely for the expedient purposes of electoral politics. Realistically, it has to be faced that black elected officials (BEOs) "fear they can't do much to help their people." In an interview sponsored by *The Wall Street Journal* in 1980, one prominent black state representative admitted, "I have a sensitivity towards poor people [and] Blacks are No. 1." But when pressed to cite specific ways he helped black people, he pointed to his authorship of a bill that made Martin Luther King's birthday a legal holiday in his state. "Many of the 4,600 black elected officials in the U.S. share [this] feeling of helplessness." The interview continued: "Perhaps more than others, they understood the size and complexity of the problems facing black Americans." "Problems don't go away when you elect a black," said another BEO. "*Even the most powerful black leaders can't change very much.*"[6] (Italics added.)

Here, the official was alluding to the powerful black leaders on the civil rights front. It is not simply that the continuing vacuity of these leaders' civil rights and welfare programs represent the diminished end products of their futility; it is that the *sheer size and complexity of black America today* reduces all pretenses and pretexts of black leadership, an exercise in verbal-protest symbolism that harks back to the heydays of past achievements when civil rights redress was the order of the day on the national agenda. But for BEOs as the new black political class, electoral politics has ended as a legislative and parliamentary dead-end trap. This is because black elected officials are both latecomers to mainstream politics and functional captives of the liberal-Democratic party alliance. "By the time blacks move into important posts," said a black member of Congress, "they've got too much work ahead of them to get it done."[7] Left unsaid by this black representative was that by 1980, there was little political leverage left in the liberal-Democratic alliance to accomplish whatever political work lay ahead. The most obvious obligatory work that loomed was more concentrated political organization by blacks, but *not only* for the elevation of more officials to political office. The organization of blacks into an independent political party could belatedly help make up for the abysmal lack of organizational achievements by blacks over the last sixty years in all areas—political, economic, cultural, educational, etc. The black woman's complaint cited earlier was far from being an idle exercise in complaint-mongering about the "black man's dilemma." Translated into its broader social meaning, *it is a dilemma of the entire black minority group,* a dilemma of black leadership.

With the end of the cycle of civil rights advocacy, only one basic option remained for the black leadership. This was internal organization and consolidation of the minority group within a multiracial, multicultural society. This imperative meant that the traditional black civil rights leadership had reached a societal void lacking a road upon which to lead its constituency. The situation called for a new black leadership consensus that was capable of *redefining* the plausible place of the black minority within the societal complex in which blacks, as a *group,* found themselves by 1980. Such a redefinition of the legitimate place of the black minority within the system had to take into full account the meaning of *plurality.* It meant the systematic *reorganization* of many areas of black life into, first a *political bloc,* then cultural blocs, and then into whatever internal economic organizations are possible within a capitalistic, free-market system. In this context an independent black political party becomes the initial step toward a total reorganization of black life over the remainder of the twentieth century. Without such a *total* political, economic, cultural, educational, and *institutional* reorganization of black life, the American black minority will *not* be able to survive into *whatever* system American society becomes by the year 2000 and after.

However, this attempt at a total reorganization of black life means that organizing the black political consensus becomes the *first priority.* In this process the traditional civil rights leadership (mainly the NAACP) *must arbitrarily be bypassed inasmuch as this leadership, which exists as the basis of a vested interest, will not voluntarily step down.* The official, institutionalized civil rights leadership will not (cannot) voluntarily vote itself out of existence. The official, institutionalized civil rights leadership cannot face the reality that it is passé. It is *not* passé simply because of the coming to power of the conservative, Reaganite, right-wing Republican party hegemony. It is passé because under the auspices of the Democratic party, civil rights legislation over the years has gleaned maximum power from the Fourteenth Amendment to the Constitution to redress the historical civil rights wrongs heaped on the heads of the blacks. Thus, black aspirations are trapped within the ambiguities of the constitutional meaning of the equal protection clause. Continued agitation and leadership confrontations on this issue at the national level of public policy are not only fruitless but counterproductive. The traditional civil rights leadership that aims at perpetuating this mode of agitation is *detrimental* to future development in the political, economic, educational, and cultural dimensions of the black cause. More than that, *the traditional civil rights leadership will oppose any attempt on the part of an alternate leadership to organize blacks into an independent political bloc.* As pointed out earlier, this was demonstrated in 1972 when the NAACP damned the objectives of the first black political convention at Gary, Indiana, by refusing to support the independent political party plank.[8] The traditional civil rights leadership remains the most highly influential body of black opinion. This leadership has the support of white liberal opinion across the board, whether Big

Labor, Big Government, Big Welfare State, Big Liberalism, or Big Public Policy of the type that has philanthropized blacks into being, as a group, a semidependency, half liberated, half victimized by disabilities and problems that are beyond the capabilities of present public policy to either redress or solve. Organizationally and politically, blacks require a brand-new set of public policy priorities. Although most blacks are loyal to the Democratic party, the Democrats are no longer capable of accommodating black social priorities, present or future. The decline of the Democratic party's viability represents a turning point in the traditional two-party system's monopoly over national electoral politics.

By implication, Jesse Jackson challenged the sacred hegemony of the two-party system when he proposed the Rainbow Coalition. Jackson, however, could not venture far enough into the uncertainties of party politics fully to define the ramifications of such a coalition. That is to say, Jackson, like civil rights leaders and the great majority of black elected officials, did not really savor the risk of breaking cleanly with the Democratic party. Just about one hundred years ago, Frederick Douglass thought in terms of "political integration" by declaring that the Republican party was the ship, and all else was the open sea. By 1984 blacks had been long programmed to believe that the only ship of state for political survival was the Democratic party, even though the ship had sprung menacing leaks. In this political debacle, the Republican party cannot represent the party of rescue today. What is needed is a brand-new alignment. As political and electoral matters evolved in the 1980s, the black electoral consensus emerged as the only potential base on which a Third, or alternate, party could be built to compensate for the faltering Democratic organization. The problem was that neither the Democratic party leadership nor the black leadership would have *dared* even to contemplate such a sacrilegious political assertion. Black leadership shares with the white electorate much of the same mythology about the two-party system. Black leaders (civil and political) must see civil rights as a *constitutional* mandate. They also share much of the same unspoken, subliminal beliefs that there is something sacred about the two-party system that is also *constitutional.*

Jackson's concept of the Rainbow Coalition was an embryonic political idea that reflected the essentially pluralistic makeup of American society. While this essential pluralism exists outside the theoretical framework of constitutional ideals, it is a social, economic, and cultural condition that cuts across all ethnic, racial, cultural, sex, and geographical lines. This obstinate fact would in the Seventies help eclipse and circumvent most of the social policy expectations of the black civil rights movement. It would activate the responses that would ultimately cut the political supports upon which the Democratic party had rested since the New Deal. In the process the impact of pluralism would thrust into competitive contention a catalogue of submerged or otherwise suppressed minorities. The question posed by Jesse Jackson's Rainbow Coalition was: Which of these variegated minorities would, in their supposed self-interest, enter into a definitive political coalition with the blacks? *This was a crucial question in the 1984 election.*

Jesse Jackson's Rainbow Coalition envisioned a minority-group alliance based on the mutual interests of blacks, other minorities, and women. But not unexpectedly, none of the vocal leaders of the other minorities answered the call. The refusal of both Hispanics and women,—the latter represented by the National Organization of Women (NOW)—to align themselves publicly with the Rainbow Coalition indicated that Jackson had misread the political signals of minorities and women for 1984. Women (as represented by NOW) and minorities are not as solidly committed to the Democratic party as are blacks, which throws into considerable doubt the assumption that minorities and women share mutual interests with blacks. There is no telling how many Democratic party dissidents among the minorities and women either supported Gary Hart over Walter Mondale or bolted to the Republicans. For Democrats like Hart, the black civil rights cause was the main bone of contention over the question of the Democratic party's advocacy of "special interests." Thus, Jackson was forced into paying campaign lip service to the media's portrayal of the Democratic party's special-interest civil rights contenders as composed of minorities and women.

Women represent more than one half the national population, but Jackson, caught in the net of the liberal consensus on minorities and civil rights, could not openly declare that they do not constitute a minority. Thus, similar to the entire liberal-Democratic party consensus, he could not openly speculate what this misapplication of the gender population ratios would mean for blacks. If the total population is measured on a percentage scale of 100, women would make up 51 percent. In view of the conservative white shift to Reaganism, it cannot be determined what percentage of women is in favor of the extension of civil rights supports for minorities—especially blacks—and particularly *in the arena of economic rights,* the *real* battleground where substantive civil rights issues are at stake.

An eventual ratification of the Equal Rights Amendment (ERA) would *constitutionally* submerge the *nonwhite minority group,* effectively burying it as a political and/or legal issue. The black minority group, in particular, would be left constitutionally stranded in the legal mire of the ambiguities of the Fourteenth Amendment's equal protection clause. The ERA is meant to transcend the equal protection clause as being an insufficient safeguard against sex discrimination practiced against a *class*. As one consequence, the ratification of the ERA would justify the argument that another constitutional amendment be placed on the political agenda: *an equal rights amendment to the Constitution that would bar economic, political, and cultural discrimination against a minority group based on race*. The idea of such an amendment would not only reassert the *original* substance of the Fourteenth Amendment, but reopen to debate the social policy implications of the equal protection clause's ambiguities. Such an amendment *could* become one of several planks for an independent black political party. It could also become *one* point of organizational departure for realizing the potential of the Rainbow Coalition. The ERA, aside from its social policy gender implications, raises more fundamental questions about the Constitution. The American Constitution is *not* the most advanced document in the world today. Moreover, it thrives off its past accomplishments in extending its democratic ideals and egalitarian principles. As written, the Constitution cannot mandate any further privileges or egalitarian promises to American blacks than it has already allowed. Thus, as the largest and most important nonwhite minority, blacks can no longer deceive themselves into believing that the Constitution can offer any additional unrealized benefits *without being amended*. Whether the American Constitution will ever undergo an overhauling, which in the opinion of some is long overdue, is a matter for speculation. However, barring any amendment process, the only hope left for the political, economic, and cultural survival of blacks into the next century is self-organization.

As American society, representing a national entity of just over two hundred years, approaches the year 2000, the social and economic conditions of American blacks as a group reflect disturbing indications that they might become, racially and ethnically, *an endangered species*. Black social, economic, political, and cultural survival is *not* guaranteed. Even the American nation *in toto*, as *constitutionally* premised, is not guaranteed to survive without some drastic reordering of its domestic priorities. As for the blacks, the only guarantee of group survival lies in reorganizing along political, economic, cultural, and institutional lines.

The end of the civil rights cycle, beginning with *Brown*, left blacks in the Eighties holding the heavy bag of an immense economic problem. This economic problem weighed down the black upward mobility toward the economic parity that the civil rights movement promised but could not deliver. Hence, the fundamental issue facing the black minority for the remainder of the twentieth century is not the fruitless contention with the unresolvable, ambiguous, open-ended legalisms of equal protection, but the reality of the closed, privileged arena of economic competition for the rewards of social status through economic parity. It is true that blacks have made the kinds of advances that would have seemed impossible in the 1890s. To compare the position of blacks in the 1980s with that of the 1890s, the pre-NAACP era, would be even more difficult than to compare the state of race relations of the 1980s with that of the 1920s. Compared with the pre-New Deal era, blacks have made unprecedented advances in politics, culture, economics, and, especially, education. On the all-important economic front, blacks have made a remarkable *relative* advance against the ravages of poverty in a rich society, the wealthiest the world has ever seen, that irresponsibly tolerates and abets that poverty. The century-old struggle against poverty has been harder, as said before, for native-born blacks than for European immigrants, and it has exerted a tremendous assault on the stability of the black psyche. Blacks' struggle for education has been disoriented and misdirected because the struggle took place in an unprecedented rich society whose intellectual tradition has neither understood nor sanctioned the true educational needs of nonwhite minorities. One of the profound consequences of this ongoing "miseducation" of the blacks has been the cultivation and encouragement of the kind of black "value system" that is generally detrimental to coping successfully with the exigencies imposed by a paternalistically racist, economically predatory, and culturally irresponsible society.

The reality of the black economic situation today is the extended but aggravated situation that W. E. B. Du Bois described in 1934 when he prophesied the unavoidable consequences of the NAACP's civil rights philosophy: "This [NAACP] program of organized opposition to the action and attitude of the dominant white group includes ceaseless agitation and insistent demand for equality: the equal right to work, civic and political equality, and social equality. It involves the use of force of every sort: moral suasion, propaganda and where possible, even physical resistance." But "there are, however, manifest difficulties with such a program. *First of all it is not a program that envisages any direct action of Negroes themselves for the uplift of their socially depressed masses: in the very conception of the program, such work is to be attended to by the nation and Negroes are to be the subjects of uplift forces and agencies to the extent of their numbers and need.* Now for obvious reasons of ignorance and poverty, and the natural envy and bickering of any disadvantaged group, this unity is difficult to achieve. In fact the efforts to achieve it . . . during Reconstruction, and in the formation of the early Equal Rights League and the Afro-American Council, were only partially successful."[9] (Italics added.)

Note the reference to the Afro-American Council (formerly called the "League"). This outcome, which was of course unavoidable in view of the ideological origins of the civil rights program, left the NAACP (and the National

Urban League) stranded at the waning of the last civil rights cycle. What Du Bois described in 1934 as the black "socially depressed masses" are the magnified black millions of the Eighties existing below the poverty line—the black unemployed, the fatherless families, the high school dropouts, the petty criminals, the urban homeless, the unskilled, the welfare survivors whom the nation and its uplift agencies cannot rescue. Civil rights organizations are immobilized with no other recourse or rationale for their continued existence but to berate the political establishment for its failure to eliminate unemployment and poverty. There is not the slightest indication that these protests will ever cease to fall on the closed ears of the neoliberal and/or neoconservative conscience of the nation and its uplift forces and agencies.

With the coming of the Eighties, the ameliorative powers of the liberal consensus to assuage the economic disabilities of the black masses were politically spent. As the largest nonwhite minority, blacks as a group bear the brunt of the well-entrenched coercive economic power wielded by politically powerful groups that function at the summits of white society. Thus, white society in general benefits in varying degrees from the "trickle-down" dissemination of economic privileges that are indispensable for the operation of the free-market economic system. In the United States, as in all societies, "coercive power is a mighty economic force," as one unconventional and reconstructed white liberal, Theodore Cross, put it:

> There appear to be few records in history of any tribe or nation where the largest share of economic goods and valued positions has not been claimed by those individuals and groups that were economically and politically strong and that had the most secure hold on society's instruments of coercion.[10]

The writer further advises that blacks "must shape their policies and build their lives not on myths and slogans published by the powerful, but on truth and experience about themselves and about how the world around them actually distributes its economic rewards and penalties."[11] One of the distressing corollaries of the civil rights movement was the creation of empty slogans and the propagation of myths: the myth about the ultimate meaning of racial integration, the myth about the redemptive powers of moral suasion, the myths surrounding the legalities of equal protection regarding race and economics in a free-market economy. A proliferation and apotheosization of myths by the official black leadership followed the Supreme Court Decision of 1954 to the effect that the millennium in complete racial democracy would be realized in just one more decade. However, the reverse occurred. *By 1980 blacks had collapsed and were deteriorating politically* as a result of having been goaded and lured by a set of false assumptions, plus having been driven to march forward under the banners of conflicting and mutually negating priorities. By skirting around the self-evident necessity of organizing politically, civil rights and political leaders would also evade the responsibility to counsel *collective enterprises* among blacks, to inspire *collective determination,* to engage in *cooperative economic* efforts on *both corporate-business* and *commodity-distribution levels.* Theodore Cross continued:

> In the tradition of many other ethnic outsiders who have achieved rank equal to the majority, blacks must also become competent in all the accepted forms of economic and political power that a democracy holds open to its citizens and protects for their benefit and advancement.[12]

However, in the face of this persuasive American economic reality, both white-inspired noneconomic liberals and radical left-wing socialist advisers beguiled blacks into believing that they had neither a legitimate nor a functional stake in the power-sharing prerogatives of the capitalist free-market system. Thus, from the black vantage point:

> It would be a seriously inhibiting mistake . . . to treat America simply as an ideologically flawed society that somehow needs a new set of human values and incentives. Rather, the United States should be seen by them for what it is, a liberal but traditional society which, like almost all societies before it, is responsive to the self-seeking needs and wishes of those groups and individuals who, through competence or position, have the ability to persuade others to share or part with valued positions and resources. The struggle by blacks to take an equal place in the economy must not be seen as an effort to overturn or humanize capitalism but rather an effort to move onto its playing fields, become part of its powerful institutions, and to share all the prerequisites and prerogatives of those who run and regulate it.[13]

Civil rights justice, for all intents and purposes of the United States Constitution, had been won; there are no more frontiers to conquer; no horizons in view that are not mirages that vanish over the hill of the next Court decision on the meaning of equal protection. The bottom line for the next black political manifesto is *economic justice,* without which there will be no future black survival. *The truth is, however, there exists in black America no such organized black leadership consensus that is either willing or able either to replace, oppose, or simply*

ignore and bypass the organized remains of the old, institutionalized civil rights and
social welfare leadership:

> Once more, blacks in America must turn to the politics of ethnic solidarity and
> self-help. As a group, black people must determine in caucus or convention
> what goals and tactics are going to serve their interests for the balance of the
> century. They must find and certify a trailblazing leader who will lay down a
> proper set of marching orders and make the black agenda effective by
> connecting it with public interest and the American sense of fair play.
> Awakening to the pleasures of elective politics, blacks must multiply their
> political and economic strength by making political and economic alliances
> with other groups that share common burdens and aspirations.[14]

On the crucial question of the role of contemporary black leadership, the
above statements are those of a major commentator on the present black political
and economic situation. They advocate a new black leadership that would
emerge out of a consensus expressed through a "caucus" or a "convention." Even
though the format (caucus, or convention) is understated, the substance of the
procedure is correct. But what is really needed is a new black leadership
organization of *national* dimensions. More than that, this organization requires
another concept of black leadership. The age of the *single* Big Leader Spokesman
has passed, since no single black leader today is capable of reflecting the many-
sided complexities of political, economic, cultural, educational, and institutional
needs of American blacks. What is required, in fact *demanded*, for black survival
is a form of *national council of collective leadership—a new concept of leadership.*
The nearest approximation to a single trailblazing leader was Martin Luther
King, Jr., whose martyrdom was the tragic consequence of being driven by
idealism to invoke a "new set of human values" in a society whose moral reflexes
are not attuned to social change. Following King came Jesse Jackson, bearing
the outlines of black leadership ideals involving both economic and political
activism. But even though he was a black leader with a pronounced degree of
charisma and national appeal, Jesse Jackson squandered too much of his
potential by opportunistically following the imaginary bait of electoral politics
at the presidential summit, while neglecting the more crucial and fundamental
and *obligatory* task of political organization at the bottom, *the independent black
political party.* Jesse Jackson's presidential bid was, in black political terms,
politically premature. While Jackson's concept of the Rainbow Coalition was
commendable, in his haste for the laurels of political notoriety, he forgot that
the sought-after prize of real black political power lies at the "end of the rainbow,"

not at the beginning. Only the blacks are in a position to form the organizational base of a "third force" departure from the Democratic party's monopolistic hold on the left-wing position of the two-party system. Yet it would be tactically incorrect to premise a black push for an independent political party on the basis of a coalition at the outset. Black political mobilization of any kind that does not aim to transcend mere electoral conventioneering, that does not outline strategies for economic elevation, is, for blacks, dead end politics. The ultimate goal of any group politics in a pluralistic society had to be self-interest, especially if the self-interest is economic. In this regard, Walter E. Williams, one of the more modish black conservative critics of civil rights who declare that the blacks' poor economic condition cannot be wholly attributed to "racial discrimination," offers this advice:

> If the evidence bears out the argument that there are laws that eliminate economic opportunities, then political resources should be expended in the direction of modifying those laws. The government, at various levels, can exert its authority to ensure that all people have unrestricted access to legitimate markets.[15]

The immediate question is *what* political resources are in fact available to be expended? And how would such political resources be mobilized? True to their twentieth-century origins, such conservative arguments do get to the heart of the black economic situation. These arguments originated with Booker T. Washington in his clash with the civil libertarians led by Du Bois, and with an NAACP imbued with Joel A. Spingarn's noneconomic liberalism. Although Du Bois would abandon noneconomic liberalism in the 1930s, the essentials of these arguments remained embedded in the ongoing ideological evolution of the black protest movements. Today one of the most extreme extensions of these arguments is reflected in the views of the black conservative Republican Clarence Pendleton, and civil rights debates that divided Washington and W.E.B. Du Bois still cast shadows over the black 1980s.

Now that the civil rights cycle has truly waned, a black conservative Pendleton, Thomas Sowell, or Walter E. Williams can challenge the legitimacy of the liberal consensus that "the past gross denial of basic rights of and gross discrimination against blacks in the U.S." is the reason for the continued discrimination in the economic sphere. In the black conservative view, "racial bigotry and discrimination is neither a complete nor a satisfactory explanation for the *current* condition of many blacks in America."[16] The catch here is that the black conservatives claim the option of delegitimizing the *social* results of civil rights legislation because of black *economic* disabilities. However, black conservatives themselves are the prime beneficiaries of precisely those maximum social, educational, and professional advances resulting from civil rights legislation. Thus, at this late date, *both* the conservative and the liberal consensus regarding the present black *economic* situation have become rhetorical, open-ended, and nonconclusive because their views reflect the racial politics of the post-civil rights era, i.e., the *end* of the civil rights cycle. Clarence Pendleton, in his zeal, got caught in the administrative net of ambiguous definitions over what minority rights are civil or economic (or, perhaps, *both*). When Pendleton went out on a "constitutional" limb to declare federally sponsored appropriations on behalf of minority business enterprises (MBEs) were not only unjustifiable, costly, riddled with corruption, nonproductive "shams," but also conducive to "reverse discrimination" against deserving *white* competitive bidders, he was attacked by other more liberal members of the Civil Rights Commission. More than that, Pendleton was *not* publicly upheld in his conservative views in this the matter by the Reagan administration! The key to unraveling this anomalous political debacle over civil rights interpretations is that the program of "minority set-asides" for disadvantaged entrepreneurs among "blacks, Hispanics, Aleuts, Orientals, Indians or other minorities" was *not* a legislative product of a Democratic party administration. The program was created through an executive order by President Richard Nixon, a Republican, in 1969! This political party history helps explain the curious phenomenon of black Republicanism in the 1980s. It is a *class* phenomenon that reflects *class* interests that are much less "civil" than they are "economic" and are *similar to those of Booker T. Washington.* Thus, it was ironic that among the main critics of Clarence Pendleton's actions against the legitimacy of the Nixon-inspired program for the MBEs were *black Republicans!* [17]

Black conservatism does express the view that some of the causes underlying the restrictions that limit black economic opportunities are certain "laws," that is, *legal* restrictions. However, the modification of such laws, if such is possible, can be achieved only through *black political organization.* The problem is that this new-style political leadership must emerge from the black middle class or, at least, from the political elites of the black middle class. It is evident that the economic consequences of the civil rights cycle produced the new, contemporary black middle class or the repository of new versions of what Du Bois described as the black Talented Tenth. Du Bois saw the Talented Tenth as the source of quality intellectual, political, educational, and cultural leadership that blacks would require in the struggle for racial, social, and economic parity with other groups in American society. But by 1940 W. E. B. Du Bois had to give up his idealistic notion about the black Talented Tenth. It became demonstrable that the class origins and affinities of the black elites were *nonnationalistic.* "The upper-class Negro has almost never been nationalistic," wrote Du Bois:

> He has never planned or thought of a Negro state, or a Negro church or a Negro school. This solution has always been a thought up-surging from the mass, because of pressure which they could not withstand and which compelled a racial institution or chaos. Continually such institutions were founded and developed, but this took place against the advice and best thought of the intelligentsia.[18]

The same social and ideological conditions still prevail in the post-civil rights era of the Eighties, especially with regard to the creation of *political* institutions. Black political leadership for any goals, economic or otherwise, must emanate from the black middle-class. However, the economic gains that accrued from the benefits of the civil rights cycle, limited as they were, became the bases of affluence for the contemporary black middle class. This new class, over the last twenty-five years, had been the beneficiary of a quantity and quality of higher education, professional and technical training, employment, upward social mobility, corporate ingress, governmental patronage, cultural and artistic expression, and entrepreneurial opportunity that New Deal middle-class elites couldn't even hope to dream of. But measured against Du Bois's assessment of the "upper-class Negro" of the 1930s, their contemporary progeny are even *less nationalistic* than their predecessors. At least, the "black bourgeoisie" whom E. Franklin Frazier berated thirty years ago was guiltily and painfully conscious of its social powerlessness and its inabilities and shortcomings as a class, and aware of the social responsibilities it either refused or was unable to assume. By contrast, and stated in socioeconomic educational, intellectual, political, and cultural terms, the new black middle class, and its elites, is an *empty class* that has flowered into social prominence *without a clearly defined social mission* in the United States. With a scattering of exceptions here and there, the new black middle class, and its elites, is an unprecedented product of specific civil rights conditioning that renders it not intrinsically incapable, but mindless of its own potential or else reticent to mobilize it through any organizational channel that is plainly open to it.

One critical gauge in assisting the general societal deficiencies of this new class is the puny results of its intellectual, scholarly, and creative output compared with the achievements of its predecessors from 1900 to the 1960s. Despite all the referential benefits bestowed upon it via extended educational opportunities, this new class has revealed only a flickering glimmer of intellectual or creative or scholarly potential reminiscent of the achievements of Du Bois, Woodson, Rayford Logan, Alain Locke, Booker T. Washington, Abram Hill, Sterling Spero, E. Franklin Frazier, Sterling Brown, Mary McLeod Bethune, Jessie Fauset, Allison Davis, Lorenzo Green, Langston Hughes, Ralph Ellison, and other notables of the Twenties, Thirties, and Forties. This is not said in condemnation of the new class, but is a general assessment that, as a class, *it does not aspire to achieve.* Lacking even a clear consensus of a social mission, except more of the same vague and evanescent idea of "civil rights," the new middle-class is *empty,* it is an indulgent "Me" generation, a class that has ingrowing psychic troubles over portents of an uncertain future.

Because of its unprecedented and unexpected social and economic evolution, this class and its various spokesmen and spokeswomen cannot admit in a political and/or economic fashion that, for all intents, it has written off the contemporary condition of the black underclass as a lost cause. (Apropos of Du Bois's critique of 1934, only the state and the uplift forces and agencies of the nation can help save the black underclass.) Flushed with the civil rights optimism of the liberal consensus, the emergent new class both denied and evaded the self-evident existence and the growth of a permanent underclass with its ominous signs of black family disintegration as outlined in the controversial Moynihan Report of 1965, *The Negro Family–A Case for National Action.* Related to this issue of the black family, the successes of the civil rights cycle ushered in new features in the evolution of minority issues such as *gender politics.* In addition to the proliferation of other minorities, the politics of gender traps the black community into political immobilization. The introduction of *gender politics* into the post-civil rights era seriously compromises, retards, and threatens the black minority's ability to maximize its organizational potential, especially *political organization.* At the crucial class level where upward economic mobility has created the maximum affluence, a "silent war" between the sexes has become a serious internal liability for black leadership fortunes. A prominent example of this silent war between the sexes over the definitions and imperatives of black leadership is displayed in the controversies over the leadership role of Coretta Scott King, who, in the words of one black male critic, is "out of place in such a post" as Martin Luther King's successor. Another male critic declared: "She anointed herself; no one ever gave her a crown. Black people aren't prepared at this stage in history to anoint anyone with Martin Luther King's crown." These black male critics of Coretta Scott King's role assert that the "grieving widow" does not merit being anointed as the successor to the real essence of Martin Luther King's goals, which is of course debatable. However, Mrs. King's telling reply to her critics was that neither she nor other "civil rights leaders have found a way" to achieve Martin Luther King's civil rights goals.[19] Hence, of all the nonwhite minority groups, the black minority finds itself at the end of the civil rights cycle as the one most compromised. Because it is and remains the largest minority, economic, political, family, educational, and other problems are magnified by its size—when its size should, in fact, become its innate advantage.

The end of the civil rights cycle has left the black minority without a leadership consensus or even a leadership forum that can claim to speak on behalf of the entire black minority inclusive of class, gender, ideological, and factional divisions. It has even been argued on occasion that such an all-inclusive black leadership consensus is neither required nor justified. That raises the crucial question, In what organizational, political, or economic manner should the future destiny of American blacks be determined or guided? Despite the fifty-year history of New Deal political traditions, the United States remains the world's most powerfully organized capitalist society—*and will remain so.* And despite the conservative right's determined political thrust to obliterate the entire corpus of the New Deal legislative record, such a goal *cannot* be fully achieved. Whether the conservative political results of the Eighties are good or bad in terms of the implied social *ethics* of national policy is beside the central point. From the particularist point of view of the American black minority, one salient historical fact has to be kept in mind. No matter how competing political, economic, educational, and minority establishments care to interpret the meaning of traditions, history, and constitutional legality, the United States still has a rendezvous with both the past and the future of its destiny as a nation. In the future context, the blacks must struggle to save themselves because allies are not promised. In organizing to save themselves, any political allegiance blacks would consider extending to other minorities would have to be purely conditional. Despite the false promises of the most recent civil rights cycle of the Sixties and Seventies, American blacks still represent the most crucial minority group, the most strategically positioned to impact on the institutional structures of the total society. What is lacking is the quality of black leadership capable of harnessing black potential.

NOTES

1. Barbara A. Reynolds, *Jesse Jackson—The Man, The Movement, The Myth* (Chicago, Nelson-Hall, 1975), pp. 23.
2. Ibid., p. 9.

3. Ibid., p. 100.

4. Esward Cowan, "The Humphrey-Hawkins Bill," *The New York Times,* November 19, 1977.

5. Ibid.

6. David J. Blum, "Minority Report—Black Politicians Fear They Can't Do Much to Help Their People," *Wall Street Journal,* October 29, 1980.

7. Ibid.

8. See *Crisis,* Vol. LXXIX, August-September 1972, pp. 229-230.

9. W. E. B. Du Bois, *Dusk of Dawn—Autobiography* (New York: Harcourt Brace & Company, 1940), pp. 192-193.

10. Theodore Cross, *The Black Power Imperative—Racial Inequality and the Politics of Nonviolence* (New York: Faulkner Books, 1984), pp. 837.

11. Ibid., 838.

12. Ibid., 840

13. Ibid.

14. Ibid.

15. Walter E. Williams, *The State Against Blacks* (New York: McGraw-Hill, 1982), pp. xvi-xvii.

16. Ibid.

17. James J. Kilpatrick, "Minority Set-Asides—Set Them Aside," *Detroit Free Press,* April 22, 1985.

18. Du Bois, p. 305.

19. John Herbers, "Coretta King Struggles with Weighty Legacy," *The New York Times,* January 18, 1986.

PART SEVEN

Interview with Harold Cruse

CHAPTER TWENTY-SIX

Interview with Harold Cruse

(Conducted by Van Gosse, *Radical History Review,* May 1997)

VG: *Were there family or cultural traditions that influenced you?*

HC: Well, they were very ordinary working-class blacks in Virginia. Our only claim to any kind of a career thing was that I have two grand uncles in the Army who were officers, two brothers of my grandmother. And one became an officer in the corps with Pershing, in Mexico. He carried a scar. He used to sit around and boast of it. Some soldier in Villa's army tried to kill him with a machete. He ducked the wrong way or the right way and it came across his face, it left a big scar there. The younger one became an officer in the World War I, when they set up an officer's training school out in Des Moines.

VG: *This was the distinctive thing in your family?*

HC: Yeah, we had one distinctive thing. The other is that my father's brother, Herman, left Virginia early, went to New York, and became an auto mechanic. And ultimately in the twenties, he became the first black to ever have a repair franchise in a big garage in the Bronx. He was real mechanically minded. He went on from there and he claimed he invented the first speedometer back in the twenties. But he became embittered, he couldn't get a patent. [. . .]

VG: *Is this how you got to New York, because you had an uncle there?*

HC: No, this becomes one of the more painful experiences. My father married my mother and my grandmother didn't approve of it, broke it up. And he took me and sent me to a foster home in Queens.

VG: *How long did you live in Queens?*

HC: I lived in Queens from about the middle twenties until 1930. With these foster people, a distant aunt's became my foster home. Then, around 1930, I was transferred back to my family, those who had come to New York. And in 1931 I was sent back [to Virginia]. In 1930 I had reached junior high school in Harlem. My foster aunt and her husband lost their house in Queens and moved to Harlem. I wound up in Harlem's Junior High School, PS 139, that was the same school Baldwin went to, had some of the same teachers that Baldwin had.

[. . .]

VG: *Who are your earliest teachers, not necessarily in school, but people you learned from?*

HC: In all of this, I must confess that one positive thing was I was fortunate, as I look back at it, to have encountered a number of very good teachers. As a matter of fact, when I was growing up in Queens as a youngster, I remember a white teacher saying to the kids in my class that "Harold is going to be a writer." Because I was best at composition, for some reason, because of natural talent. I didn't know what she meant by becoming a writer, [laughs] I mean, writing letters, what does she mean? [. . .] We used to have these intimate discussions, what are you going to be when you grow up, that sort of thing. And she referred to me as being a writer, a potential writer. That stuck with me. [. . .]

VG: *My impression is that your interest in the theater, specifically in the black musical theater, started early.*

HC: Started very early because [my] aunt in Queens was a strict black vaudeville fan, and she used to take me from Queens to Harlem at every opportunity. This was in the twenties. I had my first introduction to the theater when my Aunt Henrietta used to take me on weekends. Saturdays in particular, to Harlem on the streetcars, to go to the black vaudeville theaters. And I loved it.

VG: *In the introduction to* Rebellion or Revolution? *you list all of the acts, Cab Calloway, Chick Webb and so on. This was something you really absorbed.*

HC: That was my first intellectual absorption of aesthetic ideas, without even knowing the meaning of it. It was not until I grew up and became more acquainted, not just with blacks but more acquainted with racism, segregation and what people said about blacks, the general feeling. And I remember that by 1940, just before I went into the Army, or even before that, I had come to my own conclusion. I used to say, "no matter what they say about these blacks, these people are very talented." And that stuck with me, and led me eventually to attempt to get into the theater.

[Cruse discusses his early life in Harlem and his employment downtown.]

VG: *You couldn't get a job in Harlem?*

HC: No, there's no jobs in Harlem, not to any random kid, who didn't know anybody. So I got a room in Harlem and started out on my own. I learned, for example, how to go to the Bronx and get random jobs, polishing floors or lugging groceries, pick-up jobs, enough to pay the rent. And I had relatives in Harlem, used to go see them. . . . I remembered that we had a white teacher at PS 139, named Mrs. Hemstreet, I'll never forget her. Hemstreet used to take us down Lenox Avenue to the Schomburg Collection. That's how I discovered the Schomburg. She used to take us down Lenox Avenue from PS 139 four blocks to 135th Street [to] the Schomburg Collection. And took us into the junior section and told us, "Now, you kids, whenever you need books, you come here." I used to go to the junior section on my own and get books and read, and then I noticed here was a senior section— "I'm going to get in there! [laughs] I'd go in there unannounced, sit down, and read books. I couldn't take them out because I'm a junior. But I could go in there, sit down. It was in the senior section of the Schomburg that I stumbled on aspects of black history, right there. This was between 1935 and 1940.

VG: *Who were you reading?*

HC: Everything! I was reading magazines, *Opportunity,* I was reading *New Challenge.* That was an intellectual magazine, with Richard Wright, Ellison and those people. [When] I was drafted, [I hoped] that I would be rejected because I had flat feet, I didn't know any better. And I went and signed up. "They're not going to take me anyway," I said to myself. But I was wrong. They did. And that ended that period in my life, that early period.

HC: *It was a sharp break?*

VG: Sharp break. From my early rearings, particularly the 1930s, I was just beginning to emerge as an understanding adult. I was reading, I was training at the YMCA in Harlem, I joined the theater movement, I was usually up there to train in the gym. We got into all kinds of arguments and lectures in Harlem, at the Harlem YMCA. All kinds, all factions, Communists, Garveyites, it was a hotbed. I could walk down any street in Harlem, particularly in that section, 131st Street between Seventh and Lenox Avenue, and pass by old men sitting on the stoop, arguing politics.

[. . .]

VG: *Then you came back to New York [following World War II]. And this leads up to the period that you've written about a lot, and joining the party.*

HC: Italy becomes a factor there. Because in Italy, we got into conflict with the partisans, and that was part of my indoctrination.
　　[. . .] We had to have contact with the partisans to survive, best we could.

VG: *You mean just to get supplies, or for protection?*

HC: No, no, protection. You know the Army is a very crass experience. We, naturally, being supply troops, we got into trouble, we got into a very bad situation with the black market. They preyed on us, you see.

VG: *You could be hijacked?*

HC: Oh yeah, we were hijacked in Italy. Not in North Africa, that's another story. This has political implications, and this is something that I tried at one time to do research on to find out, to get some information from untold sources. What happened in North Africa was this: we, the black troops, mainly were in charge of supplies. We were in charge of that stuff, not the white troops. And the black market cued in on us, as conduits. That's how we got involved illegally in the black market thing, because as I began to understand—and this is something that I know happened, but can't prove—black marketeering in North Africa was what helped finance the Algerian underground against France. No evidence of that.

[. . .]

VG: *You needed [the Italian Communists] for protection?*

HC: They could show you the ropes, or to put it vulgarly, they could show you the best whorehouse. The best underground facilities [laughs]. All-night bars, underground bars, underground whorehouses, underground friends, underground this, underground that.

VG: *When you came back this was part of the reason you went into the CPUSA, because you'd met all these Communists?*

HC: I had met the Harlem Communists before, in the YMCA and elsewhere. And I knew these people, because in Harlem, nobody gave a damn who you were, what your politics were. We used to have those debates in the YMCA, there were Communists debating, black nationalists debating, [. . .] NAACP-ers [debating], the whole spectrum of critical opinion was being aired. So in those days—I used to tell people—anybody that couldn't argue Marx or Engels was considered a goddamn dummy!

[. . .] Anyway, first thing I did, I went to what was then called the George Washington Carver School, on 125th Street, between Seventh and Eighth. It's gone, it's wiped off the record. That was the Communist Party's cultural base in Harlem.

[. . .] It was run by Gwendolyn Bennett, the Harlem Renaissance poet, and the wife of Otto Huiswood, who had been exiled in Europe. That's where I first heard Du Bois lecture. [. . .]

VG: *I'm wondering, at this point in '46 and '47, were you reading the pragmatists, or did people in the party not like James and Dewey at all?*

HC: They didn't like them. I began to understand the implications of Marxism as it was being taught. Basically, these other philosophies, other schools, I didn't understand fully, but I knew there were these other schools, differences of opinion—the materialists and idealists—and [Howard] Selsam was very enlightening on this question. Cleared up a lot of foggy thinking on my part, about philosophical questions. And that led me, very frankly, to take up the challenge of joining the CP officially, at the Carver School in 1946.

VG: *Weren't people often in the party and then left, but without becoming anticommunist, just floating in and out?*

HC: Frankly, I floated in with the intention of one day being forced to drop it. I understood this, I had no illusions. I had been indoctrinated in Italy, and I was steadfastly pro-Russian in the war.

VG: *Were a lot of people?*

HC: We were overjoyed after Stalingrad. The Russians could do no wrong in our eyes.

VG: *There's some time here before you start writing for the* Daily Worker?

HC: What happened was that when I joined the party in '46, I joined as a veteran. Veterans were high on the list, for favored treatment. Veterans like me were very outspoken. [Laughs] And I joined a Harlem neighborhood club, the Lincoln-Douglass Club. And I said I want to see what these people, these Communists, are all about, in terms of practical politics. And I began immediately to observe what I considered some serious flaws in terms of strategy and tactics. I said so, right from the beginning. On my own, I began to sense that something was a little off here. Nevermind the rosy words of working-class unity. There's something off here, which I don't like. I'm not an anti-communist, I'm not anti-Marxist. I'm with you people, but there's something about your program here that doesn't sit well with me. And I said so. I was a new voice from the Army, coming in with his big mouth, saying things, got everybody shrinking—"What's he going to say next?"

VG: *Did they call you a Negro Nationalist?*

HC: Whatever they were calling me, I'm a dissident. "He's a dissident, what's his problem? Harold, what is it?" They called me in to have a talk. So I fell out with the party people in Harlem. In order to get rid of me, they sent me down to the *Daily Worker*. That's how I got on the *Daily Worker*.

[. . .]

VG: *Thirty years after* The Crisis of the Negro Intellectual, *there's a new historiography on the party, by scholars like Mark Naison, Robin Kelley, Maurice Isserman and others. Given the passage of time, do you now think that the Communist Party contributed anything positive to black politics? At the time you wrote* The Crisis *you regarded it as the major problem of black politics.*

HC: Well, that was a problem. And it remained a problem. In thinking the thing through, all these years, I have been formulating a new thesis on this. Now I'm beginning to see all those experiences in their proper historical context, neither to be condemned or deplored or heroized. No, I see it in a completely different light. I see it in the light of going back into history and realizing, more fully now than I ever could, that the problem with the Marxist movement in this country was that they could not make Marxism a part of the United States. That's what it was all about. They tried, they just couldn't: they didn't have the dialectical ability that Marx and Engels talked about to make Marxism applicable to America the way it was applicable to Europe. That was the big catch. They were off on the wrong tack. They tried to make an American Marxism composed of obdurate ingredients that didn't work. That was the basic problem. It was not simply that I had to disagree on the spot, against certain tactics, and certain ideas. I had no idea of why I was disagreeing, given what I had understood about Marxist philosophy. I came to the conclusion without being able to prove it empirically, that this does not represent an extension of Marx's real thinking. Why, I don't know. I'll find out—I think I found out.

VG: *There isn't any mention in your writings about the effect of McCarthyism on you personally. Did you get visited by the FBI?*

HC: I did, I was visited, that's a story in itself. See, I officially quit the party around 1953.

VG: *As late as that, I thought it was earlier.*

HC: It took me from 1950 to decide to quit.

VG: *And they never kicked you out?*

HC: No, I was never kicked out. They disowned me, but they didn't kick me out. As a matter of fact, I had to go out and hustle and work again, after leaving the *Daily Worker.*

[. . .]

VG: *At what point did you decide to become a playwright? Were you involved with the American Negro Theater? Did you know people who were involved, or were you in it?*

HC: No, I was not in it. I was a constant visitor then, it was in Harlem. That's where I got the notion from Abram Hill, who wrote a famous play about Harlem's 139th Street crowd, called *Strivers Row.* And I saw it in Harlem. When I was at the YMCA they had Abe Hill's play there, *Hell's Acres.* I helped to work on that crew, for his play. That tied in with my interest in black vaudeville, early on, when I started reading Shaw and Ibsen, thinking I'm going to try my hand at playwriting, which I did, I wrote four plays.

[. . .] I was interested in doing what I wanted to call "an indigenous Harlem musical play." Because my theory about the black theater was that straight legitimate drama was alien to blacks. Real black theater is a combination of music, theater, dance, acting, singing. That's my theatrical theory that I tried to bring into life. But it was a flop.

VG: *Was it ever staged?*

HC: No, I never staged a single play.

VG: *Why do you think that is?*

HC: I didn't pursue it enough. You see, the secret of theater is basically this: plays are not written, plays are rewritten. The play you see on the stage, it's not the version the playwright wrote. Never.

VG: *They put it on the road and you keep revising?*

HC: No, before it gets staged. It's got to be tried out with a director and all of that. Workshops, then changes have got to be made. It's got to be revised and revised and revised. But you can't do that profitably unless somebody takes it up. I couldn't get anybody to take anything up.

[. . .]

VG: *I gather you were involved with Paul Robeson's paper* Freedom *after you left the CP?*

HC: When I had decided to break with the party downtown, I went back to Harlem because Robeson had established *Freedom* newspaper. And it became clear to me that Robeson himself was being disenchanted with the Communist Party. They were trying to control him. I sensed this, I knew it.

VG: *Did you write for* Freedom?

HC: No, they wouldn't let me. I had a bad name downtown, because in order to combat the Communist Party's apotheosization of Jackie Robinson, I tried to apotheosize Willie Mays.

VG: *This was not quite the correct black sports hero?*

HC: No, he was not, and I knew that, so I told the editor, Lou Burnham, "I'll do you a piece on Willie Mays." I wanted to combat them on Jackie Robinson, I didn't like Robinson, for a number of reasons, I won't go into that. I wrote this piece on Willie Mays and tried to give it to Burnham, and they turned it down. They also turned down my article—I tried to write articles about the Apollo Theater, remember that?

VG: *You've written about it, that they were not engaged with what was happening in Harlem, and issues of white ownership.*

HC: No, they wouldn't engage with it, and they're only two blocks away. And here is Paul Robeson, the leading black theater person, wouldn't touch the theater problems in the community.

VG: *Did he ever give you any reason why?*

HC: "No, we're not going to do that"—it's because the Communists didn't back it, that's why. That's how much he was under their control. After all, the

Communists financed *Freedom* newspaper, so where are your loyalties? But anyway those are the things that just turned me out.

VG: *A friend suggested to me a different question: to what extent in* The Crisis of the Negro Intellectual *were you consciously taking up Du Bois' project in the thirties and forties, that particular cultural critique of where African Americans fit into America?*

HC: No. I'm going to straighten that out in my new book if I can, that question. I was influenced by Du Bois, very much so. That's part of it, not the whole question. I was, at that point, probing for possible theoretical explanations of the black position.

[. . .]

VG: *To some younger people who are reading your work now, it seems as if there's an affinity between what you were writing in the sixties and the rethinking of Marxism, especially the Marxist approaches to culture of people like Gramsci (who was just published in English in the sixties) or Raymond Williams. Had you read Gramsci or Williams?*

HC: No, I don't read philosophy that much. I didn't because I didn't believe much in European philosophy. I still don't. That's part of my argument with Marxism. In my view, in terms of philosophical thinking, there is room and there's a necessity for a truly American form of philosophy other than Pragmatism. Pragmatism is the American philosophy. That's it. But that's because we are a young nation which was formed pragmatically in terms of politics and economics and culture. It had nothing to do with Europe. Nothing, as far as I'm concerned. Now I can be shown otherwise, but I don't believe it. I believe that the functional philosophy of the American nation is Pragmatism. And everybody follows it one way or another. And it's only the intellectuals, some of them, who attempt to find sustenance in European philosophy, like Cornel West. I couldn't be like Cornel West, forever quoting some European philosopher. I just don't believe in that.

VG: *What is your attitude towards Pan-Africanism?*

HC: That's a funny question for me because I like the notion of Pan-Africanism, in a romantic way. But in terms of practical politics, no. I just don't see it. My thesis here is that the American black is a specific product of Americanization.

That he's not an African, he's an Afro American. Like a German American is a German American, he's not a German.

VG: *Perhaps even white people are also in a sense "Afro-American," on a cultural level all Americans are.*

HC: Well, you can deal with that, but they're not African in the African continental sense. I don't think American blacks are either. And that's part of their hang-up. They're talking about bloodlines, and I think the bloodlines have been too contaminated with Americanism, to put it in a vulgar way. They are strictly Americans of a special kind. And their future lies in the solution of their American situation, not their African situation. That's my basic belief. And that does not mean I have no interest in Africa.

VG: *You haven't written about it, though.*

HC: I see our only connection with Africa that makes any political sense is political, in a sense that unless we are involved as black Americans directly in the development of Africa, which we are not, then Pan-Africanism means nothing.

VG: *You're often cited as the theorist of cultural nationalism, but to me that doesn't seem to fit.*

[...]

HC: Because I wasn't too clear, I muddle that question myself. Put it this way— when I wrote *The Crisis of the Negro Intellectual,* I had retained some of the aspects of the Marxian dogma. The basic idea of the Marxian dogma about revolution is simply this: that the growth of capitalism creates a working class. The capitalist system has political control, economic control over the working class, mainly because it has control over the communications media, which is the newspapers. They control the newspapers, they control the workers' minds. By using this strategy, they can better dilute and otherwise confuse what would ordinarily become a class struggle. It is not a class struggle purely because the capitalists, in the simplest terms, by their control over the information, the media, can control workers. But there's one fact that we don't take into account, that coming out of the nineteenth century there was another factor added into this communication issue. And this was because of the addition of technological mass communications media, in addition to the press. The capitalists ruled both of them, not just the press, all of it. Now, the whole question becomes more complex than my simplistic way of putting it. And I concluded that we can talk all we want about revolution in this country, me and everybody else, but until we are able to take the communications media, cultural media, the apparatus, out of capitalist hands, there ain't going to be any revolution. That has to also be revised in its own way and brought up to date but that's my basic belief. It's an extension of Marxism. Since I must also believe in revolution, at that time that was my theoretical conclusion, now that has to be revised also. See, my ideas of culture came from C. Wright Mills's description of the cultural apparatus. I got my ideas from him, a lot of his ideas fortified what I had originally been thinking but couldn't spell out.

VG: *I wanted to ask about your critique that the black bourgeoisie has not played the role of a national bourgeoisie. Do you think anything has changed in the last thirty years?*

HC: Nothing's changed. That basically is correct. They are a lumpen bourgeoisie. They were from the beginning a lumpen bourgeoisie. But this lumpen character has been, in recent years, augmented or influenced by the fact that it's grown larger, because of or in spite of the welfare state, in spite of what the Civil Rights Movement has accomplished, they've grown larger, but that does not mean that they are any less a lumpen bourgeoisie with no political consciousness whatsoever as being a bourgeoisie: "We just some other black people out here suffering from racism. . . ." So that complicates the matter for us blacks who are trying to concoct theories about this stuff, about American realities.

[Cruse then describes the need for the historian to be "a partial social scientist, a cultural theorist, you've got to be all these things wrapped into one."]

VG: *But it is the goal that one should seek—to be a historian, in this complete sense?*

HC: Why? Because if Marx proved anything he was all of these things at once. Or else there could not have been any consistent Marxian philosophy, if he hadn't been all these things thrown into one category, infused. And used as a fusion of disciplines to describe the real world. I'm saying that overall, black academicians, including myself, have not been trained to think that way.

VG: *But it is what you attempt.*

HC: I attempt, but only in my limited way. I'm saying that this is ultimately the problem of the black intellectuals. We are going to have to overcome this difficulty because they have been trained under the rubric of the separation of disciplines. And that separation of disciplines cannot apply to the black experience. Cornel West is still a theologian, no matter what he says. But none of these people see the interconnectedness of their different disciplines. They don't see it, they can't think that way. That limits them, in my view.

VG: *The "new black intellectuals," so-called—you don't see it as a successful enterprise?*

HC: It has the potential of becoming that. That's the question I'm dealing with right now.

VG: *Let's turn to Baraka. You knew him for a long time, even before you went to Cuba together in 1960, and he asked you to teach at the Black Arts School in 1965. Did you stay in touch with him after that, during the Congress of African Peoples period?*

HC: No, I wasn't involved.

VG: *You were severed from all that?*

HC: My complete severance takes place in 1968 when I'm invited out here [Ann Arbor, MI]. That was another watershed development in my personal career. I was lifted out of New York. It was only supposed to have been for a year. They extended it, automatically. In New York, as you well know by now, all my activities, whatever they were, led ultimately to writing *The Crisis.* That summed me up. Now, in many ways, I should never have left New York. What happened was, when the book came out, I started being noticed, and I was getting all these invitations, which actually meant that my financial career was being solved. I was on the map. This is all new to me. I wrote back to the University of Michigan and thanked them very much, said to them I was highly honored to be invited by a great university. I mean, after all, you can't put this stuff down. If you're invited to one that means you do have some substance to what you're saying. And I wrote back and thanked them very much and said I didn't want to come because I was really afraid to come out to the sticks. [. . .] But I was highly honored and I thanked them very much. It took less than two weeks. They bounced a letter back to me and offered me, guess what? In 1968, $18,500 for one year.

VG: *That's terrific money for those days.*

HC: For one year! And all the people who I had been arguing with: "Don't go out there" they told me, "don't get involved in the university," and I partially agreed. So when the second letter came I said, "Look, I can do that year standing on my head; $18,500, you're going to turn that down? Not on your life, I'm going out there."

[...]

VG: *When did they give you tenure?*

HC: They gave me tenure in '77, and they gave me emeritus in '85.

VG: *Speaking of that period in the early '70s, why do you think that all of the energy and unity around the Gary Conference dissipated?*

HC: Truth to tell, if there's anybody that could be accused of derailing it, it was Baraka.

VG: *Even when he writes about it himself, he confesses to an enormous amount of sectarianism.*

HC: *His* sectarianism—it was Baraka. That's the one who fouled up the possibility of the Black Caucus–type politicians to link up with the black nationalist people in the streets, and form an alliance.

[...]

VG: *Is that possibility [for an effective black political party] related to the Rainbow, or Jesse Jackson? The fact that he is able, when he wants to, to surface a kind of mass politics?*

HC: No, he is a carryover of the same problem of the black political party. Why does he stay in the Democratic Party? Anyway, the elements, the ingredients are still there. My thesis is that, based on all these developments we've been fleshing out here, it comes down to this as far as I see it: the unsolved problem of the sixties and seventies in particular, and the eighties when Reagan comes on the scene, the significance of that period's failures was brought out, in bold relief, in the collapse of the NAACP. There it is. I see it clearly.

VG: *Are you talking about the form of leadership, one-man rule and all that?*

HC: Whatever the case, it's a leadership problem, in the collapse of the NAACP. The very organization that they want to reject over the years. The ingredients of the collapse of the NAACP, are those that were left unresolved after Black Power, after Gary, after the Rainbow Coalition, after all of these movements. It is encapsulated in the uncompleted theory of leadership that comes about with the collapse of the NAACP. There's your point of departure. Now, from here on to the twenty-first century, and I'm laying it at the feet of the black intellectuals, the NAACP is not going to be revived until it changes its organizational and political format. The question is: Who's going to change it?

VG: *When people read this, they're going to say, "I thought Harold Cruse thought that the NAACP was the problem all along, because of its commitment to integrationism."*

HC: That was only part of the programmatic evolution of the NAACP. A lot of people didn't belong to integrationism. That became their official philosophy only because of their antecedents: racial democracy, integration, racial equality, all that kind of stuff. But now it's been shown, you're not going to solve anything with integration. It took time for that to become clear. They won everything that was possible for them to win in the 1960s. *Brown*, the Civil Rights Acts of '64-'65. They won everything that it was in the cards for them to win. Now we're talking about the coming twenty-first century, about the necessity of a new kind of leadership coming to the fore. This new leadership has to be based on the ingredients of past failures and new forms. You've got to deal with that, what form is it going to take? It's been foreshadowed already, in terms of black intellectuals. The whole leadership evolution becomes clear to me now, within the context of the twentieth century, with the beginning of the NAACP, on down to the sixties, seventies, eighties, and nineties. What becomes clear is that although time and tide have disemboweled the NAACP as an effective organization, it only means that the NAACP's goals have, for all intents and purposes been achieved. Now, in order for them to continue, they've got to change the organization's program and format and they don't want to, they can't. I have notes at home on the statements made by West, Gates, [. . .] Farrakhan, Chavis, everybody. What they can't grasp is that what is needed here is a new paradigm, because the old paradigm of 1909-1910 that brought the Civil Rights Movement to be, has lost its effectiveness. There needs to be a new paradigm. The question is, who's going to build it? I'm taking statements made by a number of people at the time the collapse of the NAACP took place. One of them that I am using is a statement of Roger Wilkins. At the height of the NAACP crisis he came out with a long article in *The New York Times* saying, it is now or never for the NAACP. He outlined what he believed they had to do. This is Roy Wilkins' nephew. He said, we have got to bring in new people to replace the current leadership. If we don't do that and we can't do that, then we have go to go to outside forces to bring to bear on the NAACP in its present state, and force them to change. That outside force is the new black intellectuals.

VG: *So their time has come in a sense?*

HC: The other part is the chapter in the NAACP's history that the historians have left out. They have left out the key figure of Kelly Miller. Kelly Miller attempted to be the moderating influence that sought to bring Du Bois and Booker T. Washington together. He wrote a book called *Radicals and Conservatives.* These radical and conservative blacks were contending with each other over how to set up what I call the first new Civil Rights paradigm for the twentieth century, in 1903. Now historically speaking, the curious thing about the new intellectuals—they come on the scene, and they're divided between conservatives and radicals. In the same way that the crowd that started the NAACP and the Urban League were divided. The Urban League became a product of Booker T. Washington. And Du Bois became a product of the radicals. Kelly Miller pointed it out, that nothing's going to happen, that these radicals and conservatives must in time come together and resolve that.

VG: *This is the one really major mass black organization and its history is more central than anything else? Because that breaks the centrality of Du Bois.*

HC: Well, one of the problems there is that the centrality of Du Bois by itself is a manufactured centrality. He is now representing all of the ingredients of the first paradigm. Because he couldn't come to terms with Booker T. Washington and Kelly Miller, whom I name in my book as "The Big Three." It's a historical crime to date that none of them mentioned Kelly Miller's name. He described it, and it's happening again. The whole significance of the new intellectuals is that they are divided between radicals and conservatives, and they come at a time of the collapse of the first paradigm, created by Booker T. Washington and Du Bois. The mistake here is that the over-idealization of Du Bois. He is highly important, but he came from the North, not the South. So far the black intellectuals, particularly Gates and West, are beginning to take a critical stand on Du Bois. You read *The Future of the Race,* you see Gates and Cornel West and Stanley Crouch are beginning to reassess Du Bois the way he should be assessed because, in my view, as great as he was, the problem with Du Bois is he was an overarching idealist. Du Bois is a philosophical phony. That double-consciousness thing is phony. It's *his* double consciousness. It's philosophical romanticism. That's what that is. It's got to be called such.

VG: *In your writings there are several places where you say, "I have never had any doubt about my Blackness, any doubt about who I am." Double consciousness for you doesn't mean anything?*

HC: It's meaningless. It's an extension of Du Bois's egotistical idealism. In reality he was trying to refashion the whole Negro race in his own image. That's what he was trying to do and it doesn't fit. The double consciousness thing is philosophical romantic crap. It's been handed down as a verity, and it's not. It had nothing to do with those blacks he met when he went to Fisk University, nothing. They had no goddamn double consciousness, they knew who they were.

VG: *You think it's an evasion?*

HC: No, not an evasion, it's a concoction. He explained it himself. Here was a near-white mulatto. Born in the North, educated along the lines of European philosophers, who early on discovered that, "I've got to choose races here." He says to himself, "Who do I really identify with? Well, they wouldn't let me be an individual intellectual operating on universal grounds, like Hegel. I can't be that, they won't accept me as that. Well then, there's only one way out for me to legitimize myself. I am choosing to be black, to be all black." It's the only world open for him, no way to be anything else. "But in order for me to do that successfully, I have got to attempt to re-create the black image or the black mind or else I've got to attempt to over-idealize and transform blackness in terms of myself." Hence double-consciousness, which nobody else had that was born in the South. Now, some of those New England mulattos might have felt that way but. . . .

INDEX